Schools for the Future Europe

Also available from Continuum

Comparative and International Education: An Introduction to Theory,
Globalization and Internationalization in Higher Education,
  edited by Felix Maringe and Nick Foskett
Method, and Practice, David Phillips and Michele Schweisfurth
The German Example, David Phillips

Schools for the Future Europe

Values and Change Beyond Lisbon

Edited by

John Sayer and Lynn Erler

continuum

Continuum International Publishing Group

The Tower Building   80 Maiden Lane
11 York Road   Suite 704
London SE1 7NX   New York NY 10038

www.continuumbooks.com

British Library Cataloguing-in-Publication Data
A catalogue record for this book is available from the British Library.

ISBN: PB: 978-1-4411-6573-2
       HB: 978-1-4411-3194-2

Library of Congress Cataloging-in-Publication Data
A catalog record for this book is available from the Library of Congress.

Typeset by Newgen Imaging Systems Pvt Ltd, Chennai, India
Printed and bound in India

Contents

Part 2

Part 3

Introduction

John Sayer and Lynn Erler

Background perspectives

Europe, the great peace project, hope and expectation, the confederation of nations where human beings have spent, irrespective of boundaries, the last one and a half millennia killing one another, has shown itself a model of co-operation and harmonization for the world. We are looking at the unifying values of this spirit of working together. At the same time, we distinguish between the Council of Europe and the European Commission, to draw out what has been learned, promoted and supported with respect to education as opposed to legislated for it. We do this in order to establish where we are now, into the second half century following the calamity of World War II. From an analysis of values which underlie a vision of where next, we have invited authors and experts to discuss their views of the structures and programmes they know have attempted to put those values into practice, aiming to bring about a concrete vision of the future of our schools in Europe.

There are still among us here people who knew the exceptional trauma of World War II and the postwar stress of rebuilding, only to have further divisions and threats. These people were witness to Europe being conceived and brought together as a community. The last 60 years have demonstrated a period of growth, a wrenching apart and a pasting together underlaid by indefatigable spirits of idealism, hope and human dignity. It is time to review these spirits, to highlight what is already here and to work actively and with clear aims on what has been proposed in the policies, guidance and treaties involved.

Among the key themes that have arisen during the past decades and that must serve as reference points for the future are:

- honour and respect for the individual who is also a negotiator and force for co-operation beyond his immediate concerns and environment, all the while free and encouraged to preserve those concerns and environs
- mobility of European Union (EU) citizens
- educational policies and structures that affirm human rights, political rights, individual self-esteem and a sense of the freedom and the responsibilities of being part of the EU
- outlining contents of the general education an EU citizen is entitled to
- identifying the unifying experiences that can be provided for young people that help them to establish personal relationships across nations and languages
- identifying the education required to prepare teachers to provide that guidance and instruction
- distinguishing between cooperation and competition among nation–states with regard to education, for instance, taking a step back from knee-jerk policy reactions to the results of international tests such as those the Organization for Economic Co-operation and Development (OECD) has been carrying out recently and being armed with secure policy and structures in order to take that step back
- promoting language entitlements

Behind all these themes are the philosophical, moral and intellectual ideas and concepts that *are* Europe. These ideas and concepts have cross-pollinated Europe, and have involved travel and study exchanges at several points in European history. These are now again possible and being undertaken. It is important to attempt to range the kaleidoscope that is Europe so that the underlying principles can serve as a clear guide for the future and can make education far more than an arena for training future economic donors and emphasizing competition. Global and international pressures could force that to become the principal aim of a European education. Yet what lies behind and within Europe is so much more human and humane. This is what Europe has to offer the world as well as its own citizens. It is what we aim to identify, condense and exemplify in this book, to be individually and in other respects collectively interpreted in schools and classrooms throughout Europe.

Europe is a peninsular continent stretching from Iceland to the Ural Mountains, from the Bosphorus to Gibraltar, from the Arctic Ocean to the Mediterranean Sea, with 50 sovereign states, most of them members of the Council of Europe, half of them, together with Malta and South Cyprus, members of the European Union. Each country has its own history, but none can be understood without the context of European history. More than 40 different working languages are spoken, a majority the official language of their country. The history of Europe has been one of power struggles and wars among major nation–states and empires, projects for peaceful trade, interchange and harmonization at last being the result. The cultural heritage has been dominated by the thought, literature and science of ancient Greece, the language, literature and law of ancient Rome, the influences of Hebraic religions from the Middle East and thereafter such major episodes as the schisms that affected the medieval church, the Renaissance, the advent of scientific method and the age of discovery, the eighteenth-century Enlightenment, the eighteenth- and nineteenth-century Industrial Revolution and the major conflicts that marked the twentieth century. All of these episodes have affected the major European countries. No school curriculum or nationally prescribed curriculum is adequate without them. Their effects were felt on all the other continents, through voyages of discovery, emigration, colonization, missionary zeal and exploitation, and European culture and heritage, for good or ill, has influenced all the inhabited continents and is in turn affected by them, particularly during the last century. So this European dimension is more than the geographical space and much more than the internal market-based and treaty-bound union of 27 political entities. It is what Europe brings and has brought to the world; it is what being European contributes to a multicultural society. It is also about what each country, not least one's own, can be proud to have contributed and be contributing to a European heritage.

Current European structures and policies

In the actions and activities of the European Union and its antecedents, however much education has become more important, it has not been at the forefront and has been considered first and foremost for its contribution to the market economy. While wider and deeper aspects receive some mention, the major impetus for the EU concept of a 'knowledge-based' European society is for economic prosperity and survival. This is why it is vital for such bodies as the Council of Europe and the European Cultural Foundation to have more fundamental priorities. No economist would argue that economics is a discipline of the first order; however vital, economics is a subdiscipline to be applied to political priorities and values for the overall good of society and humankind. The economics of education is about the efficient translation of values into the use of resources for learning: externally, in making resources equitably available to institutions; internally, in distributing resources equitably according to the aims of the school and the needs of learners. Education is not primarily about economic profit making, whether for a society, or an institution, or individual learners. Or, rather, profit making is no more than a means toward realizing values, and it is shared European values that the Council of Europe has managed to keep in the forefront.

There are those who now challenge the view that education for a knowledge-, skills- and competence-based national or regional economy is the key to future survival. What has become of the Lisbon 2000 aspirations to become 'the most competitive and dynamic knowledge-based economy in the world, capable of sustained economic growth with more and better jobs and greater social cohesion'? 'The Global Auction: The Broken Promises of Education, Jobs and Income' (Brown et al., 2011) is one example of voices preparing for future shock to the Western dream and examining how we might see education as a good in its own right. The earlier calls for more vocational skills to be introduced in primary and secondary schools or for courses to be relevant to the world of work as currently practised have been replaced by the advice that schools should provide a broad general education and a window on the world before focusing on specific training and skills. So it is important that the EU should continue to try to ensure that all its programmes, however vocationally oriented, also include general priorities such as language learning and citizenship, strongly supported and shared more widely by the Council of Europe's sustained output. We applaud the recent report 'Living Together' (Council of Europe, 2011) and its emphasis on the rôle of education, which now needs detailed interpretation and implementation by schools. It also reminds us that Europe is not just the Western Europe of EU origins. The report's authors include prominent thinkers from Serbia, Poland, Russia and Turkey. Their history is a shared European history, their future a shared future.

Our approach and purpose

Other books, though now overtaken by recent events, have treated in general terms the main thrusts of European policy making in education, but this has been dominated until now by the EU's promotion of vocational training and qualification, including higher education, for a professionally mobile trading union of member states. Some have explored particular topics in greater depth. This book is distinctive in its post-Lisbon focus on schools and in its look beyond the economy-driven EU to the heritage and future of Europe as a whole. Unlike any book on this topic in the last two decades, it will project a controversial and challenging perspective on future developments affecting schools. This is not just another book analysing EU policy and showing how differently or indifferently it has been interpreted and implemented in practice. It is not a neutrally comparative study. It is more about action that will make sense for our children. The book was prompted by the conference of the same title organized for the same reason by a voluntary body, the English Trust for European Education, which offers a platform for the range of views developed more fully here, the thoughts and findings of our contributors. They often focus on the needs of schools in Great Britain, which however serves to illustrate priorities throughout Europe.

In debates about Europe, there are constant polarizations between co-operation and competition, or frameworks of co-operation created in order to be globally competitive or to help others become competitive. Let us think of Europe as a classroom in a school. We know as teachers that a climate of co-operation in the classroom is conducive to individual learning, even though individuals learn differently and have different needs for learning. We organize friendly competition or rivalry within that overall framework of co-operation as an added inducement to learning, and we organize competitions and rewards for that purpose. We also know that, if personal success becomes more than a means and becomes an end in itself, rivalry and competition can lead to a sense of failure and can halt co-operative learning altogether. This applies to individuals in a classroom and to classrooms in a school as well as to schools in neighbourhoods.

Yet our whole school system is geared to individual success and failure, individual rewards and sanctions, systematized selfishness, competition among schools not as friendly rivalry but for survival of the fittest and motivated by fear of failure rather than a love of improvement. There is no place for cooperation in a framework of competition. Co-operative learning ceases when learners are fighting one another for promotion or reward. Co-operation across schools does not work unless they are convinced that they are mutually supportive.

The learning classroom Europa is not helped by the political misuse of outcome indicators taken from the Programme for International Student Assessment (PISA)[1], pointing the finger at an individual country's apparent underperformance as an excuse for assuming more national government powers to do something about it. Nor is it roused by the threat of overseas competition. It is helped by mutual understanding, an awareness of individual needs and helping hands. In the social market economy, it is social cohesion that comes first, as a framework and condition of profit making. In global terms, Europe's survival will be determined by what it has to offer the world rather than by its own profit.

Throughout this book, there will be differing uses of spatial descriptors such as outer and inner, bottom-up and top-down or subsidiarity. Terms will be used that have specific meanings for some: Europe, European, education, European education. We will not always be offering definition of terms used, simply alerting the reader to that fact.

One term that requires specifying here is 'subsidiarity', because it is key to this book. The use and abuse of the principle of subsidiarity constantly recurs. In the EU, it is limited to national ministries and the commission and/or European Parliament. It is also often used interchangeably with centralization and decentralization or even confused with the different uses of federation and federalization. But the principle of subsidiarity does not rest with national sovereignty, nor is it, as it might at first seem, a top-down movement, as though the human being were at the bottom of some pile. Yet it is constantly explained in terms of levels. The concept, on the contrary, centres on the primacy of individuals, with decisions being taken as close as appropriate to the individual citizen. It implies respect for the individual, for nonstatutory groups, for local, regional, national and international governance and an understanding by all of what can best be handled by each of these. That understanding is part of education for citizenship. Subsidiarity also implies, therefore, individual responsibility of the kind presented by Montesquieu.

> Si je savais une chose utile à ma nation qui fût ruineuse à une autre, je ne la proposerais pas à mon prince, parce que je suis homme avant d'être Français ou bien parce que je suis nécessairement homme et que je ne suis Français que par hasard.

Si je savais quelque chose qui me fût utile et qui fût préjudiciable à ma famille, je la rejetterais de mon esprit. Si je savais quelque chose utile à ma famille, et qui ne le fût pas à ma patrie, je chercherais à l'oublier. Si je savais quelque chose utile à ma patrie et qui fût préjudiciable à l'Europe, ou bien qui fût utile à l'Europe et préjudiciable au genre humain, je la regarderais comme un crime.[2]

(Masson, ed., 1941, pp. 9–10)

Issues addressed

This book tries to mirror that mutual respect and shared responsibility in matters affecting schools, with examples of local educational initiatives that have been given a managed European framework and of schools within European projects that may become models for wider adoption. The former have been accompanied by European permissive policy formulation, the latter require national and local recognition. This interplay of inner and outer activity, of practice leading to policy leading to extended practice, is far from notions of policy imposed and variously implemented.

We begin in Part 1 with a challenge from outside the school system: What is the entitlement of all our children to have access to the heritage that is Europe, and how as a parent generation can we transmit that experience on which to build? It is a heritage of culture and of language, a part of the human rights that have become fundamental to European education. How have they become the foundation for the future, and how can they be promoted? This includes personal historical perspectives from the school workplace and from within promoting agencies, charting stages in European policy and practice since World War II, reviewing where we are now, and offering pointers to where we are or should be going.

Part 2 addresses specific issues of citizenship education and language learning, both key elements of declared European policies. It shows how particular initiatives, not least by civil society groups, can bring to life a European dimension, both in term of general knowledge and understanding and in the uphill task of matching the policy and aspirations of European language-learning initiatives, especially through bilingual modes of education, through preprofessional mobility, and through the preparation and continuing development of teachers .

In Part 3 the position of European Schools and of the European Baccalaureate, which all EU member states share in directing and have agreed to recognize, is scrutinized not only because of the European Parliament's call for wider access, but because they represent a coherent understanding of what is meant by European education, firmly held within the schools themselves but not necessarily shared more widely and needing scrutiny for the future. Can such a framework be adapted and extended to meet future needs and encompass them? These are questions we address from within the European Schools system, with a view as well to the European Baccalaureate, and with a case study of the attempt at Culham to bridge the European Schools and the national system, from which we hope there may after all be solutions both there and elsewhere. Initiatives such as the United Kingdom's Anglo-European School at Ingatestone and Hockerill Anglo-European College at Bishop's Stortford, the Europa-Schulen accredited locally in several German Länder, or bilateral agreements to recognize bilingual European examinations such as the Abi-Bac may need a framework of wider recognition.

The conclusions are our responsibility and not necessarily shared by our contributors, to whom we are most grateful for their insights. Our aim has been to provide a challenging volume, readable from outside systems, and within reach of the reality of classrooms in Great Britain and across Europe, one that points to specific reforms and reconstructions which we consider to be vital to the future of education for Europe and achievable within a generation.

Notes

1 PISA was devised for OECD and used since 2000 for measuring attainments in mathematics, science, and literacy among 15-year-olds, and ranking the results of national samples.

2 If I knew of something useful to my country which would be ruinous for another, I would not propose it to my monarch, because I am a human being before being French, or indeed because I am human in essence and French only by chance. If I knew of something which would be useful to me but prejudicial to my family, I would cast it out of my mind. If I knew of something useful to my family but not to my country, I would try to forget it. If I knew of something useful to my country but prejudicial to Europe, or useful to Europe and prejudicial to the human race, I would consider it a crime. (authors' translation)

Putting Europe into Education

Frank Furedi

Chapter Outline

It is evident that it is far easier to create a European Union than to make people think of themselves or identify as Europeans. It is often said that one of the main reasons European identity is so feeble is because of the strength of national sentiment. However, despite the periodic success of nationalist populist political parties – for example, the advance of the True Finns party in April 2011 – the EU is not overwhelmed by an upsurge of strident nationalism. On the contrary, numerous societies in Europe – Belgium, Great Britain, France, and Holland, to name a few – are confused about the meaning of their own national identity. So if people who inhabit the EU do not have strong attachments to Europe it is not because they possess a powerful national identity. There are of course many reasons for the relative weakness of a European identity. However, one of the principal reasons for this state of affairs is that Europe as an idea, as an important constituent of our culture, has little meaning for children.

The estrangement of young people from a European identity is not surprising since this subject plays a relatively marginal role in their curriculum. In part, the relative absence of Europe from the classroom is due to the diminishing significance of the role of knowledge-based subjects like history and literature. Educational initiatives designed to promote Europe tend to have an institutional and propagandistic character. Take, for example, *The EU Explained: A Toolkit for Teachers,* published by the Hansard Society.[1] This toolkit is entirely focused on providing pupils with an understanding of the EU's institutional framework. Its underlying objective is to outline the pragmatic calculations for being in the EU. It offers no insight into what it means to be a European and contains only one short paragraph that touches on the historical legacy of the continent: 'After the Second World War, the countries of Europe were left devastated and they were determined not to let such destruction happen again. Europe began thinking of ways in which future conflict could be prevented.'[2]

A review of educational resources with regard to the EU indicates that *The EU Explained* is typical of a tendency to discuss Europe outside any historical, philosophical indeed intellectual context.[3] It is as if Europe was born in the aftermath of World War II.

Certainly from my experience of talking to teachers and children across the continent, it is difficult to avoid the conclusion that far too often Europe plays only a minimal or a ritualistic role in their education. So what are the influences that inhibit the flourishing of European-related themes in mass education?

The relative weakness of an inter-generational transmission of knowledge

Education has many dimensions, but it is most usefully understood as not simply the act of teaching or learning but as the process through which one generation initiates another into the ways of the world. Through education, adult society attempts to introduce children to the world as it is and provide them with the knowledge through which they can understand it. This generational dynamic is central to the meaning of education. It is through the institution of education that adults demonstrate their responsibility to the new generation, by introducing young people to the world as a whole.[4]

Serious thinkers from across the left-right divide have recognized that education represents a transaction between the generations. Antonio Gramsci, the Italian Marxist thinker, wrote that, in reality, each generation educates the new generation.[5] Writing from a conservative perspective, the English philosopher Michael Oakeshott concluded that 'education in its most general significance may be recognized as a specific transaction which may go on between the generations of human beings in which newcomers to the scene are initiated into the world they inhabit' (1989, p. 56). The liberal political philosopher Hannah Arendt (2006, pp. 118–89) regarded the 'realm of education' as a site governed by the 'relations between grown-ups and children', and she took the view that this relationship was far too important to be 'turned over to the special science of pedagogy'.

Arendt was not exaggerating when she stated that education was far too important a subject to leave to the experts. She took the view that education provides an opportunity for society both to preserve and to renew its intellectual inheritance. According to this interpretation education constitutes a critical phase in the renewal of humanity. What she meant when she concluded that the 'essence of education is natality, that human beings are *born into world*' was that it is through education that society both preserves and renews itself. Arendt's concept of natality is not so much a biological but a cultural metaphor, signifying the capacity to preserve and develop humanity's understanding of itself (2006, p. 171).

One of the tasks of education is to teach children about the world as it is. Although society is continually subject to the forces of change, education needs to acquaint young people with the legacy of its past. 'Since the world is old, always older than they themselves, learning inevitably turns towards the past, no matter how much living will spend itself in the present', observed Arendt (2006, p. 192). The phrase 'learning from the past' is often used as a platitude. Yet it is impossible to engage with the future unless people draw on the insights and knowledge gained through centuries of human experience. Individuals gain an understanding of themselves through familiarity with the unfolding of the human world. The transition from one generation to another requires education to transmit an understanding of the lessons learned by humanity throughout the ages. One of the main tasks of education is to preserve the past so that young people have the cultural and intellectual resources to deal with the challenges they face.

As I argue elsewhere, education in Western societies has become estranged from communicating the legacy of the past to young children (Furedi, 2009). The problem has, if anything, become more complicated in the context of the EU. Recently it was reported that the cost of the EU's proposed House of European History has doubled from its original estimate to £137 million.[6]

One could live with these rocketing costs if the project remained true to its objective of promoting an awareness of European history. But instead of serving the cause of making Europeans conscious of their historical memory, the museum is likely to institutionalize historical amnesia. Why? Because EU politicians regard the past as a source of tension and conflict and believe Europe's disunited history is an embarrassment rather than an inspiration. Consequently, the designers of this project have decided that 1946 will serve as the point of departure for the EU's history. By settling on 1946 as Europe's year zero, the EU political élite seeks to free itself of a tradition that it neither appreciates nor understands. A political culture that appears to be so embarrassed by its past is unlikely to succeed in communicating its cultural legacy to the younger generation. Of course European history contains its share of depressing and horrific episodes. It is entirely understandable that many enlightened Europeans wish to do everything they can to eliminate the regressive influences of aggressive nationalism and xenophobia. But like it or not, Europe is stuck with its past and it cannot go forward unless it consciously assimilates its experiences.

Europe's history is nothing to be ashamed of. Ancient Greece was responsible for acquainting humanity with the spirit of philosophy and opening us to the promise of science. From Judaism and Christianity, Europe gained a series of moral principles that are upheld as ideals to this day. From the Romans, we inherited an appreciation of the law and a legal system that provides security and order.

Europe's history has provided an important intellectual resource for revitalizing the thinking of humanity. The Renaissance and the Enlightenment were genuinely history-making European events: they drew on the experiences of ancients to call into question prevailing assumptions and prejudices. It is no less likely that Europeans today will need to draw on their past to revitalize their society and develop the intellectual resources necessary to face the future. The past matters. What Europe needs is not commission-sponsored mission statements about artificially constructed values, but an appreciation of its historical legacy. Paradoxically, the best antidote to petty national rivalries is a dose of historical memory. History provides Europe with experiences that transcend national boundaries but which also constitute a genuine transnational sensibility.

Sadly, it is not simply the curators of the House of European History who have decided that 1946 is the continent's year zero. In effect a reluctance to look into the past, beyond year zero dominates the culture of schooling in western Europe. In this way, important but tricky questions about Europe are evaded. In such circumstances, Europe mutates into the EU, and instead of providing children with an opportunity to acquaint themselves with their cultural legacy, they are instructed in the workings of an institution.

European education's fetishization with novelty

The year zero approach to education resonates with a tendency to regard the past as having little relevance for the present and even less for the future. A review of educational policy documents indicates a one-sided obsession with novelty and change. Change is frequently represented as an omnipotent force that by its very nature renders prevailing forms of knowledge and schooling redundant. In such circumstances, it is claimed that education has no choice but to transform itself to keep up with the times. From this perspective educational policies can only be justified if they can keep up or adapt to change. Since they are likely to be swiftly overtaken by events, such policies by definition have a short term and provisional status. So a report, 'Improving Competences for the 21st Century: An Agenda for European Cooperation on Schools', argues that the world is changing so fast that young people will 'work in jobs that do not yet exist'. It warns that 'technology will continue to change the world in ways we cannot imagine'.[7] Constant change is not merely portrayed as a fact of life that educationalists need to live with, it is also upheld as the decisive influence on the school curriculum. In the worldview of the educational establishment change has acquired a sacred and divine-like character that determines what is taught and what is learned. It creates new so-called requirements and claims to introduce new ideas about learning and encourages the mass production of an easily disposable pedagogy.

The dramatization of change renders the past wholly irrelevant. If, indeed, we continually move from one new age to another then the institutions and practices of the past have little relevance for today. Indeed the ceaseless repetition of the proposition that the past is irrelevant serves to desensitize people and prevent them from understanding the influence of the legacy of human development on their lives. Of course the constant reiteration of an argument – decade after decade – should at the very least lead an inquiring mind to question just how novel the latest version of the 'new age' is. However every new generation of school reformers imagines that it faces an unprecedented period of perpetual socio-economic transformation. The idea of ceaseless change tends to naturalize it and turn into an omnipotent autonomous force that subjects human beings to its will. This is a force that annihilates the past and demands that people learn to adapt and readapt to radically new experiences. From this standpoint, human beings do not so much make history as adapt to powerful forces beyond their control.

The reconfiguration of education around the valuation of novelty, innovation and adaptability lends it an unstable and short-termist character. Yesterday's classroom lessons soon become irrelevant to a world that never stands still. The EU education establishment often appears to communicate the idea that what children and young people learn in school cannot educate them for their lives as adults. Those who uphold the authority of the new assert that, since knowledge swiftly becomes obsolete, schools should place an emphasis on flexibility and adaptability. One policy document argues that 'challenges such as climate change will require radical adaptation'. It claims that schools should focus on helping their pupils become flexible rather than burden them with soon-to-be-outdated knowledge. 'In this increasingly complex world, creativity and the ability to continue to learn and to innovate will count as much as, if not more than, specific areas of knowledge liable to become obsolete', it states.[8] Those who uphold the authority of the new frequently assert that, since knowledge swiftly becomes obsolete, schools should place less importance on academic subjects.

European policy statements on education present change in a dramatic and mechanistic manner that exaggerates the novelty of the present moment. Educationalists frequently adopt the rhetoric of breaks and ruptures and maintain that nothing is as it was and that the present has been decoupled from the past. Their outlook is shaped by an imagination that is so overwhelmed by the displacement of the old by the new that it often overlooks important dimensions of historical experience that may continue to be relevant to our lives. The discussion of the relationship between education and change is frequently taken over by the fad of the moment and the relatively superficial symptoms of new developments. It is often distracted from acknowledging the fact that the fundamental educational needs of students do not alter every time a new technology impacts on people's lives. And certainly the questions raised by Greek philosophy, Renaissance poetry, Enlightenment science or the novels of Honoré de Balzac continue to be relevant for students in our time and not just to the period that preceded the Digital Age.

The objectification of change is symptomatic of a mood of intellectual malaise where notions of truth, knowledge and meaning have acquired a provisional and arbitrary character. Perversely, the transformation of change into a metaphysical force haunting humanity actually desensitizes society from distinguishing between novelty and qualitative change. That is why lessons learned through the experience of the past and the knowledge developed through it are so important for helping society face the future. When change is objectified, it turns into a spectacle that distracts society from valuing the important truths and insights that it has acquired throughout the best moments of human history. Yet these are truths that have emerged through attempts to find answers to many of the deepest and most durable questions facing the human species, and the more that the world changes the more we need to draw on our cultural and intellectual inheritance from the past.

If, indeed, what we know today might soon become outdated it is difficult to take seriously any knowledge that is focused on the past. In such circumstance, the legacy of European culture – which has taken almost 3,000 years to emerge – is unlikely to have a place in a curriculum oriented towards novelty. If indeed what counts is providing skills that foster adaptability to an uncertain future, the legacy of Europe becomes an irrelevance, confined to providing material for the nostalgia industry and museums.

European education's unhealthy obsession with relevance

Policy documents on education conceptualize change as the principal influence on the curriculum. From their perspective, the design of the curriculum is less influenced by any intellectually driven logic than by the amorphous influence of change. Enthusiasts of the so-called knowledge society rarely reflect on what they understand as the content of knowledge. Their silence on this subject is not surprising, since their interest is not with the content but the use to which knowledge can be put. Historically a sound formal education was associated with the provision of knowledge that was not accessible to young people through the direct experience of everyday life. In part the value of such knowledge is that it 'enables those who acquire it to move beyond their experience and gain some understanding of the social and natural worlds of which they are a part' (Wheelahan, 2008, p. 206). For those who see the task of education as the provision of skills necessary to be flexible, this type of knowledge is far too irrelevant to the project of adapting to an ever-changing environment.

So a report by the EU Commission which reviewed the implementation of its 'Education & Training 2010' work programme is far more interested in skills training than in the intellectual content of schooling.[9] Its section on 'Progress in Curricular Reforms' noted:

> There is a clear trend across the EU towards competence-based teaching and learning, and a learning outcomes approach. The European Framework of Key Competences has contributed considerably to this. In some countries, it has been key in policy reform.
>
> Significant progress has been achieved particularly in school curricula. Traditional subject areas such as mother tongue, foreign languages or mathematics and science are being treated in a more cross-curricular way, with more emphasis on developing skills and positive attitudes alongside knowledge, and with more 'real-life' applications.[10]

In others words, what the EU educational establishment means by reforms is a reorientation from a formal, subject knowledge-based curriculum to one that promotes its skills agenda. Traditional subjects like literature, history and science are treated in a 'more cross-curricular way . . . with more "real-life" applications.'

The report boasts that 'the trend in school curricula is to help learners acquire knowledge and the skills and attitudes necessary to apply it in real life situations.' Its focus on these particular situations contains the implicit criticism that traditional subject-based knowledge has little to do with real life and is therefore irrelevant. The focus on relevance also targets the formality of education. In this vein, the EU's review of its Education & Training 2010 work programme calls for a less formal, more flexible approach to schooling. It notes that the 'school consultation responses called for a more flexible learning environment that helps students develop a range of competencies, while retaining a grounding in basic skills'. These proposals are designed to weaken subject-based teaching – euphemistically referred to as developing 'cross-curricular approaches to supplement single-subject teaching' – or to diminish the formality of schooling.

Today, critics of formal education object to the fact that it is too formal and not directly relevant to the lives of young people. But education is not reducible to ideas that are directly relevant to a pupil. It is about imparting the knowledge and insights gained through the experience of others in faraway places and often in different historical circumstances. The main significance of formal education is that it provides people with the capacity for generalization and the acquisition of what Michael Young describes as 'context-independent or theoretical knowledge' (2008, p. 67). This is knowledge that is distinct from the practical knowledge that people acquire through the experience of their everyday life.

The knowledge acquired through formal education is not always useful or directly relevant. Indeed one of its characteristics is that it is the kind of knowledge that most people cannot acquire through their everyday existence. Often the knowledge provided through education is 'detached from the immediate, local world of the learner' and demands a redirection of interests away from the direct experience of the learner (Oakeshott, 1989, p. 68). Education involves providing answers to questions that the young have not yet asked. One reason why this kind of knowledge is important is that it can help students rise above their particular experience and gain insights into the wider world into which they are initiated. This type of formal education has as its premise the understanding that there are real limits about what can be learned from direct experience. Indeed we often rely on knowledge gained through theoretical reflection to make sense of our own immediate experience. As Peters wrote, reflection on the world often involves the 'postulation of what is unobservable to explain what is observed' (1982, p. 15). Since the way the world appears is often not the way it is, we rely on abstract theoretical knowledge to interpret it. In putting the case for a knowledge-based curriculum, Young observed that 'because the world is not as we experience it, curriculum knowledge must be discontinuous, not continuous with everyday experience' (2008, p. 82).

The purpose of education is to help young people develop their capacity for thinking, knowing, reflecting, imagining, observing, judging and questioning. At its best, such education provides students with an understanding of the past and with the knowledge to think about and engage with the issues of the present and the future. Of course formal education requires the acquisition of skills – reading, writing, counting – but these are aids that are necessary for acquiring knowledge.

From the perspective of an inter-generational transaction, education represents a distinct stage in the life of young people, and it has a beginning and an end. As far as Oakeshott was concerned, education proper begins with the act of 'deliberate initiation' (1989, p. 68). Through the term 'deliberate' Oakeshott pointed to the formal and institutional dimension of education.

Unlike episodes of learning from life or through emulating the behaviour of others, education is an experience that is qualitatively different to the routine of normal life. 'It begins when the transaction becomes "schooling" and when learning becomes learning by study, not by chance in condition of direction and restraint', remarked Oakeshott (ibid.). Arendt added that 'education, as distinguished from learning, must have a predictable end' (2006, p. 192). She insisted that this phase of the life-cycle had to be clearly delineated and distinguished from forms of learning that occurred later in life. She drew a distinction between learning and education, which was motivated by her conviction that this inter-generational transaction possessed features that were specific to it and it represented a particular phase of young people's development.

The idea of education as a clearly delineated phase in young people's lives goes against the grain of contemporary thinking on the subject. The premise of lifelong learning is to contest the line that separates formal from informal forms of education. Its advocates contend that there is nothing that is intrinsically special or important about schooling as such. From this standpoint, formal schooling has no special purpose. It is seen as merely a variant of other forms of learning. Yet there is an important reason for distinguishing formal education from other forms of learning. Unlike the insights that a child picks up through interactions with friends and family and from other experiences, the knowledge gained through education is not directly related to his or her life. The knowledge imparted by a teacher is based upon an intellectual legacy of humanity as a whole and is often not directly connected to questions that are of interest to the child. This is knowledge 'which is *not* immediately connected with current wants or "interests" of the "learner"' (Oakeshott, 1989, p. 68).

One of the main problems raised by the EU's review of its Education & Training 2010 work programme is that prevailing methods of assessment are too steeped in the old-fashioned ways of knowledge-based education. It decries that 'most current assessment methods have a strong emphasis on knowledge and recall and do not sufficiently capture the crucial skills and attitudes dimension of key competences.'[11] The aspiration to displace the assessment of knowledge with that of basic life skills indicates that EU policy makers have lost sight of the meaning of education. The act of training people for an adult rôle avoids tackling the more basic question of how to acquaint children with their cultural and intellectual inheritance. Instead of relying on intellectual understanding and the capacity to reason, some educationalists have opted for motivational techniques that promise to help youngsters to cope. This shift from education to training represents the downgrading of what adults expect children to achieve in schools.

It is important not to confuse the current advocacy of preparing young people for life with the idea of education as part of a generational transaction that is necessary for the renewal of the world of humans. The former represents an implicit rejection of the ideal of education that provides the young with their inheritance of human understanding. The goal of preparing young people for adult life represents a form of training whose objective is to facilitate the introduction of the trainee into society. This preoccupation with preparing young people for adult life coincides with an underestimation of the task of education. It bypasses the question of what should be the intellectual and cultural foundation upon which the preparation for adult life will take place. When the curriculum is fixated on the immediate practical questions posed by everyday life, it is difficult for teachers to cultivate an interest among their pupils in fundamental intellectual questions which have little direct connection to their circumstances.

Yet often education begins by reflecting on answers to questions never posed by the students themselves: questions that were crucial to the historical development of human understanding. That is why Arendt insists that 'the function of the school is to teach children what the world is like and not to instruct them in the art of living' (2006, p. 192).

EU educational policy, with its emphasis on relevance, skills and instrumentality has little place for teaching about a European ideal. The legacy of Europe does not count as relevant. More importantly the means available for communicating this legacy – knowledge-based subjects like history, literature, religion, philosophy – are regarded as outdated and antithetical to a curriculum addicted to skills and competences. It is worth noting that EU policy statements regard the homogenization of the curriculum and skills training as a far more important concern than its intellectual content.

Throughout modern times the subjugation of knowledge to the dicates of relevance has been the hallmark of philistinism. As the great nineteenth-century German man of letters Goethe observed, 'the philistine not only ignores all conditions of life which are not his own but also demands that the rest of mankind should fashion its mode of existence after his own'[12].

Probably the single most important driver of educational philistinism in the EU is the compulsion to render education more and more relevant.

In the name of relevance, the teaching of grammar gives way to the celebration of street language and functional skills are preferred to theoretical knowledge.

But is a curriculum that is constituted around a child's social life broader than one that is devoted to academic learning? The appeal to relevance is intuitively an attractive one; nobody, after all, would wish to provide children with an irrelevant education, and academic knowledge is often conveyed through clearly compartmentalized, formal and codified subjects. But such knowledge is anything but narrow: it is 'at least potentially universalizing knowledge' that allows children to transcend their immediate experience and learn from the lives of other cultural communities (Young et al., 2007, p. 175). An academic education is potentially more open-ended and provides more opportunities for children to acquaint themselves with knowledge and experience gained from a variety of sources than is an education devoted to relevance.

Take the subject of history, which is frequently portrayed as an outdated and irrelevant relic of the nineteenth-century curriculum. Outwardly the study of this subject is entirely unnatural and unrelated to children's experience: how can the study of ancient Greece or medieval Europe be of relevance to twenty-first-century children confronted with the challenges of a high-tech globalized world? Yet properly understood, history is the subject that probably contributes most to the broadening of the imagination. One of its purposes is to help children transcend their own immediate experience and gain an understanding of how humanity has evolved, changed and developed an understanding of itself. It is ironic that precisely at a time when policy makers are obsessed with training children to adapt to change they actually devalue the academic study of change. What can be more narrow than the current emphasis on programming children to internalize the correct personal and relationship skills? In contrast, the study of humanity's journey through time provides children with the complex motives that make people tick and with insights about the influences that make us who we are. The Roman thinker Cicero understood far more about the relationship between education and personal development than promoters of the year zero approach to Europe's past, when he stated that 'not to know what has been transacted in former times is to continue always a child'. Current thinking on rendering the curriculum broader and more relevant infantilizes children rather than achieving its aim of assisting their personal development.

So what's the way forward?

For some time, many Western societies have found it difficult to forge a consensus through which they can affirm their past and the basic values they uphold. Traditional symbols and conventions have lost some of their power to enthuse and inspire and in some cases have become irrevocably damaged. This development is strikingly illustrated through the constant controversy that surrounds the teaching of history. When a generation senses that the stories and ideals that it was brought up on lose their relevance to a changed world, it finds it difficult to transmit them with conviction to its children, and bitter disputes about historical rights and wrongs refract competing claims about conflicting interests and identities. How to continue an intergenerational conversation in such circumstances is a question that society is hesitant to pose. Nevertheless policy makers and educators intuit that this question needs to be addressed and are forced to respond to the demand for values and traditions that can be imparted to children. Such projects rarely succeed because, unlike the conventions organically linked to the past, these are artificial – albeit well-meaning – constructs that are open to challenge. Unlike customs and conventions that are held sacred, constructed values need to be regularly justified. That is one reason why EU-sponsored values and mission statements rarely inspire or motivate young people.

Putting Europe into education requires that schools take the intellectual development of their children more seriously. It is important that the question of conceptualizing the rôle of Europe in a school curriculum is not seen as a distinct, separate problem to thinking about how children should go about learning about their national cultural heritage. Once Europe is taught as an add-on, in the manner of *The EU Explained*, it ceases to have an organic relationship to children's lives. Europe is not separate from the culture and community life of its citizens. What makes people European is the capacity to interpret their shared experiences according to a mutually comprehensible narrative.

There are of course a number of different ways that the ideal of Europe can be conceptualized. Time and again Europeans have rediscovered the idea of liberty and freedom as fundamental principles that bear upon their existence. It was in Europe that the idea of toleration gained hold and the freedom of individual belief and of individual conscience was crucial in providing societies with a capacity to be open to new ideas and experiences. The conceptualization of a separate sphere of individual conscience and belief created the foundation for the distinction between public and private life. The emergence of these two separate spheres and the valuation of privacy accorded the individual affirmation and respect. One of the important legacies of the European Enlightenment is the ideal of individual moral autonomy and its attendant recognition of the importance of individual choice. Today's celebration of self-realization and of self-actualization would be unthinkable without the ascendancy of the sixteenth-century ideal of individual conscience.

The combined contribution of the ancients, specifically the Greeks and Romans, the Renaissance and the Enlightenment helped to consolidate an openness to experimentation leading to the growing influence of reasoning and science. As a result, European culture has always taken ideas very seriously. Typically religious, philosophical and scientific movements have transcended cultural and national boundaries and have always been expressions of a genuinely European imagination. The experience of the Renaissance and the Enlightenment serves as a testimony to the fact that important expressions of culture and science were from the outset genuine European events. So irrespective of the reality of the nation–states, citizens of different cultures were able also to collaborate to build a legacy that transcended their communities.

History provides Europe with experiences that both transcend national boundaries and constitute a genuine transnational sensibility. It is this sensibility that we need to cultivate among our children. To do this, we need to place a greater emphasis on the classics – including the teaching of Greek and Latin – not because of an élitist addiction to an irrelevant obsession, but because many of the questions raised in ancient times continue to haunt us.

Instead of struggling with cobbled-together citizenship classes, we would do better to teach children about those historical moments when being a citizen actually meant something: for example, the experience of ancient Athens, with its celebration of the *demos,* the agora and its valuation of rhetoric and science. Philosophy has a foundational significance for Europe and its story needs be transmitted to the younger generations.

I think that we can be fairly pluralistic and open-minded about how we teach Europe's cultural legacy, but what is important is that we do it. Why? Not because of an obsession to impose a traditional old-fashioned curriculum on pupils but because an orientation to the future requires that we attend to the questions raised through the making of Europe. Of course Europe, even one that is confused, as it is today, is a living phenomenon. Which is why we need to educate our children about how it speaks and communicates its moral and cultural values. From this perspective, the teaching of languages and literature is particularly important. What the curriculum needs to do is not offer Europe as an arbitrary extra but as an important part of the legacy that we share with one another. We may speak different languages and inhabit different parts of the continent, but through education we can draw on common moral and intellectual resources as we make our way in this world.

Notes

1   www.hansardsociety.org.uk/blogs/citizenship_education/archive/2011/05/09/3032.aspx

2   Ibid., p. 3

3   See, for example, the website of the European Commission 'Education and Training': http://ec.europa.eu/education/comenius/doc859_en.htm

4   These points are developed in Frank Furedi (2009) *Wasted; Why Education Is Not Educating*, chapter 2, London: Continuum.

5   This statement comes from Notebook 1, note 123 in: Gramsci A., 1971, *Selections from the Prison Notebooks*. Translated and edited by Quintin Hoare and Geoffrey Nowell Smith. New York: International Publishers. Gramsci was an Italian socialist-Marxist philosopher, political thinker, and linguist writing in the early twentieth century.

6   Bruno Waterfield, 'House of European History Cost Estimates Double to £137 Million', *The Daily Telegraph,* 3 April 2011.

7   Commission of the European Communities: Communication from the Commission to the European Parliament, the Council, the Economic and Social Committee and the Committee of the Regions: 'Improving competences for the 21st Century: An Agenda for European Cooperation on Schools,' 3 July 2008, Brussels. http://eurlex.europa.eu/LexUriServ/LexUriServ.do?uri=COM:2008:0425:FIN:EN:PDF

8   Ibid.

9   See 'Joint Progress Report of the Council and the Commission on the implementation of the 'Education & Training 2010 work programme', 18 January 2010.

10   Ibid.

11   Ibid.

12   Johann Wolfgang von Goethe (1807) *Gespräche mit Eckermann*, zu Riemer, 18 August: 'Der Philister negiert nicht nur andere Zustände, als der seinige ist, er will auch, daß alle hörigen Menschen auf seine Weise existieren sollen'.

Post-War Perspectives: what Europe meant for education then, what it means for us now

John Sayer

Introduction

This chapter recalls the background, spirit and intentions of key stages in the post-war movements Churchill called 'Europeanism'[1] and their implications for school education, then and now. It offers a personal view, as seen from schools, of the plethora of events: those influencing and influenced by the Council of Europe from 1949 to the present day; European Communities (EC) support from 1957 and later development projects seen as education by any other name; and the stages leading to the European Union's current involvement in education. These include its action programmes, its 1993 consultation (European Commission, 1993), the 2000 Lisbon Accord leading to the 2006 Reference Framework (European Parliament and Council of Ministers, 2006), multilingual Europe policy (Coulmas, 1991; Extra et al., eds, 2008), and the educational implications of the 2007 Lisbon Treaty enacted from 2009.

Most studies in this field are either confined to policy development (e.g. Ibánez-Martin et al., eds, 2002), actions from the centre (e.g. Hingel, 2001), European Commission (2006), vertical (top-down, from policy to implementation, e.g. Phillips et al., 2003), horizontal (comparisons of national responses, e.g. Brock et al., 2000), or a combination of these. I start from the contrary proposition, akin to the principles of subsidiarity[2], that policies are prompted by personal experiences and that their adoption depends on their resonance with people's lives and professional practice. It is the largely uncharted accumulation and interplay of personal histories that inform and sustain policies and prompt their practice, perhaps more than the reverse. There are signs in the Lisbon Treaty that this may at last be given some recognition, as in its Citizen's Initiative.[3] What leads to policy formulation is as significant as its results.

The early post-war years

The generation which came of age during World War II and determined that there should never again be such a catastrophic conflagration rediscovered a European identity to be restored, shared and treasured. Beyond the European ambitions of national dictators such as Napoleon or Hitler, proposals for a more unified Europe have been most frequently prompted by the aftermath of war and threats from outside. In the sixteenth century, Sully's grand design for Europe was born of the devastation following conflict and conquest. Victor Hugo's post-revolutionary 1849 Peace Congress vision of a conflict-free Europe would be taken up only a century later:

> Un jour viendra où la guerre vous paraîtra aussi absurde entre Paris et Londres, entre Pétersbourg et Berlin. Un jour viendra où vous France, Russie, Italie, Angleterre, Allemagne vous vous fondrez dans une unité et vous constituerez la fraternité Européenne.[4]

World War I led to the Pan-Europa Movement (Coudenhove-Kalergi, 1923), but Briand's 1929 proposals to the League of Nations for a European Federal Union were laid to rest until Winston Churchill became the first prominent post-World War II statesman to propose a united Europe, first in a broadcast to the nation in March 1943 and then on the European stage to the Youth Conference in Zürich on 19 September 1946[5]:

> I wish to speak to you to-day about the tragedy of Europe. This noble continent, comprising on the whole the fairest and the most cultivated regions of the earth, enjoying a temperate and equable climate, is the home of all the great parent races of the western world. It is the fountain of Christian faith and Christian ethics. It is the origin of most of the culture, the arts, philosophy and science both of ancient and modern time. If Europe were once united in the sharing of its common inheritance, there would be no limit to the happiness, to the prosperity and the glory which its three or four hundred million people would enjoy.
>
> (Lipgens et al., 1988, vol. 3, p. 664)

Churchill followed this by taking the lead in forming the Council of Europe, first at The Hague and then at the council's opening assembly in Strasbourg, setting an agenda still to be carried through:

> It is said with truth that this involves some sacrifice or merger of national sovereignty. But it is also possible and not less agreeable to regard it as the gradual assumption by all the nations concerned of that larger sovereignty which can alone protect their diverse and distinctive customs and characteristics and their national traditions. . . .
>
> We aim at the eventual participation of all European peoples whose society and way of life, making all allowances for the different points of view in various countries, are not in disaccord with a Charter of Human Rights and with the sincere expression of free democracy. We welcome any country where the people own the Government, and not the Government the people. (Hague Congress, 7 May 1948)

Although unrealistic about the relationship with the British Commonwealth, Churchill went further, echoing William Penn in talking of a United States of Europe and of 'the growth and gathering of the united sentiment of Europeanism'.

Those of us who had grown up during the war readily entered into that spirit, whatever our questions about Churchill's perspectives of history. As a student in the early 1950s, I was drawn to the Anglo-German Association, part of the Oxford International Committee; to the Amicale or Freundschaftsbund Europäischer Studenten; and to work camps to build homes for refugees. These were formative influences for life, and our generation of future schoolteachers was leading the way and looking for institutional support. The

World Confederation of the Teaching Profession (WCOTP) emerged in 1951 with a strong element of European-centred secondary school leaders' side, the International Federation of Secondary Teachers (FIPESO)[6], and the European Association of Teachers[7] (EAT) would be born in 1956.

The French-occupied post-war no man's land of the Saar, where our student Amicale would meet in 1951 and 1952, had become an associate member of the Council of Europe and remained so until 1958 when its future status was resolved. The initial statute of the council, drawn up by the ten founder – members, including Norway and the United Kingdom, states the aim 'to achieve a greater unity between its members for the purpose of safeguarding and realizing the ideals and principles which are their common heritage and facilitating their economic and social progress.' By the mid-1950s, the ten had been joined by Greece, Turkey, Iceland, Germany and the then neutral Austria. The council was from the outset supportive of schools and teachers working for education in democracy and citizenship, in European languages, and in particular in human rights, its most notable contributions to the European ethos. That support has continued to this day, as Hugh Starkey's chapter elaborates.

Meanwhile the economics and politics of western Europe, initially boosted by the Marshall Plan, were focused on closer economic co-operation to sustain recovery and also as a bulwark against the Soviet take-over of eastern and much of central Europe. The Treaty of Paris established in 1951 the European Coal and Steel Community (ECSC), and its six signatories, France, West Germany, Italy and the Benelux countries (Belgium, Netherlands and Luxembourg) agreed to joint financing for the retraining of employees. I was later told on good authority that I created a diplomatic incident in one European student conference, by asking coal and steel community enthusiasts whether Russians were not also part of Europe.

The Treaties of Rome in 1957 not only established the European Economic Community (EEC) and Euratom, the atomic energy community (which would later be the justification to establish the European School at Culham, to be discussed in Chapter 12), but also proposed a range of co-ordinated activities related to education and training: exchange programmes for young people, mutual recognition of qualifications, and improving knowledge of European culture and history. The proposals for technical education and vocational training went further, empowering the EEC Commission (as it had now become) to establish general principles for a common vocational training policy. This it did with the approval of the Council of Ministers in 1963. However, it was not until 1971, by which time the EEC had merged with Euratom and the Coal and Steel Community to become the European Communities (EC), that there was a meeting of education ministers to ratify a community programme to help put training policy into practice. General school education remained largely untouched by EC deliberations.

The more broadly based Council of Europe was unwieldy in its formal structure, with a merely consultative Parliamentary Assembly and a Committee of Ministers meeting only once a year. But its Convention on Human Rights, held in 1951, had come into force in 1953 for those countries which ratified it, its European Court of Human Rights was set up in 1959, and the European Social Charter was born in 1961. These encouraged and inspired educators to contribute to what later (Council of Europe, 1985) became its endorsed recommendations for human rights education in schools.

Schooling directed towards Europe

Those of us who had taken the post-war Amicale to personal union conclusions were by the 1950s and 1960s bringing up our children bilingually, and discovering not only that there was little professional knowledge about bilingualism, but that most of our convictions about methods (or 'the method') of modern language teaching were undermined by experiencing our own children's individual responses to the same approach at home.

Great Britain was making overtures to join first the EEC and then the EC from as early as 1961, even though opposition from Charles de Gaulle prevented this from happening until 1973. In the interim, British schools were strongly encouraged to promote foreign language learning and European studies, with the support of Her Majesty's Inspectorate and vigorous backing from local authorities, many of them active in European town-twinning exchanges. Learning a foreign language in British schools had been confined until the 1960s to the 20 per cent of children in grammar schools, the 5 per cent then in independent schools and the most able in secondary modern and technical schools, perhaps 30 per cent in all. It was the spread of comprehensive education which brought about language-learning opportunities for all, with much investment from government and non-governmental sources such as the Nuffield Foundation. This was accompanied by a massive increase in school exchange programmes as well as family travel. The move to decimal currency and metrication in 1971, preceded by intensive conversion curricula in schools, was all about European convergence. Most schools, including primary schools, had increased European involvement well before 1973.

In the late 1960s, running a school deep in southwestern England, and host to arts society and festival events, I was touched by the brief Prague Spring from 1968, when the Moravian String Quartet was allowed to tour this country. None of the quartet could speak English, but two had some German, so our family hosted them. Soon afterwards the Iron Curtain descended again, but we took the opportunity at a FIPESO/WCOTP conference in Zagreb, in then accessible Yugoslavia, to continue our journey across frontiers to our musician friends' homes in Brno. If the police files still contain the required secret reports about our visit, we can testify that we helped our hosts write them with considerable mirth and political correctness. Later, having moved into university work to support schools, I would return to Brno as one of six British academics allowed annually in a bilateral cultural agreement, six Czech counterparts being allowed to visit Great Britain. This and other east-west cultural interchange agreements were the result of the Helsinki Accords of 1975, when 35 east-west countries agreed to accept existing borders, on condition that all endorsed the human rights declaration derived from the Council of Europe. Without previous personal contact and trust, the difficulty of travel and communication would have made it impossible for me, as for others, to embark on the TEMPUS programmes (which I will refer to later in the chapter) which were to become my central activity for well over a decade, giving me the opportunity to work on matters which concerned our longstanding Czech and Polish friends. Their personal stories and civil courage similarly prompted their later activity in formal programmes.

The European Commission legacy of the 1970s and '80s

The EC had established a single commission and in the early 1970s the EC began to consider policies related directly to education across its enlarging membership, beyond the principles of vocational training, which was part of the common market treaties. The French minister for education, Olivier Guichard, had proposed a 'European Centre for the Development of Education', and a committee of officials had been instructed to study the proposal. There it might have stayed, but in 1972 a new directorate was formed, for research, science and education under Ralf Dahrendorf, previously commissioner for external relations and trade. In 1972 he commissioned an independent enquiry which resulted in the Janne Report 'For a Community Policy on Education' (Janne, 1973). This remains the primary background text for translating EU policy into practice. Professor Henri Janne's enquiry included exemplary consultations with a panoply of educational thinkers and enactors.

The Janne Report identified an 'irreversible recognition of an educational dimension of Europe and the irreversible initial movement towards an education policy at European Community level' (p. 10). While emphasizing the link between education and the economy, the report goes further and insists on the link between educational, cultural and science policies. It proposes that, wherever possible, education should have a European dimension, recognize diversity and avoid any kind of European nationalism. It not only urges the promotion of language learning from an early age into permanent education, but goes into detail which puts later national reports to shame. The Janne Report remains an inspirational consensus of principle and practice, much of it still to be pursued.

Alongside initiatives in higher education, Henri Janne's report also acknowledged for the first time the existence and potential of the European Schools, which has never been taken up by the commission or Council of Ministers, but which we will take up in subsequent chapters:

> European schools are functioning where the needs of a sufficient number of children of officials and technicians of Community institutions have justified their creation (but they are open to national and foreign pupils who do not belong to the category of children for which they were founded). Let us not lose sight of the fact that they constitute a prototype with regard to the conferring of the European baccalaureat and the use of several languages in teaching. (Janne, 1973, p. 10)

In 1974, the EC Ministers of Education took account of the Janne Report and the commission's recommendations, and cautiously pointed to areas for action: improved cultural and vocational education; knowledge of educational systems in Europe; recognition of diplomas, statistics and documentation; co-operation across universities and, of most direct significance to schools, encouraging mobility of teachers and students through improved education in languages and the creation of equal opportunities to all forms of education.

Although the earlier call for a European Centre for the Development of Education could not yet be pursued, a start was made with the European Centre for Developing Vocational Education and Training (CEDEFOP), set up in 1975 to provide advice, research, statistics, analysis and information and to stimulate European co-operation. Moreover, an authorized agenda was set for the Community Action Programme of 1976, from which eventually sprang the information net Eurydice in 1980 and training programmes such as the European Technologies Network (EUROTECHNET) in 1983, the National Academic Recognition Information Centres (NARIC) in 1984, Partnerships for Education and Training (PETRA) in 1985, the Community Action Programme for Education and Training in Technology (COMETT) in 1986 and Improvement through Research in the Inclusive School (IRIS) in 1988. More controversially impacting on general education were the European Community Action Scheme for the Mobility of University Students (ERASMUS) instituted in 1987, Arion in 1987, Lingua in 1990 and, in part, the Trans-European Mobility Programme for University Students (TEMPUS) in 1990. In Chapter 4, Paddy Carpenter examines some of these programmes from within, and they are briefly outlined in the appendix.

Schools and the Council of Europe

It was the Council of Europe more than the still western and still predominantly trade-oriented European Communities which provided the principal European channel for the exchange of ideas on schooling in the 1970s and 1980s. The council was and is about ideals, values and principles for the future of Europe first and for economic convergence second. It could reach out, first to the Iberian Peninsula and then to Eastern Europe, and be a channel for cultural and social rapport from which political and economic rapprochement might later come. It had moral authority, rather than constitutional force. It was free to promote and disseminate key publications on school issues: teacher education, language learning, social education, human rights education and citizenship education, including teacher resources and classroom materials. Its rapport with schools and school advisers was informal, and was the stronger for it. Its education committee, under the dynamic Maitland Stobart, was one of four set up by its Council for Cultural Co-operation and extending to non-members of the council, with the aims of promoting human rights, pluralistic democracy and an awareness of European identity and sharing common issues and challenges to European society, west, east, north or south.

Personal and professional ties mentioned earlier were channelled through professional associations and through bilateral links. There was great interest in other European countries in the development of comprehensive education in Great Britain in the 1960s and 1970s. So as a school head, I attended conferences and participated in exchanges through WCOTP, FIPESO and the EAT. I also established bilateral ties channelled through the British Council and its counterpart events, such as the 1976 Aktion der Deutschen Lehrerorganisationen; a working seminar on Gesamtschulwesen in Europa (comprehensive schooling in Europe), involving the new Mittelstufenzentren[8] in Berlin with the support of the Senate; drawing educators from Finland, Luxemburg, the Netherlands and this solitary figure from England; hosting the study tours by the Nederlands Genootschap van Leraren (NGL) in England in 1980; and leading the Secondary Heads Association presidential conference in 1980, 'Education and Europe', having invited our counterparts, still without involving the European Commission in mind. This was also an occasion when Edward Heath, by then an inspiring liberated elder statesman, could launch the Brandt Commission's North-South initiative (Quilligan, 2002) for development education, later taken under the wing of the Council of Europe. These and scores of others were activities which led towards the establishment of European Commission action programmes rather than from them. So, too, the initiative in the mid-1980s to create the European Secondary Heads Association[9] (ESHA), which as will be discussed later flourishes today, came from the heads ourselves and only later did we seek funded opportunities.

EC action programmes and schools

What the EC action programmes then offered was coherence, recognition, context, and support for initiatives. Paddy Carpenter, in Chapter 4, catches their spirit from the inside. Working from a school, my first direct contact with the EC was not until 1984, and it elicited modest but welcome support.[10] Schools did not realize through the late 1970s and early 1980s that implementation of the action programme was being blocked by the lack of an EC legal framework. Vocational training programmes had a head start, being more clearly authorized by article 128 of the Treaty of Rome and having an advisory committee on vocational training, which worked for the commission starting in 1963. To this impetus should be added the first-ever world oil crisis of the 1970s, which increased economic co-operation.

Eurydice was the first EC programme to use a name drawn from the European past, in this case Greek mythology, to project into the future. Its purpose was to enable information exchange among national governments or agencies, in order to make summaries of national education systems available. Its databank continues to be updated by a European Commission unit in Brussels. It has since developed dimensions of analysis and conducted comparative studies on key issues such as the education of migrant children and indicators of trends and future priorities. It is an awesome databank of factual information, invaluable for specialized study, but despite its name and accessibility it does not promote interest and remains largely unknown to citizens at large. School leaders, advisers and seconded teachers became only gradually aware of its usefulness.

Other programmes came with less inspiring acronyms. First came two preparatory and enabling networks: EUROTECHNET and NARIC.[11] Starting in the mid-1980s a series of EC action programmes were instituted to promote exchange and co-operation. In 1985 a modest programme for the exchange of young workers was begun, obviously within the remit of promoting professional mobility. This led to Council of Ministers legislation in 1987 and was later merged with the larger frameworks of PETRA I and II from 1988 to 1994, to supplement and give a European aspect to existing national provisions for young people to follow compulsory education with 1 or 2 years of vocational training – and under PETRA to include language and cultural dimensions – in preparation for working life. It had a larger but still modest budget of about 80 million ECUs (European currency units, the precursor of the euro) and was of direct benefit to 20,000 to 30,000 young people and 2,000 to 3,000 teachers and trainers each year, as well as prompting research institutions to work in this field. In Great Britain, PETRA funding was in heavy demand from local authorities and their technical colleges (colleges of further education), when their national resources were being restricted and when employers were scaling back their use of the colleges for training.

The 'Euro-modules' from PETRA programmes in various specialized employment areas were inherited by the much larger Leonardo da Vinci programme from 1995 to 1999, with a budget increased fivefold in annual terms for the 15 member states and with access extended to some of those about to join. The even larger Leonardo II was instituted from 2000 to 2006, with a budget of 1,450 million euros, though of course across an enlarged European Union and aspirant members, a total of 31 states. Leonardo 'mobility' projects funded travel abroad for the purpose of professional training, and pilot projects helped the cross-national development of vocational training. Other projects funded language learning and cultural understanding; and there was some funding for networks and information activities. More than 20,000 projects affected more than a third of a million young people, the figures are daunting. Yet in terms of impact, there is little evidence beyond the project reports, which of course are positive (truthfully but selectively), on the impact on the future lives of young people in Great Britain, still blocked from access to career mobility opportunities by the resistant disease of monolingualism. Leonardo, which had already encouraged vocational courses in schools and local colleges, has now been transformed into a composite programme for lifelong learning, which will be discussed in greater depth later.

EC youth action programmes of the 1980s could be accessed by those of us who in the 1970s and 1980s had fostered youth wings and community school activities. The initial Youth for Europe programme from 1988 was modest, but the Maastricht Treaty of 1992 provided impetus by encouraging youth and youth leader exchanges among member states. In 1995 a second and larger programme came into being to support second-chance education of young people outside formal education, and in 1996 there was a modest action programme, prompted by the European Parliament, to promote European Voluntary Service, which has since flourished. These were brought into a much larger Youth Action Programme from 2000 to 2006, a White Paper adopted by the Council of EU Ministers in 2001 to increase co-operation. Then in 2005, as part of the Lisbon Strategy, the European Youth Pact was introduced. Not least among the inspirers of these youth programmes was Hywel Jones, deputy director of the commission's directorate in this period. The video to celebrate 20 years of European Youth Programmes in 2008 is easily accessible and still usable, while the website Cafébabel,[12] by young people for young people, is a good and inspiring example among others of what can result. The current framework, Youth in Action Programme, supports more than 7,000 projects. The 2010 assessment carried out by the commission shows not only an overwhelmingly positive response from young people and those working to support them, but such 'spin-off' or value-added indicators as 60 per cent of participants having voted in the 2009 European Parliament elections, as compared with 29 per cent of 18- to 24-year-olds who had not been involved, 43 per cent in the population as a whole.

Three more EU vocational training programmes from the 1980s deserve mention. Arion, which for two decades from 1987 funded study visits for leaders and specialists in education, was subsumed into the later Socrates programme. Arion was a well-conceived opportunity; its main weaknesses were the failure at national level to influence political action and its misuse as an incentive for officials. School leaders were included in these visits, though with a maximum of two from any one country, their involvement was minor. IRIS was a modestly funded promotion of networking across vocational training projects for women, in existence for a decade starting in 1988. COMETT was a major action programme for 8 years from 1986, with a significant budget to fund links between higher education and enterprises in technology training. Again, direct impact on schools was not involved, but all schools are affected by shifts in priority in post-secondary education, both in their preparation of young people and gradually in the background experience of graduates coming into teaching.

ERASMUS, school leaders and teacher-training

The 1980 Oxford school leaders' conference on education and Europe was hosted by New College, where Erasmus himself had spent 6 months. This humanist scholar had moved across Europe, and was at one time vicar of Aldington in Kent. His name was aptly chosen for a student mobility programme, the ERASMUS action programme which at first caused controversy, being challenged as not falling clearly within the vocational training remit of the commission. Following 5 years of piloting, the 1986 proposal for ERASMUS also had a difficult reception from the big three, France, Germany, and Great Britain, because they had their own bilateral exchange programmes. Even when a compromise was reached by an EC majority in 1987, there were procedural challenges in the European Court of Justice, but the proposal survived and in the next 20 years, inherited by the overarching Socrates in 1994 and Lifelong Learning (2007) programmes, ERASMUS involved more than two million students. Its main impact on schools has been through university teacher training, curriculum development and school management training programmes, which often involved partner schoolteachers as associates.

British involvement has been less intensive than other nations', but most universities have an ERASMUS co-ordinator working with the British Council as national co-ordinator, and some universities and other higher education institutions are substantially committed, with such subject areas as law, politics and international relations being notable. Periods of study are funded for 3 months or more, usually recognized as part of a student's home university course. However, in Great Britain, France and Germany, the EU scheme still accounts for only a small minority of study visits by foreign students or even those of other EU nationality.

The ERASMUS scheme has, since 2004, been extended through ERASMUS Mundus, with the focus on non-EU students. This encourages co-operation with non-EU countries and promotes and exports European forms of higher education, usually offering a 2-year postgraduate European masters degree in specific subject areas. An offshoot, Mundus Urbano, is linked to international development for African and Asian countries, promoting postgraduate inter-disciplinary urban studies, but Great Britain has yet to become involved in its co-ordinating consortium.

Towards TEMPUS

By the time the ERASMUS programme was announced in 1987, I had moved into university work in London to set up an education management unit running management training courses for heads of schools and other institutions. I had immediately committed London to an ERASMUS project on developing school management co-ordinated from Amsterdam. ERASMUS, though principally targeted at students, also had a sub-section, university teacher mobility, for those directing their studies. This Amsterdam project itself did not survive, but three of us continued its work and set up the European School of Educational Management (ESEM), which continued to run courses and expanded into a European research network on education management, the European Network for Improving Research and Development in Educational Leadership and Management (ENIRDEM)[13], on the collapse of the Iron Curtain and subsequently into our TEMPUS programmes. The experience of the Amsterdam project was a good grounding: future activity would be guided by knowledge derived from the inside.

Friendship ties in the late 1960s and early 1970s led me to renewed contact beyond the Iron Curtain. That renewed contact was contrived by extending international conference journeys, by hosting our Czech violist friend's daughter in a permitted mid-1980s visit to us, yielding a student's view of education in Brno, and in 1987 by a formal visit to the principal Czech centres, through the post-Helsinki cultural accord, to study school organisation and teacher training as seen from the national ministry. That led to more friendship ties with educators. Our Czech interpreter had been in Hamburg during the Prague Spring, and had chosen to return home in 1973 rather than relinquish citizenship; his wife, we learned, was distributing leaflets, which later we realized were the underground precursors of *Lidové Noviny*[14] reborn, the paper directed pre-war by her grandfather and suppressed in 1952. As soon as it could be printed legally, starting in November 1989, I would be contributing occasional articles on education.

The 1989 Velvet Revolution in Prague took western Europe by surprise. There were already moves to aid Hungary, with its less restricted academic community, and the Solidarnosc-inspired 1989 elections in Poland – with a background of Chernobyl in the air and in their mushroom clouds, Gorbachev, perestroika and glasnost – presented a challenge to which the EU was able to respond readily, with aid programmes including TEMPUS-PHARE (Trans-European Mobility Programmes for University Studies, Poland and Hungary Action for Economic Reconstruction). Czechoslovakia could now be included from the outset. TEMPUS-PHARE was not focused on education as such: urgent needs were to bring safety to nuclear energy, to infra-structures, to polluted towns and land and to financial institutions beyond state control. However, education and social services were present, too, competing with the more obviously collapsed systems. So in collaboration with my ERASMUS colleague from Leuven, both now able to ply the commission systems, and with a former school head colleague with similar links in Kraków, I could apply in the first round of 3-year TEMPUS programmes, from Oxford University and partner schools, and with universities in Brno and Kraków, proposing the overarching topic, 'Developing Schools for Democracy in Europe'. We were among the 10 per cent of project proposals accepted. The Flemish Studiegroep Authentieke Middenscholen (STAM) movement for progressive schools, and the schools-university partnership in Oxfordshire found their Czech and Polish counterparts; our programmes for teacher-training curriculum development based on study visits and working groups have been documented elsewhere (DSDE, 1993, Sayer et al., 1995), and led to a second 3-year project in Kraków related to schools and social services (Vanderhoeven, ed., 1998), more fraught with complications, but opening the way for Kraków to take initiatives when Poland joined the EU.

Meanwhile, events in the Soviet Union had transformed Eastern Europe, and a similar programme was offered, Technical Aid for the Confederation of Independent States (TEMPUS-TACIS), and two further programmes were proposed from Oxford, this time with my ERASMUS colleague from Amsterdam and new partners in Halle, itself just released from Soviet control. The DSDE group applied to work with colleagues first in Kiev and then in the Urals, in Perm Pedagogical State University, whose current Rector we had met in Oxford as a result of individual contacts made as soon as Mikhail Gorbachev ended Perm's era as a closed city. We joined in helping create the Oxford-Perm city twinning partnership, built before Perm gained access to the internet and other new media. Here again, the EC programme created an enlarged opportunity; the conditions and the motivation had to be pre-existing. Our Perm projects (Sayer et al., 1999, 2001; Sayer, 2002, 2005) continued from 1991 to 2006, just three examples among hundreds of aid projects across many priority fields.

The TEMPUS programme as a whole was massive, responding more to the identified needs of 'beneficiary' countries than to EC internal priorities. It was designed to ensure stability and economic viability along the borders of the EC, and establish a solid basis for future economic social and cultural interchange. Much of this was happening before the Maastricht Treaty gave extended legitimacy to education and training programmes. Aid later extended from 2004 to the Balkans, in the Community Assistance for Reconstruction, Development and Stabilisation (CARDS) programme, and was matched with parallel programmes targeting Mediterranean nations. With similar aims, TEMPUS continued in the new frameworks, TEMPUS III and the current TEMPUS IV (2007–13) moved to include business and voluntary sectors.

After Maastricht: schools on the map

The ambiguities between training and general education continued to cause friction throughout the period of action programme expansion in the 1980s, and clarity was badly needed. The Maastricht Treaty not only replaced the Treaty of Rome's Article 128 with its own, numbered 127, on vocational education and training but for the first time covering general education in the article that preceded it

> The Community shall contribute to the development of quality education by encouraging co-operation between Member States and, if necessary, by supporting and supplementing their action, while fully respecting the responsibility of the

Member States for the content of teaching and the organisation of education
systems and their cultural and linguistic diversity

(Article 126)

So in this general education field, Maastricht continued the rôle of the
European Communities in promoting and complementing co-operation
among member states, respecting their cultural autonomy, but now also not
just permitting but requiring such a contribution where necessary. This, however, did not go as far as Article 127, which for vocational training required
the EC to implement a supplementary and supportive policy.

The treaty was followed by the 'Delors White Paper' (European Commision,
1996) with much stronger emphasis on education and training at the heart of
policies for growth, employment and competitiveness. This led to a re-shaping
of overarching Socrates and Leonardo da Vinci programmes. Socrates inherited
and continued Lingua, Arion and ERASMUS, but added Comenius, a relatively
small but increasingly significant programme for school partnerships, as discussed in Chapter 4. Leonardo brought into a single framework and extended
the earlier vocational training programmes. Both moreover emphasized the
'European dimension' in education, not least of all the teaching of EU languages. The European dimension is an expression that had been used in the
Janne Report, and an attempt was made to secure agreement of what it meant
in a Council of Ministers resolution of 1988 and then in the 1993 'green paper'
(op. cit). The British responses were so few and the Department for Education
and Skills so apathetic that it sent them on to Brussels with no more than a
covering note. By contrast, other countries took the opportunity to provide
national frameworks for regional and local initiatives. The Europa-Schulen[15] in
several German *Länder* provide one such example, prompted by their federal
government.[16]

Mobility continued to be a watchword of post-Maastricht programmes, but
the priority which would develop even more strongly would be e-learning to
ensure that a knowledge-based economy commanded competences in information and communication technologies (ICT). Youth and adult education
were no longer to be seen as separate; all education and training activity would
be viewed as part of lifelong education. The White Paper of 1996 (op. cit), in the
European Year of Lifelong Learning, was issued jointly by the Commissioners
for Education and Employment. By 1997, the Education Council set out a common view for the future, in the Lisbon Accord, giving itself a stronger guid-
ing and co-ordinating rôle, with emphasis on agreed concrete objectives and

benchmarks in monitoring progress. Accordingly, in 2007, the Socrates and Leonardo programmes were merged into the present Lifelong Learning programme, with its four strands of COMENIUS (schools, including teacher-training) Leonardo (vocational), ERASMUS (higher) and GRUNDTVIG (adult education), with language learning and ICT seen as 'transversal' across all four, and Jean Monnet actions to continue to stimulate debate on European integration.

Each of the four strands is blessed with targets: by the end of the current programme extending to 2013, COMENIUS aims to have involved 3 million pupils, ERASMUS 3 million, Leonardo to have achieved 80,000 placements per year, and GRUNDTVIG more modestly to have supported 7,000 adults per year in mobility projects. These targets far exceed previous levels. The programmes are all now managed, together with TEMPUS and bilateral international partnerships – Media, Culture, Europe for Citizens, and Youth in Action – by an agency set up in 2006, the Executive Agency, that is, Education, Audiovisual and Culture Executive Agency (EACEA), jointly supervised by three EC commissions. It is fortunate for users that most programmes are channelled through or assisted by national bodies. Those that are not, such as TEMPUS, have become more unwieldy as their curtailed funding is stretched across more beneficiary countries.

What was all this co-operative and co-ordinating activity set to achieve? The Education Council at Lisbon and thereafter had asked for a reference framework of competences, and in 2006 the European Parliament and Education Council formulated a Reference Framework (EU, 2006) setting out eight key competences seen as essential for education in Europe:

- communication in the mother tongue
- communication in foreign languages
- mathematical competence and basic competences in science and technology
- digital competence
- learning to learn
- social and civic competences
- sense of initiative and entrepreneurship
- cultural awareness and expression

The key competences are all considered equally important, because each of them can contribute to a successful life in a knowledge-based society. Many of the competences overlap and interlock: aspects essential to one domain will support competence in another. Competence in the fundamental basic skills of language, literacy, numeracy and information and communication technologies (ICT) is an essential foundation for learning, and learning to learn supports all educational activities. There are a number of themes that are applied throughout the Reference Framework: critical thinking, creativity, initiative, problem solving, risk assessment, decision taking and the constructive management of feelings play a role in all eight key competences.

The 2007 European Commission paper 'Schools for the 21st Century', a public consultation paper, was the first from the EU to focus on compulsory education systems and institutions, acknowledging that whereas the European Union had previously concentrated on vocational education and training and on higher education, it is in schools that

> the majority of Europeans spend at least nine or ten years of their lives; here they gain the basic knowledge, skills and competences, and many of the fundamental norms, attitudes and values which will carry them through their lives. Complementing the key roles of parents, school can help individuals develop their talents and fulfil their potential for personal growth (both emotional and intellectual) and well-being. If it is to prepare them for a life in the modern world, school must set people on the path to a lifetime of learning. A sound school education also lays the foundations for an open and democratic society by training people in citizenship, solidarity and participative democracy. (p. 3)

It is noteworthy that the statement could emanate from the commission, inviting responses not only about co-operation at EU level but about needs to improve compulsory schooling within national contexts, in a framework of key questions relating to headings in the document. The EC benchmarks for 2020 are accompanied with annual monitoring reports, including tables for each country. It is why this book in turn focuses on schools for the future.

The Lisbon Treaty from 2009

Article 165 of the 2007 Lisbon Treaty confirms that EU action shall be aimed at developing the European dimension in education, particularly through the teaching and dissemination of the languages of the member states; encouraging mobility of students and teachers, by encouraging *inter alia* the academic recognition by all countries of diplomas and periods of study; promoting co-operation between educational establishments; developing exchanges of information and experience on issues common to the education systems of the member states; encouraging the development of youth exchanges, the exchanges of socio-educational instructors and the participation of young people in democratic life in Europe; encouraging the development of distance education and developing the European dimension in sport, by promoting fairness and openness in sporting competitions and co-operation between bodies responsible for sports. Importantly, it adds that the EU and the member states shall foster co-operation with third countries and the competent international organizations in the field of education and sport, in particular the Council of Europe. Article 167 requires that the EU contribute to the flowering of national and regional cultures and to bring the common cultural heritage to the fore, and should where necessary support action to improve knowledge and the dissemination of the culture and history of the European peoples.

On vocational training, the treaty confirms again in Article 166 that the EU shall implement a vocational training policy which shall support and supplement the action of the member states, while fully respecting their responsibility for the content and organization of vocational training. EU action should also aim to facilitate adaptation to industrial changes, in particular through vocational training and retraining; improve initial and continuing vocational training in order to facilitate vocational integration and reintegration into the labour market; facilitate access to vocational training and encourage mobility of instructors, trainees and particularly young people; stimulate co-operation on training practices between educational or training establishments and firms; and develop exchanges of information and experience on issues common to the training systems of the member states. Again it asserts that the EU and the member states shall foster co-operation with third countries and the competent international organizations in the sphere of vocational training.

This is largely a transfer of text from Maastricht, but more important is the demand for an open method of co-ordination (OMC) and the follow-up[17] inviting the commission to develop a coherent framework of indicators and benchmarks to harmonize with the objectives set by the Education Council for 2020. This will extend the involvement of researchers seeking commensurability and unfounded governmental illusions of progress through the dead hand of targets, competitive comparison, control and accountability.

Perhaps more significant to schools will be the treaty's adoption, after a half century, of the European Convention on Human Rights (despite the shameful options for Great Britain and Poland) and the articles on citizenship, discussed in Chapters 3 and 6. It is clear that citizenship is by direct representation in the European Parliament, without discrimination and with freedom of information, that citizens have equal rights of movement and employment in any member state, other than in its civil service. Equally important for schools will be the strengthening of the European Parliament's powers, for it is through the parliament that non-governmental concerns can best be raised and pursued. Moreover, the introduction of Citizen Initiatives brings an element of direct democracy.

So the EU has brought into binding treaties what the Council of Europe had instigated as informal conventions and charters. As Hugh Starkey shows in Chapter 3, the council continues to take a principled lead in education, with the non-binding adoption of declarations of good practice which take account of the increasing need to combat racism, intolerance and xenophobia. Its 2009 'White Paper' on Intercultural Dialogue was adopted by the Council of Europe's Foreign Ministers. The 2010 Charter on Education for Democratic Citizenship and Human Rights is strengthened by manuals for teachers.

Conclusion

The 2007 consultation and the Treaty of Lisbon together for the first time bring schools centre stage for the future of the European Union. Much sustained work has been going on, both centrally in the EU and the Council of Europe, and in and among nations for the purpose of distinguishing the lines and actions needed for a European conceptualization of education. It is unique in the world for so many individuals and countries to co-operate across borders to accomplish such aims. For the next 20 years, that heritage will depend on the active engagement of schools themselves, not just in or through the EU or through the wider and more direct support of the Council of Europe's accords and publications.

It will depend on such initiatives as currently being taken by ESHA, with 24 national associations of 86,000 school leaders, to create a managed learning community throughout Europe, creating from spring 2011 their Wiki community and web portal[18] to work on the common issues that school leaders have identified, and to disseminate input and information across schools and to policy makers, and to share their own experiences, not yet funded by the EU or any national government, a voluntary activity untouched by government regulations. Whatever the framework or the enabling agreements, the impetus remains with teachers, and Paddy Carpenter shows them taking advantage of the e-learning programmes. But British schools managing their own budgets, with diminishing local authority influence and with little more than rhetorical support for language learning, are finding increasing difficulty in promoting staff and pupil mobility, the other major thrust for schools in the COMENIUS programme. British school participation in language-related mobility projects is far lower for both staff and pupils than in any other large EU country[19], even taking account of non-COMENIUS bilateral activity.

How much of all this figures in current British teacher-training programmes or requirements in school curricula? Virtually nil. As Chapters 6 and 9 will show, the initial training of teachers has been enslaved to the extraordinarily insular national curriculum, and continues to be so assessed even though the national curriculum itself is in a state of constant confusion. It is doubly ironic that an English secretary of state for education, on presenting to parliament his intention to abolish the 'arm's length' national curriculum agency (QCDA), should have scoffed at its very mention of knowing about the European Union,[20] even though this was a minimal application and mere shadow of EU government agreements since 1988. In the latest deliberations on the 2011 Education Bill, whether in public debate or at committee stages, there has been not a single further mention of the European dimension, only of enforced school participation in OECD league tables. This insularity is equally apparent in the government response to the Wolf Report.[21] British governments have yet to fulfil their treaty obligations in relation to school curriculum and teacher training. Schools will not be able to wait for government provincialism in order to fulfil their obligations to the coming generation.

Notes

1   Address to Council of Europe opening assembly, 17 August 1949.

2   Subsidiarity is the idea that a central authority should have a subsidiary function, performing only those tasks which cannot be performed effectively at a more immediate or local level. The individual is the highest point. The concept has become wrongly limited to questions of national

sovereignty. See Jover, 2002, and *Protocol on the Application of the Principles of Subsidiarity and Proportionality*, Official Journal of the European Union 16.12.2004, C310/

3 Regulation (EU) No. 211/2011 of the European Parliament and of the council 16 February 2011 on the citizens' initiative, to start in 2012, requiring 1 million signatories from at least seven member states within 1 year, to invite the European Commission to bring forward proposals within its powers. Well, a start at least!

4 Opening address to the Peace Congress (Paris, 21 August 1849) The day will come when war will seem to you just as absurd between Paris and London, between Petersburg and Berlin. The day will come when you – France, Russia, Italy, England and Germany – will merge in unity and you will constitute European fraternity.

5 In a speech before the League of Nations in Geneva, 5 September 1929, Briand proposed the creation of a federation of European nations.

6 FIPESO: Fédération Internationale des Professeurs de l'Enseignement Secondaire Officiel [International Federation of Secondary Teachers].

7 The European Association of Teachers (Association Européenne des Enseignants), founded in Paris in 1956, an organization promoting understanding of EU issues among educators in all member states.

8 Intermediate school centres. These non-selective community schools were massive investments in Berlin (at 35 times the permitted building costs for English schools), now largely demolished because of asbestos.

9 Later extended as the European School Heads Association.

10 Before EC education and training action programmes began, the EC Bureau for Action in Favour of Disabled People could fund the 1983 Otzenhausen European Forum on Integration, the 1984 Oxford seminar on Teacher Training and Special Educational Needs, and production of the book with the same title (Sayer et al. (eds), 1985).

11 The Council of Europe had already set up as early as 1974 its NEIC information centres to help inform on transnational recognition of post-secondary educational and professional training qualifications. This was extended in 1979 by UNESCO, and eventually in 1994 the two merged to form so-called ENICs (European Network of National Information Centres on Academic Recognition and Mobility). Since 1999 they now share a website as ENIC-NARIC, prompted by a newly accessed EU member state, Estonia.

12 The website www.cafebabel.com, initiated in 2001, is now the multilingual European current affairs magazine of the 'Erasmus generation', networking across 32 centres, including cafebabel.co.uk.

13 ENIRDEM was created from a strand of the ESHA conference in Utrecht in 1991.

14. *Lidové Noviny*, the oldest Czech newspaper, founded in Brno 1893, suppressed in World War II and from 1952, reappeared clandestinely as a monthly newssheet in 1987 and 1988, reopened legally in November 1989, from 1990 a daily.

15 Not to be confused with the 14 European Schools directed by the ES Board of Governors under the aegis of the European Commission. *Europa-Schulen* are accredited by each of several *Landesministerien* (province government ministries).

16   Recommendation of the German Federal Conference of Ministers of Education on the European Dimension in Education, 8 November 1991.

17   Council Conclusions of 12 May 2009 on a strategic framework for European co-operation in education and training (ET 2020) [Official Journal C 119 of 28.5.2009].

18   See http://eshacommunity.wikispaces.com.

19   Latest figures available, from 2006. Annex 4. DG Educ & Culture, Socrates II programme, http://ec.europa.eu/education/lifelong-learning-policy/doc/report09/annexes_en.pdf.

20   While introducing the Education Bill 2011, recorded on BBC parliamentary programme archive 8 February, but discreetly removed from Hansard.

21   *Wolf Review of Vocational Education* 14–19: Government Response, May 2011. www.education.gov.uk/publications.

Europe, Human Rights and Education

3

Hugh Starkey

Introduction

This chapter examines and discusses European education policies and activities intended to promote understandings of citizenship, human rights and languages. The creation of a European economic community requires social and cultural policies that develop in the population understandings of the principles of democracy and fundamental freedoms that mitigate the inequalities inherent in capitalism. Schools and teachers, therefore, have a central role in helping to foster commitment to the foundational ideals and principles that underlay the creation and constitution of the Council of Europe in 1950 and the European Economic Community, predecessor to the European Union (EU), in 1957. The principles that underpin European co-operation and institutions are clearly articulated in the European Convention on Human Rights and Fundamental Freedoms (ECHR), itself explicitly derived from the Universal Declaration of Human Rights (UDHR). While these provide a vision of freedoms, justice and peace in Europe and the world, the realization of this project requires common understandings by citizens and residents as well as a capacity to communicate effectively in this multilingual community. Policies for education for democratic citizenship and human rights education (EDC and HRE, respectively) and for language learning are thus linked and offer a challenge to schools and teachers to play a central role in the development of a European consciousness and identity.

Education policy at the European level is developed by two major institutions. The Council of Europe, an intergovernmental organization of 47 member states in 2011, was founded with a view to furthering European unity in order to achieve a peaceful continent in a peaceful world. It consequently requires its member states to be fully democratic and protective of the human rights of all individuals living in Europe, whether citizens or not. These principles are also accepted by the 27 member states of the EU, all of which are also members of the Council of Europe. While the Council of Europe's mission prioritizes culture, including education and human rights law, the EU aims to develop as a major economic bloc. However, since member states acknowledge that education is essential to sound economic development, the EU also funds research and educational projects, increasingly working in collaboration with the Council of Europe.

Other aspects of the Council of Europe's work include education, cultural heritage, sport, youth, the media and local government (Coleman, 1999). Since 1983 there has been a particular emphasis on human rights education and education for democratic citizenship (Starkey, 1991; Osler et al., 1996, 2010). Another major strand of the education programme of the council has been the development of the teaching and learning of languages (Sheils, 1996; Byram et al., 2002). These educational programmes and initiatives aim to promote a culture of human rights as basic European values in order to safeguard fundamental freedoms.

Education for Democratic Citizenship and Human Rights Education

Through its education directorate, the Council of Europe has been particularly active in promoting human rights education since the 1980s. Political stability in Europe is considered to be founded on effective political democracy, which in turn requires a widespread understanding of the procedural principles essential for living together in the common European home. However in encouraging a European consciousness or sense of identity, there is a danger that education programmes encourage Eurocentric attitudes or feelings of cultural superiority. The policy response has been to propose a cosmopolitan perspective encouraging schools to help young Europeans see themselves 'not only as citizens of their own regions and countries, but also as citizens of Europe and the wider world' (Shennan, 1991, p. 229).

The Council of Europe thus stresses the role of education in developing an active commitment to human rights and the principles of pluralistic democracy. This logically extends to combating challenges to democratic values such as intolerance, xenophobia, anti-Semitism and racism. The secretariat, with the political support of the Committee of Ministers of Education, has initiated a succession of programmes intended to develop and disseminate good practice. The outcomes of the different phases of this work are published and disseminated in the form of policy recommendations and also accompanying materials that provide practical help, support and materials for teachers and school leaders. However, since education policy is devolved to national, regional and local levels, the recommendations can only be advisory.

One recommendation that exercised considerable influence was Recommendation R(85)7 of the Committee of Ministers of Education of the Council of Europe on 'teaching and learning about human rights in schools', which was adopted in 1985 (Council of Europe, 1985; Starkey, 1991). In their preamble the ministers reaffirm democratic values in the face of intolerance, acts of violence and terrorism; the re-emergence of the public expression of racist and xenophobic attitudes; and the disillusionment of many young people in Europe who are affected by the economic recession and aware of the continuing poverty and inequality in the world. The recommendation emphasizes that 'throughout their school career, all young people should learn about human rights'. It identifies certain skills they should acquire such as the identification of bias, prejudice, stereotypes and discrimination; recognizing and accepting differences; establishing positive and non-oppressive personal relationships and resolving conflict in a non-violent way.

Students, the recommendation suggests, should learn about 'the main categories of human rights, duties, obligations and responsibilities'. They should know about 'the various forms of injustice, inequality and discrimination, including sexism and racism'. As a result, 'the study of human rights in schools should lead to an understanding of, and sympathy for, the concepts of justice, equality, freedom, peace, dignity, rights and democracy. Such understanding should be both cognitive and based on experience and feelings'.

As well as defining the attitudes, skills and knowledge associated with human rights education, the recommendation has a section on school climate. It is not sufficient for individual teachers to be committed to promoting human rights, but there are implications for the whole school. The argument is that learning democracy cannot be dissociated from learning in a democratic setting. While schools are not fully operational democratic institutions, they can be places where democracy is a key value and where freedom of expression is encouraged and opportunities for participation provided.

The 1985 recommendation provided the impetus for extensive development work in human rights education, focusing initially on newly democratizing Greece, Portugal and Spain, subsequently central and eastern Europe and then the Balkan region. By the late 1990s the emphasis evolved to include citizenship education (Council of Europe, 1999) and a new phase of the programme began at the turn of the century (Birzea, 2003, 2004; Council of Europe, 2000, 2002, 2005). The conclusions and recommendations demonstrating the close relationship between EDC and HRE were published in the form of a Charter on Education for Democratic Citizenship and Human Rights Education (Council of Europe, 2010). The charter defines education for democratic citizenship as:

> education, training, awareness-raising, information and activities to equip learners with knowledge, skills and understanding as well as the development of attitudes and behaviour, to empower learners to exercise and defend their democratic rights and responsibilities in society, to value diversity and to play an active part in democratic life, with a view to the promotion and protection of democracy and the rule of law (p. 7).

Human rights education covers parallel educational processes which similarly empower learners to 'contribute to the building and defence of a universal culture of human rights in society, with a view to the promotion and protection of human rights and fundamental freedoms' (p. 7). According to the charter, EDC and HRE are understood to be inter-related and mutually supportive, differing in focus and scope rather than in goals and practices.

Importantly, EDC and HRE are seen as a lifelong entitlement for all people living within the jurisdiction of member states and as a responsibility in which a range of stakeholders are involved, including policy makers, learners, parents, education professionals, youth organizations and the media. Recognition and respect for diversity is seen as being at the heart of EDC and HRE. The charter identifies an essential element of such education as: the valuing of diversity; the promotion of societal cohesion; the development of skills for intercultural dialogue and the promotion of skills to reduce conflict, enabling learners to cross cultural and faith boundaries and respect human dignity.

The charter highlights pedagogy, emphasizing the need for democratic learning practices among the young and in the training of teachers and other professional groups. It acknowledges that democratic principles and human rights need to be taught in a democratic way. Significantly, the charter recognizes that learners need to be empowered to take action in society in the defence and promotion of human rights, democracy and the rule of law.

While recommendations, including the charter, define and promote EDC and HRE, the declaration of policy does not necessarily result in its enactment (Maguire et al., 2010). Certainly, governments sometimes make significant efforts to ensure the dissemination of recommendations. The French minister of education circulated the 1985 recommendation to all schools with his own accompanying letter of warm endorsement. However, enactment of these policies also depends on the actions of NGOs, teacher unions and networks of activists as well as regional and local authorities (Osler et al., 2010).

Language learning and inter-cultural education

A clear example of the complementarity of the education policies of the Council of Europe and the EU is the extent to which EU funding has enabled teachers, academics and non-governmental organisations (NGOs) to develop materials and projects to promote EDC and HRE, particularly in the context of teacher education (Osler et al., 1995; Osler et al., 1996, 1999; Holden et al., 1998; Roland-Lévy et al., 2002; Ross, 2008). EU funding for research and curriculum development projects through its COMENIUS, ERASMUS and GRUNTVIG programmes has often prioritized proposals addressing issues of living together in diversity, including antiracism (Osler et al., 2002; Starkey et al., 2009). Interestingly, but perhaps not entirely surprisingly, the need for a high level of communication skills in a multilingual environment has meant that language teachers have been disproportionately represented in such projects. This has made possible the development of practical approaches to forms of language teaching and learning that complement EDC and HRE. Studies commissioned and published by the Council of Europe have developed a rationale and theoretical framework within which grassroots initiatives can flourish.

An instrumental case for the role of language teaching as an important site of learning for democratic citizenship is that even where citizenship education is a formal curriculum requirement, the relatively small amount of time allotted and the prestige of more traditional, examined disciplines tends to minimize its impact. A study for the Council of Europe concluded that:

> [l]anguage teaching, on the other hand, requires and is given substantial curriculum time and benefits from the prestige of an established university discipline. Moreover, the content of language teaching has for long been flexible, including literature, cultural awareness, media studies and debates of topical issues. (Starkey, 2002, p. 15)

The study goes on to analyze the reciprocal relationship of EDC and languages. For example, when citizenship topics, such as questions of peace, gender relations, racism, and social and cultural movements, are included in the curriculum for languages, motivation for many students is likely to increase. It goes on to suggest that 'the pedagogy associated with language learning since the development of communicative methods is in itself democratic' (p. 17). The skills developed in language classes are directly transferable to citizenship education. In the communicative language classroom, learners are often required to speak and discuss in pairs and groups, having the freedom to express their own opinions and develop ideas and new ways of thinking. They can develop the skill of listening to others and, with encouragement, skills of critical engagement with ideas.

The cultural and intercultural dimensions of language learning also complement EDC and HRE. The importance of this dimension is stressed in a recommendation on modern languages (Council of Europe, 1998) which stresses 'the particular importance of the intercultural component in creating awareness of and respect for cultural differences'. This approach has been characterized as critical cultural awareness (Byram, 1997) and requires the ability to evaluate critically and on the basis of explicit criteria perspectives, practices and products in one's own and other cultures and countries. Human rights principles constitute appropriate criteria for making such judgements.

Examples of inter-cultural skills to be developed include identifying and interpreting explicit or implicit values in documents and events in one's own and other cultures. This may require using a range of analytical approaches to ensure contextual and ideological dimension factors are considered. Students thus learn to interact and mediate in intercultural exchanges, being aware of potential conflict between their own and other ideological positions and attempting to find common criteria or negotiate agreement on the acceptance of difference.

It can be argued that language teaching in Europe, particularly at the school level, has been heavily influenced by considerations of how to communicate, often at the expense of what to communicate about or for. However, citizens in a democracy need intercultural skills for living in communities where cultural diversity is the norm. They need critical cultural awareness to understand the world around them and challenge injustice, complacency, social exclusion and unwarranted discrimination. The construction of a peaceful, democratic and multicultural Europe requires multilingual citizens.

Imagining a peaceful Europe

The chapter now traces some of the origins of European principles and shows how they have been applied to policy as both intergovernmental organizations have expanded and developed. Given that European ideals inform strategic development at intergovernmental and member state levels and that they consequently influence regional and local policies, education is a key means for enabling citizens to understand the rationale for the existence of the Council of Europe and EU. Knowledge of the foundational principles can also act as a standard against which to judge policy. These founding principles are claimed in the Statute of the Council of Europe to be the 'common heritage of their peoples' which would arguably constitute a defining feature of European identity. This chapter now traces the origin and development of this conception of what it means to be European and demonstrates some of its manifestations in education policy. It argues that education has the capacity both to promote understanding of European institutions and to enable citizens to critique their actions.

At the height of World War II (1939–45), far-sighted leaders and political activists from a number of countries made intense efforts to ensure that the outcome of the war would be the establishment of strong international institutions capable of promoting and preserving peace. At a global level, Great Britain and the United States signed the Atlantic Charter in August 1941 and 26 states signed the Declaration by United Nations in Washington, DC, in

January 1942. The charter and declaration consisted of eight common principles to define a world order worth fighting for. These included the right of all peoples to choose the form of government under which they live (democracy) and proposed the goal of people living in freedom from fear and want. The declaration also specifically included the preservation of human rights and justice as a war aim, introducing the key concept of human rights to international diplomatic discourse (Borgwardt, 2005).

In 1945 representatives of 50 states met in San Francisco to draw up the Charter of the United Nations which came into force in October that year (United Nations, 1945). The UN Charter sets out mechanisms and organisational arrangements based on the equality within UNO of 'nations large and small'. This is represented and symbolized in the UN General Assembly, a periodic meeting to which all members are invited to send delegates. Underpinning this apparatus is a set of beliefs including, specifically 'faith in fundamental human rights, in the dignity and worth of the human person, in the equal rights of men and women'.

In Europe, the failure of the well-intentioned League of Nations to prevent a second war between European states gave impetus to the creation of continental as well as world institutions. By the early 1940s movements of resistance to fascism and Nazism, elaborating their post-war strategies, were actively promoting the idea of European unification. One of the most influential documents in circulation was the Manifesto of Ventotene, named after the prison camp on the island of Ventotene where the anti-fascist resister Altiero Spinelli drafted *Towards a Free and United Europe* from 1941 to 1942 (Surhone et al. 2010). This text became the founding document of the Italian Movement for European Federation, one of a number of similar movements in Europe at this time. The manifesto is informed by Enlightenment principles as developed by Immanuel Kant, recognizing the essential equality of all human beings and their entitlement to be considered as subjects with agency and never as objects to be used by others. It is this intellectual inheritance that, as John Dewey ([1916], 2002) observed, had become stifled in Europe by the mid-nineteenth century when nationalism became the dominant ideology. The preparations for a post-war Europe sought to re-connect with traditions of democracy, humanism and cosmopolitanism (Starkey, 2003).

The vision of a peaceful and united Europe was strongly promoted by conservative British prime minister Winston Churchill. In a wartime broadcast in 1943, he proposed a regional Council of Europe to complement the United Nations. Even when out of power in 1946, Churchill, still leader of the opposition in the British parliament, continued to argue for the creation of a United States of Europe. He delivered major speeches in The Hague in May 1946 and in Zurich in September 1946 in which he argued for a regional structure, the Council of Europe, as a contribution to strengthening the United Nations (Canadine, 1990). In December 1947 Churchill convened an International Committee of the Movements for European Unity, which organized the Congress of Europe in The Hague (Netherlands). This met for 3 days in May 1948 with Churchill as honorary president. Six hundred sixty-three delegates from 16 European states attended, along with observers from other European states and from the United States and British Commonwealth. The main work of the congress was conducted in three committees: political; economic and social; and cultural. Each committee produced a resolution, and each was adopted unanimously in plenary session, along with a Message for Europeans, which summarized the main policies that resulted (Congress of Europe, 1949).

The Resolution of the Political Committee of the Hague Congress unequivocally recommended the pooling of sovereignty and proposed a union of member states open to democratically governed European nations which undertake to respect a Charter of Human Rights. The Cultural Committee argued that there is a European culture that overrides the all too apparent national, ideological and religious differences. This culture is defined as based on both a common heritage of 'Christian and other spiritual and cultural values' and a 'common loyalty to the fundamental rights of man, especially freedom of thought and expression'. Although Christianity is singled out, the defining common heritage includes other spiritual and cultural values. Thus traditions including humanism, Judaism, Hinduism and Islam, while not mentioned specifically, are not excluded from this definition of European culture.

The second dimension of a European common culture is defined as a 'common loyalty' to principles codified in the late eighteenth century as 'the rights of man' (sic). In this resolution the emphasis is on those rights that are essential for cultural expression, namely: 'freedom of thought and expression'. These are expressed in articles 10 and 11 of the French *Declaration of the Rights of Man and Citizen* (1789) as follows:

10. No one is to be disquieted because of his opinions, even religious, provided their manifestation does not disturb the public order established by law.
11. Free communication of ideas and opinions is one of the most precious of the rights of man. Consequently every citizen may speak, write and print freely,

subject to responsibility for the abuse of such liberty in cases determined by law
(Laqueur et al., 1979, p. 119).

This formulation went much further than the English Bill of Rights of 1689,
which merely guaranteed freedom of speech in parliament. It was included
in successive constitutions of the French republics. However, this encoding
of rights was restricted to national laws and constitutions until 10 December
1948, when the Universal Declaration of Human Rights was proclaimed by
the United Nations (United Nations General Assembly, 1948). This was the
first international declaration defining human rights, providing the basis for
future conventions and other more legally binding instruments.

The Cultural Committee of the Congress of Europe made a confident
statement about common European values without necessarily being able to
justify it fully. That said, its aspiration to present the achievement of intellectual, religious and cultural freedoms as a common European heritage quickly
found mass public support in Europe and is demonstrably in the spirit of
the European Enlightenment. For European culture to flourish, fundamental
freedoms, which had been absent from parts of Europe during the 1920s and
1930s and from virtually all of Europe during the war, had to be protected.
Hence the emphasis at The Hague was on a charter to codify human rights
and a supreme court to uphold them.

In drawing up its resolution, the Economic and Social Committee proposed the creation of a humane economy, one that is 'reconciled with the
integrity of human personality'. In other words, the economy should support
'better conditions of life, both material and cultural' rather than be an end
in itself. Freedom is an objective of the economy, but this is not the freedom
of unfettered economic development. Rather it is freedom as applied to individuals and groups aimed at producing 'a harmonious society in Europe'.
Such a Europe will be a model, seen 'as a constructive element and a force for
peace'. To achieve this harmonious society requires 'free association of individuals and groups', including cultural groups, political parties and trade
unions. Individuals should be given the opportunity 'to develop in freedom
and concord a full and balanced personality'. This implies that individuals
are not just workers, but that they have opportunities for rest, leisure and
cultural activities. Certain categories will require special consideration, as
expressed by guarantees of 'the protection of the weak and infirm'.

The first of the post-war European institutions, the Committee for European
Economic Co-operation (CEEC), had been created in Paris in July 1947.

Following the ratification by the U.S. Congress of the Marshall Plan, in April 1948, the CEEC became the Organisation for European Economic Co-operation (OEEC, precursor to the current Organisation for Economic Co-operation and Development OECD). The mission of the OEEC was to co-ordinate the application of Marshall Aid and was therefore strongly influenced, if not entirely dominated, by the United States. The resolutions of the Hague Congress can be seen as an attempt to offer Europe an alternative vision to that proposed by the Americans, namely an insistence on political, economic and cultural rights as the basis for the reconstruction and development of Europe.

The late 1940s was, for Europe, a time of intense diplomatic activity resulting in the establishment of a powerful body of international law. Belgium, France, Luxembourg, Netherlands and Great Britain signed the Treaty of Brussels (17 March 1948) titled the Treaty of Economic, Social and Cultural Collaboration and Collective Self-Defence. In the Treaty, the heads of state resolved:

- to reaffirm their faith in fundamental human rights, in the dignity and worth of the human person and in the other ideals proclaimed in the Charter of the United Nations
- to fortify and preserve the principles of democracy, personal freedom and political liberty, the constitutional traditions and the rule of law, which are their common heritage

The reference to 'common heritage' is another example of a group of European states defining a collective identity, built on human rights, democracy and the rule of law.

Article 3 of the Brussels Treaty was cited in the Cultural Resolution of the Congress of Europe. It committed contracting parties to 'make every effort in common to lead their peoples towards a better understanding of the principles which form the basis of their common civilisation'. While this may appear to admit that the leadership in Europe is possibly running ahead of public opinion, it clearly mandates public education about human rights, democracy and the rule of law.

The conclusions of the Congress of Europe were summarized in a final Message to Europeans which pulled together the main recommendations of the three committees. It contains five pledges, the first calling for a 'United Europe' and the last promising support for this aim. The other three pledges are about an institutional structure on which European unity can be built, namely a Charter of Human Rights, a Court of Justice and a European Assembly.

The message contains a further assertion both of European identity and of the potential of this as a contribution to the wider international community:

> Human dignity is Europe's finest achievement, freedom her true strength. Both are at stake in our struggle. The union of our continent is now needed not only for the salvation of the liberties we have won, but also for the extension of their benefits to all mankind.

This understanding and belief informed the founding of the Council of Europe.

The founding of the Council of Europe (5 May 1949)

The resolutions of the Congress of Europe at The Hague were developed by the European Movement, an unofficial body set up to maintain the momentum of the congress. The European Movement formally presented its proposals to the five member states of the Brussels Treaty Organization: Belgium, France, Luxembourg, Netherlands and Great Britain. In March 1949 a further five nations (Denmark, Ireland, Italy, Norway and Sweden) were invited to join the Brussels Treaty Organization with a view to preparing a formal constitution for a body to give institutional weight to European unity.

These ten founding member states met at St James's Palace in London on 5 May 1949, to formally establish the Council of Europe. The Statute of the Council of Europe is thus also known as the Treaty of London (1949). The founding members were joined by Greece and Turkey in August and Iceland and the Federal Republic of Germany the following year (1950). The founding member states agreed that the headquarters of the Council of Europe would be the frontier city of Strasbourg, on the Rhine, symbolizing reconciliation. The first meeting of the assembly was held in the Great Hall of the University of Strasbourg on 10 August 1949. By 4 November 1950, the European Convention on Human Rights and Fundamental Freedoms was ready for signature by the 14 member states meeting in Rome. The assembly (which became the Parliamentary Assembly) and the European Convention on Human Rights are still two pillars of the Council of Europe.

The founding constitution of the Council of Europe, the Statute, commits its members to respecting 'the spiritual and moral values which are the common heritage of their peoples and the true source of individual freedom, political liberty and the rule of law, principles which form the basis of all genuine democracy'. Again the authority of tradition is invoked in an attempt to define a collective commitment to democracy based on shared values and principles as the means to achieving peace with justice. The vision is largely that of the Enlightenment and what Klug (2000, p. 71) calls 'First-Wave Rights' whose defining feature is liberty from state tyranny and religious persecution. There is little in the preamble to prioritize social and economic rights in addition to these political rights. A broader view of rights may, however, be discerned in the proposition that economic and social progress is a goal also to be pursued through the proposed closer association of European states.

The remit of the Council of Europe, defined in its Statute, is on the one hand, 'economic, social, cultural, scientific, legal and administrative matters' and on the other hand, 'the maintenance and further realisation of human rights and fundamental freedoms'. Thus the scope of the council is broad but does not include defence, which had been the subject of the Treaty of Washington, signed in April 1949, creating the North Atlantic Treaty Organisation (NATO). The Statute makes specific reference to the United Nations emphasizing the key role of the European organization within the UN and in support of the UN's Charter and aims, as Churchill had proposed in his 1946 Zurich speech.

The ten founding members had grown to 18 by 1970. In order of accession, Greece (August 1949), Iceland (March 1950), Turkey (April 1950) and Germany (July 1950) joined as the institutions were still being created. There was then a gap and Austria (April 1956), Cyprus (May 1961), Switzerland (May 1963) and Malta (April 1965) formed the next wave. In 1967 a putsch in Greece brought to power an undemocratic military regime and the other member states decided to act under Article 8 and expel Greece, but the colonels' regime had anticipated the decision and withdrew. Greece re-joined in November 1974 after the restoration of democracy. However in the summer of 1974 the intervention of Turkish forces in Cyprus led to the partitioning of the island, at a time when Greece was suspended and the Council of Europe was unable to have an impact on the situation.

Around this time, first Portugal and then Spain emerged from long periods of dictatorship and joined the Council of Europe in September 1976 and November 1977, respectively. This illustrates the specificity of the Council of Europe as a democratic and cultural organization. Portugal was able to be a founding member of NATO, for example, in spite of being a dictatorship. The only other occasion on which Article 8 has been invoked was in 1981, when the Turkish delegation to the Parliamentary Assembly was refused the right to take its seats. Turkey was re-admitted following free elections in 1984.

The fall of the Berlin Wall in 1989 and the dismantling of the Soviet Union led the way to a doubling in size of the Council of Europe in the 1990s, following the accession of Finland in 1989. Formal admission to the Council of Europe on the signing of the European Convention on Human Rights has been granted as follows: Hungary (1990), Poland (1991), Bulgaria (1992), Czech Republic, Estonia, Lithuania, Romania, Slovakia and Slovenia (1993), Albania, Latvia, Moldova, FYR Macedonia and Ukraine (1995) Croatia and Russia (1996), Georgia (1999), Armenia and Azerbaijan (2001) Bosnia Herzegovina (2002), Serbia (2003), Monaco (2004) and Montenegro (2007).

European Convention on Human Rights and Fundamental Freedoms (4 November 1950)

The European Convention on Human Rights and Fundamental Freedoms (ECHR) is a powerful treaty, binding on its signatories (Council of Europe, 1950). It sets out to provide strong protection for all the inhabitants of member states, whether or not they have formal citizenship. The preamble re-affirms the claim that there is an essentially European identity based on a 'common heritage of political traditions, ideals, freedom and the rule of law'. European countries, including the early signatory Turkey, are said to be 'like-minded', a phrase also used in the Statute.

The ECHR develops previous concepts of European identity by asserting that it is founded on a commitment to human rights. The preamble begins with a reference to the Universal Declaration of Human Rights (UDHR) and affirms that the ECHR is intended to be the first step 'for the collective enforcement of certain of the rights stated in the Universal Declaration'. European human rights are thus also universal human rights, but, in 1950, the governments of member states were not prepared to commit themselves to a legally binding obligation to all the rights in the UDHR. In particular, they were wary of collectively guaranteeing rights to health and social security, preferring to reserve such commitments for national legislation which allowed them to discriminate between nationals and others in the provision of welfare benefits.

The ECHR guarantees, through Article 14, that the enjoyment of rights is equally available. It specifically outlaws discrimination on the grounds of 'race, colour, language, religion'. In summary the rights covered by the convention are first personal rights, particularly the right to life, liberty and security of person, including the enjoyment of family life, possessions and privacy in the home and in correspondence, the right to a fair trial and the right to education. Secondly, the ECHR guarantees fundamental freedoms, particularly: freedom of thought conscience and religion, freedom of expression (including for the press) and freedom of peaceful assembly and association including the right to form trade unions. Finally, the ECHR prohibits governments of member states from resorting to torture and inhuman or degrading treatment, including slavery and forced labour, and bans retroactive criminal legislation, the death penalty, the expulsion or refusal of entry to nationals and the collective expulsion of aliens.

As proclaimed in the preamble, the aim of the ECHR is the promotion of peace and justice in the world. The collective belief is that this will be protected by, on the one hand, 'effective political democracy' and, on the other, by a 'common understanding and observance of the human rights upon which they depend'. An explicit statement of European human rights is in itself a requirement for a common understanding. A further implication of 'common understanding' is that there should be public education, in and out of school, about the rights and fundamental freedoms provided and protected by the ECHR.

The Council of Europe and the European Economic Community and its successors

The promotion and protection of human rights in Europe is one major function of the Council of Europe. The institutional mechanism for this is the European Court of Human Rights, based in Strasbourg. This is a busy and effective court since member state governments are bound to implement its judgements.

The institutions aimed at promoting the economic development of Europe developed in parallel to the cultural work of the Council of Europe. In 1951, Belgium, France, Italy, Luxembourg, the Netherlands and the Federal Republic of Germany signed the Treaty of Paris which established the European Coal and Steel Community. This led directly to the European Economic Community founded by the Treaty of Rome in 1957. Although all member states of the ECSC and the EEC were also signatories of the ECHR, it was not until 1986 that the European Community explicitly acknowledged that its unity and identity is also based on human rights. The Single European Act (1986) signed by 12 member states makes specific reference to the European Convention on Human Rights in its preamble. The subsequent Treaty of European Union signed at Maastricht in 1992 states in the preamble that member states confirm an 'attachment to the principles of liberty, democracy and respect for human rights and fundamental freedoms and of the rule of law'. The subsequent Treaty establishing the European Communities (TEC) contains several references to the Council of Europe, notably Article 149 on co-operation in education, Article 151 on co-operation in cultural matters and Article 303 on general overall co-operation (European Communities, 1997).

The fact remains, however, that the EU has no human rights instrument of its own and since it is not itself a sovereign state it cannot be a state party to the European Convention on Human Rights. Another difficulty is that the Treaties of the European Communities have no provision for the EU as a body to sign international treaties or conventions. The EU is, nonetheless, profoundly concerned with promoting human rights and a number of policy initiatives and regulations to strengthen, in particular, the struggle against discrimination on grounds of sex, race and disability. The European Parliament (not to be confused with the Parliamentary Assembly of the Council of Europe) adopted its own Declaration of Fundamental Rights and Freedoms on 12 April 1989. This consists of 28 articles laying down the basic principles of a common legal tradition based on respect for human dignity and fundamental rights (Duparc, 1993). A convention of representatives of the European Communities, including members of the European Parliament also drafted a Charter of Fundamental Rights of the European Union, which is intended to reaffirm those rights already found in EU provisions. Under the 2007 Treaty of Lisbon this became legally binding for member states. It is another instrument intended to reinforce the perception and the self-perception of a European culture defined as being founded on a commitment to human rights. The preamble to the charter states:

> The peoples of Europe, in creating an ever closer union among them, are resolved to share a peaceful future based on common values. . . .
>
> Conscious of its spiritual and moral heritage, the Union is founded on the indivisible, universal values of human dignity, freedom, equality and solidarity; it is based on the principles of democracy and the rule of law. It places the individual at the heart of its activities, by establishing the citizenship of the Union and by creating an area of freedom, security and justice.

The development of European institutions from the 1940s onward, while having a highly significant economic dimension, building prosperity and promoting higher standards of living, has also been founded on the creation of what is essentially a useful myth of European values. By definition a community based on fundamental freedoms accepts diversity, including the freedoms to create political parties or disseminate religious doctrines that fail to accept the equal rights of others. By ensuring that commitments to human rights are prominent in the major treaties, instruments and institutions of Europe, the European establishment promotes a sense of European identity that is more homogeneous than it may appear to residents on the ground. Given the continued dissonance between rhetoric and reality, the role of education is crucial in helping European residents to understand the principles on which Europe is founded and to create societies in which these principles are in fact the basis for living together.

Conclusion

By adopting a cultural rather than an economic approach to European unity the Council of Europe is a less politically contentious international organization than is the EU. Nonetheless the moral authority of the Council of Europe is strong and, since 1949, it has promoted the development of a European culture of human rights which it has defined as forming part of European heritage. The widening of the definition of Europe to include all 47 member states makes sense essentially because the claim to cultural unity is sustainable. For this reason, the Council of Europe's programmes of education, youth work and cultural heritage can be seen as contributing to the democratization of the continent and to peace and stability. At the educational forefront of this cultural development of peoples who are learning to live together (Delors, 1996) are teachers of EDC, HRE and of languages. Attacks on European institutions by populist nationalist politicians, whose essentially xenophobic pronouncements may get wide media coverage, tend to undermine what was established precisely to avoid the disastrous effects of ultra-nationalism. An understanding of something of this historical background, as well as of the principles that have broadly kept the peace in Europe and allow personal and cultural flourishing, will serve teachers well as they inevitably encounter prejudice and intolerance among their students and even their colleagues. The development of a European home that is truly respecting of human rights is a long-term project that can never be fully accomplished. What is certain is that teachers and schools are at the centre of this inspiring programme.

School Links Across National Cultures: a personal experience of Europe in the school curriculum

4

Paddy Carpenter

Chapter Outline

Island mentality . . .

The seas that surround us have provided more than just a moat around our castle home and an anti-invasion ditch against potential enemies. They have also built into the genes of our island race a view of ourselves and a self-sufficiency which our foreign neighbours have sometimes described as smug or even arrogant. Although originally intended as a compliment, the 'splendid isolation' of Great Britain, whether by choice at the end of the nineteenth century or by dint of circumstance in 1940, has served us less well in recent times. Our misreading of what our neighbours were up to in the 1950s, resulting in the creation of the European Economic Community, led to the humiliation of having our suit turned down on two separate occasions when we applied for membership[1] and was not a felicitous start to our post-war relationship with the rest of Europe. And in spite of various prime ministers declaring that they wanted Great Britain to play a central rôle in Europe (yes, even Mrs Thatcher, although in her case not quite the Europe foreseen by its founding fathers), we have often been seen by the others, not always without reason, as the least willing and least 'European' of all its member states.

More than a quarter of a century has passed since we joined the then European Economic Community in 1973, and our leaders are still divided as to whether it was a good idea. One political party and, no doubt, a number of back benchers from other parties would like us to pull out entirely. So it is not surprising if the ordinary citizen is ambivalent about our membership and still refers to 'going to Europe' and the 'Europeans and us', and where at least two of our national newspapers cannot resist poking fun at whatever comes out of Brussels, especially if it looks like a straight banana or has a French accent.

The phenomenon is not unknown in other member states where a sense of European citizenship to match national or regional loyalties is still a long way off. Creating a common market or economic community is a much easier business than creating what President Mitterrand called at the summit in Fontainebleau in 1985 '*l'Europe des citoyens*', a people's Europe, dropping the word 'economic'. Administrative changes can be brought about in a relatively short time, but changing the hearts and minds of people, with their inherited sense of identity, can take generations.

. . . and a world language

If our seas have helped to shape our character and our attitudes, the more recent use of our language as a world language has distorted yet further our view of ourselves and how (and in what language) we should relate to other cultures.

English has become the de facto world language. More people are now learning English in China than live in the United States and, according to statistics provided at the Frankfurt Book Fair, some 64 per cent of the published translations in the world are now from English into other languages, with under 3 per cent from other languages into English. A number of parents in South Korea, which spends approximately $3 billion a year on English tuition, have reportedly taken this to the extreme by submitting their children under 5 to an operation on their tongues to make them more flexible and 'better able to pronounce such notorious English tongue teasers as rice without it sounding like lice'.

Things have not gone quite so far in Europe, but most EU member states no longer look upon English as an optional language in schools but as an obligatory core subject, along with maths and the national language. English, in fact, is no longer looked upon as a foreign language. In higher education, countries such as the Netherlands, the Scandinavian nations and Germany have promoted a deliberate policy of internationalization and offer degree courses entirely in English.

For us on these islands, the phenomenon is a mixed blessing, a poisoned chalice. On the one hand, the increasing global importance of English has given certain clear advantages to native-speaking countries such as Great Britain and Ireland. For some years now, the world's need for English has been an enormous source of revenue for Great Britain and increasingly for the Republic of Ireland. It has been called the 'cultural North Sea oil' and there are few signs that the oil is drying up. The effect that the newly acquired economic strength of China, India and Brazil will have on the pattern of language use in the world is still to be determined and for the moment their entry into world markets seems to have strengthened the need for English as the language of communication[2].

Until recently, the native speaker of English has had privileged access to a number of employment possibilities, and the relative ease we have in communicating throughout the world using our own language, whether it be to order a beer or to intervene at an international conference, gives us the impression of being at home and, for some, a feeling of superiority over those whose languages are less widely spoken. But the linguistic researcher David Graddol predicts that 'monolingual speakers of any variety of English – American or British – will experience increasing difficulty in employment and political life, and are likely to become bewildered by many aspects of society and culture around them'.[3]

On the other hand, this feeling of being at home has meant that we only learn about the non-English speaking world through translation (or not at all), and it is not without significance that the so-called coalition of the willing in Iraq was almost entirely English speaking. At a different level, our lack of motivation to learn other languages has bedevilled our attempts to operate effective language teaching strategies. In any survey carried out by the EU on language proficiency[4], Great Britain ranks at the bottom of the league table, with Ireland as runner-up for the wooden spoon, the only two English-speaking members of the union. The number of students studying A-level French in Great Britain has dropped by two-thirds over the past 10 years and the latest EU survey reveals that only one out of three Britons is able to speak a language other than English. The oft-quoted assessment by the late lamented Professor Eric Hawkins still holds true that teaching foreign languages in an Anglophone country, such as Great Britain, is like 'gardening in a gale' (Hawkins, 1981). This has a debilitating impact on the culture of our country and the attitudes of its people toward the rest of the world community.

Not surprisingly, our crisis in language teaching has an impact on the supply of native English speakers with competence in foreign languages in a number of specialist professions. The EU interpreting and translation service can no longer find sufficient British or Irish candidates to fill available (and lucrative) posts, and the work is now being done by recruits from other EU member states which produce competent (but not native) English speakers. The latest profession calling out for more linguists is our own secret service which cannot fill its vacancies at Government Communications Headquarters (GCHQ) in Cheltenham without launching a promotion campaign throughout the country – not that I can remember James Bond ever using a word in a foreign language!

Are we alone in having problems?

We are not of course unique in having problems to solve connected to attitudes and complexes inherited from history and geography and all the other influences on national character. To take a significant example, France, the country where I live, retains attitudes toward language learning, based on the historical importance of French as the language of diplomacy, spoken by most of the crowned heads of Europe and until recently the lingua franca of most Latin countries and a number of nations in central and eastern Europe.

The creation of l'Organisation Internationale de la Francophonie in 1970 was an attempt to maintain respect for a language which had been such an effective vehicle for so many advances in Western culture.

Like us, the French have an idea about themselves based on their imperial past and tend to punch above their weight. Unlike us, they are extremely protectionist about their language and culture. Where Europe is concerned, as a founding father, their concept of Europe is the one we have at the moment and understandably therefore their attitudes toward it are not as hostile as ours sometimes are. In fact when their concept of Europe is 'threatened' through enlargement, they give a resounding '*Non!*' as they did twice to the British in the 1960s and as they are currently saying to the Turks.

France also has an education system which, because of its very highly centralized, top-down character, finds it difficult to react swiftly to change. I once heard Education Nationale described as the world's third-largest employer after General Motors and the Red Army, which, with the demise or down-sizing of the latter two, makes it now the world's number-one employer and a '*mammouth à dégraisser*' ('mammoth to be scoured'), to quote Claude Allègre, a French minister of education. Our education system, on the other hand, seems to have the opposite problem and is constantly moving the furniture.

What are the implications of these challenges for schools?

We did not wait for the EU to cope with some of these challenges. British schools have a fine record of initiatives devised to raise an awareness of the outside world among their pupils. Great Britain helped to pioneer school links and exchanges, and the government showed its commitment by setting up and financing the Central Bureau for Educational Visits and Exchanges in 1957. Mrs Thatcher, when secretary of state for education in the 1970s, called it the world's leading organization for international education. Now part of the British Council, its work continues in helping schools to set up contacts with the rest of the world. Look at their website; it really is your oyster![5]

In the days before the European programmes and their budgets existed, schools had to use their own resources to create links and set up a programme of activities for pupils and teachers. And they did, or many of them did, particularly in France, Great Britain and Germany. Links were created between schools dating back to the 1960s and in some cases much earlier within the framework of a town twinning which had taken on a new lease of life after World War II. The three countries each had an agency which acted as a clearing house and the Central Bureau, working with colleagues in the Pädagogischer Austauschdienst in Bonn and the international section of the ministry of education in Paris, registered hundreds of links of this kind and published ways of using the link imaginatively.

The links were usually bilateral, focusing principally on the foreign language needs of the school. In all three countries mentioned (known as 'the golden triangle'), English, French and German were taught in schools and so the arrangement was suitably reciprocal. The cooperation between the ministry agencies in the three countries encouraged initiatives to be taken, creating opportunities for others in the school service, such as headteachers and administrators, to learn from opposite numbers abroad. An initiative setting up links between local authorities and similar authorities abroad goes back to the 1970s when, for example, the education authorities in Leicestershire signed a protocol with the Seine-Maritime in France and the Saar in the former Federal Republic of Germany and Hertfordshire set up a similar triangular relationship with the Académie de Dijon and Rheinland Pfalz. By 1980, there were some 30 authorities linked with one or more authorities abroad, providing a framework for constructive cooperation between senior executives, education committee members, schools and the youth service[6].

Preparing young people for life and work in the EEC was the aim of the so-called Rippon funds[7] made available through the British Council following EEC membership in 1973, which supported multilateral youth exchanges with the other member states. A similar bilateral exchange scheme, CAUSEWAY, was set up in the late 1990s at the initiative of the Irish and British governments to contribute to better understanding between the young people 'of these islands', reflecting government faith in the effectiveness of exchanges to dispel prejudice and build for the future.

The French and British authorities celebrated recently the one hundredth anniversary of the language assistant scheme which dates back to the Entente Cordiale in 1904. By the mid-1970s approximately 5,000 assistants were being exchanged with up to 50 countries throughout the world. This imaginative arrangement, aimed mainly at future language teachers and at the same time bringing a (usually young) native speaker into schools, is now also part of one of the European cooperation programmes[8] and more than 1,000 are financed every year by Brussels. Let us hope that governments of today or tomorrow will not see fit to cut this scheme which has contributed so much to language teaching and to good relations with people throughout the world.

We are now tied by treaty to the European Union, living in an increasingly globalized society where future generations will wish to or have to seek work far from home. How do our school systems prepare the young for this new environment where the one thing we are certain about is rapid change, change brought about by advances in technology, by the migration of people and the altering climate of the planet on which we live? What are the core skills required for a mobile society? And how do we go about forming attitudes towards the outside world which are not based on fear of the other and inherited prejudice or worse still, based on the patrician views formed in the flush of a former empire, on which 'the sun never set' ('because God didn't trust the Brits with the lights out' my French friends might well insist!)? But with or without an imperial past, being now an EU member state, we have a remarkable opportunity to find answers to these questions through joint research with other member states, the sharing of good practice and resources and through the consultative frameworks and programmes of cooperation in education and training established by the services of the EU.

Europe and education

Cooperation between the members of the Community in the field of education is essential. In fact it was the rule in Europe for centuries. Until the 19th century, ideas, teachers and pupils moved freely and frequently between our countries. It is only recently that our national education systems became more inward-looking.

The then French minister of education wrote these words in an article in *Le Monde* in 1971 and for the next 30 years statements of this kind can be found in speeches and writings of the great and the good, culminating in the declaration at the Lisbon Council in the year 2000 that the EU was to become, by the year 2010, 'the most competitive and dynamic knowledge-based economy in the world, capable of sustainable economic growth with more and better jobs and greater social cohesion' in which education was to play a pivotal role. We all now know that some of this has been achieved and some of it has not, particularly Lisbon's economic ambitions, overtaken, as they say, by 'events'.

At a more practical level: 'If I were invited to devise a simple mechanism to facilitate cooperation between schools in Europe and thereby provide a

European dimension to the curriculum I would propose the setting up of a European Network of School Projects'. Not by one of the great and the good and not a very revolutionary proposal, but when I wrote it in January 1989[9], soon after starting work as a soldier-monk[10] in Brussels, it met with no response from the Education and Training Task Force of the EU Commission to which I had been seconded. It was written in the days when creating a European programme for schools was out of the question. The word 'education' had yet to be used in any treaty between member states which virtually barred the commission from entering the school gates, its sole access to 'education' being limited to programmes in support of training. Even ERASMUS, which became the flagship of educational cooperation programmes, was shoe-horned through to adoption in 1987 because it was established that it contributed to the training of young people and not their education.

Ideas such as the one I developed in my paper were disregarded until such time as the commission acquired the necessary legal competence to create programmes for the educational world. The school systems were jealously guarded by member states as their private gardens where they grew their citizens and cultivated their own distinct national identity. In fact, as one Europe watcher put it, 'the member states at the time seem to have adopted toward education the attitude that the French politician, Léon Gambetta, suggested that his compatriots adopt towards the loss of Alsace in 1871 – "*Y penser toujours, n'en parler jamais.*"' ('Think about it always. But speak of it never'; Neave, 1984).

The main reason I had been seconded to the EU Commission Brussels in 1988 was to set up a team to create a programme in support of language learning and even that programme (which came to be known as LINGUA), whose objectives were fundamental in a multilingual community, fell foul of the same limitations referred to previously. When the programme was adopted in 1989, we were not allowed to support language teaching in general school education, only in schools where technical training took place, and then only for pupils older than the school-leaving age!

1992 and all that

All this was to change with the signing of the Treaty of Maastricht in 1992, 'a landmark in the history of Community cooperation in the field of education' (European Commission, 2006). By the inclusion of two new articles, (127 and 128, it provided at last a legal basis for what had already been achieved 'out of wedlock' and prepared the way for the massive growth in EU support for co-operation in education and training between member states in the 1990s and beyond. Subsequent treaties have not changed that position and the Treaty of Lisbon, finally agreed upon in 2009, recognizes the strategic importance of cooperation in education as pivotal to achieving its economic and social ambitions.

The Education Council's[11] three broad aims are currently: individual development, by ensuring that each individual reaches his or her full potential; social development, by reducing inequities and promoting cultural diversity and economic development, through ensuring skills correspond to needs. These are broad aims which the EU pursues by creating high-level consultative procedures and setting up expert groups to study together subjects of special concern, such as the education of migrant children and the position of maths and science in primary education, just the sort of co-operation foreseen by Olivier Guichard, French minister of education, in 1971.

Not surprisingly, among the basic skills listed by the European Council, alongside traditional literacy and numeracy, are information and communication technology (ICT) and foreign language skills. Added to these are competences such as social and problem-solving skills, flexibility and adaptability. When member states are invited to share with others their experience in these fields, it is remarkable from reading reports how much of this is transferable. Each culture has its own strengths and weaknesses and, as a Flemish Belgian friend suggested, 'you learn from each other's strengths, but also from their weaknesses'.

Europe gets through the school gates

On a recent visit to the medieval Cistercian Abbey at Fontenay in Burgundy, founded in 1147, I came across a plaque on the wall in the abbey's ancient forge proudly announcing that the massive hydraulically controlled hammer, originally built by the monks in the Middle Ages, had been totally restored by young people from seven technical schools around Europe in an EU-funded project. Some 20 years after I had written my piece for the *ESHA Journal*, here was the cast-iron proof, literally, for all to see and admire, of one of the benefits of linking schools from different countries around a common project, in this case participating in restoration work on a European heritage site.

The project had been financed under the COMENIUS programme, a chapter of the SOCRATES programme directly targeting schools, which was adopted in 1995 as a direct result of the empowering articles in the Treaty of Maastricht. The school gates had at last been flung open and projects of cooperation covering the whole curriculum, and involving establishments from pre-school to the end of schooling or initial training, were eligible for support from Brussels. Since the programme was adopted, thousands of schools have benefited from EU grants to set up a network of links throughout the EU, involving approximately 2.5 million participants. The European Network of School Projects, which was just a pipe dream back in 1989, when I wrote my article, now exists and a whole generation of young people will have had an experience of Europe in their schooling.

Similar to its older sibling, ERASMUS, in higher education, the COMENIUS programme sets out to bring a European dimension to almost all aspects of school education. As it has developed over the past dozen years, it has touched the lives of thousands of pupils, teachers, parents and others who work for schools,[12] by helping to finance partnerships with schools in other EU member states and by creating an environment in which pupils and teachers learn from one another.

The amazing achievement of the seven technical schools that rebuilt the forge hammer at Fontenay is symbolic of how the COMENIUS programme reaches young people who were neglected in the past, students in technical and vocational education. As noted above, exchange opportunities were often restricted to young people following academic courses, particularly languages, and COMENIUS has done much to broaden access to international experience for all students.

During the late 1980s and early 1990s another EU programme, PETRA[13], specifically targeted initial vocational training and funded placements around Europe for trainees in further education (FE) and similar institutions elsewhere. Survival language and, just as importantly, an awareness of cultural difference were considered of the utmost importance and some hard lessons were learned by some of the young participants: 'I might as well have been a nine-month-old baby; in fact I was worse off – at least a baby can sob, grunt and coo' was how a young lady described the experience of not being able to communicate on her transnational placement. And a young man offered: 'At home I'm best at woodwork but out there I was terrible'. Something, however, of real value will still have been gained by those young people, if only an awareness that the world is full of difference and the opportunity to measure oneself against others in unfamiliar circumstances.

Looking at the British Council's website on COMENIUS, one obtains an idea of the range of educational establishments and themes covered by the programme. 'Products of the land and gastronomy' by a day nursery for 2- to 4-year-olds, 'We are the world' by a primary school, 'Migratory Processes in European History' by a comprehensive school, 'Health and Sport – Exploring What Unites Us' by a girls school, 'European Citizenship' by a further education college, 'Designing a Training Course on Cross-Currents in European Literature' for future teachers. All of these projects are carried out with a minimum of three schools or colleges in other member states. Sometimes up to a dozen or more schools are involved. The challenge is to sustain the link when the funding runs out.

On a less happy note for language teachers in Great Britain, experience has shown since these programmes were set up that transnational activities indeed highlight the need for foreign language competence but, sadly, in most cases (in fact in the case of all but the two Anglophone member states) the perceived need is to learn English. For example, English is often used as the lingua franca for communicating within a transnational project financed by COMENIUS, even though no Anglophone country is a participant. The more Europe gets together the more the use of English is reinforced with all the ill effects on the motivation of Anglophones described above.

Two activities with a bright future

E-Twinning

'Information technology is the great enabler'. So concluded a working group at a Council of Europe colloquy on 'Using the New Technologies to Create Links Between Schools Throughout the World', held in Exeter in 1988. This followed the aptly named colloquy 'The World in the European Classroom' held in Haiko, Finland, in 1986, and preceded the colloquy in Stockholm, Sweden, on 'School Links and Exchanges' in 1993, which took discussions a stage further. Informed by these Council of Europe-led deliberations, the Swedish government, on joining the EU in 1995, sponsored the establishment of a major electronic network linking education systems throughout the EU.

The proposal eventually led to the creation of EUROPEAN SCHOOLNET, which operates today under the sponsorship of the 32 ministries of education of EU and European Economic Area (EEA) member states. It fulfils, at a European level, some of the functions of the former Central Bureau in Great Britain, particularly in finding partners for schools in other countries and helping them to create links based upon projects. It has taken Europe by storm. Some 35,000 links between schools have been created since it was launched in 2005, and the action is now part of the COMENIUS chapter within the EU's Lifelong Learning Programme. SCHOOLNET's website[14] provides a rich anthology of 'kits' which can be used to animate projects for all levels of schools and colleges. And it is all done at minimal cost through the internet and the use of Skype.

CLIL

Another initiative of the last 15 years, also not dependent on a grant from Brussels and which has greatly contributed to building intercultural knowledge and understanding in schools, has been the development of content and language integrated learning (CLIL), the rather cumbersome way of describing the teaching of another subject through the medium of a foreign language. Originating from early attempts to set up bilingual education and *sections bilingues* in the 1970s, it provides a rich environment for initiating intercultural learning. Monitored by the great and the good among European linguists and other subject specialists and supported by the EU through its Lifelong Learning Programme, it has begun to revolutionize the curriculum throughout the school system in Europe, in some countries more than others. It has serious implications for teacher training and for the internal organization of subjects within the school but with its record of success and the support it now enjoys at every level of education, its future seems assured. Sadly, although some of the significant pioneers and current thinkers are from Great Britain, there are few examples of CLIL being used in British schools. It would seem an effective way forward to combat the gale which is raging even more strongly.

What do our neighbours think?

I keep in touch with a number of friends around Europe and often discuss their views on what for them have been the achievements and mistakes of the past and what we should be focusing on in the future.

Cooperation and learning from each other

All of my friends have welcomed the principle of cooperation on which EU programmes are based. It has greatly helped to break down the barriers we have built around our nation states, allowing ideas and examples of good practice to flow between us and our institutions. This spirit of cooperation has also counterbalanced the competition, which also seems to have become more prevalent, especially in Great Britain, with its league tables which tend to pit school against school and which skew the choice of subjects and methods of work.[15]

A Danish friend, who has a long track record running European projects in the field of language learning and the use of ICT, welcomed the opportunity of working with the 'other half of Europe', in his case the Catholic south. 'We work on Nordic time up here. We're even more clockwise than our German neighbours. So working with southern Europe, is a real education for us'. It opened his eyes to other values and to ways of solving problems he had never imagined.

A young Catalan friend from Barcelona spent her ERASMUS placement in Wales and felt an immediate kinship with people whose native tongue is a minority language within the country in which they live. It has created a special bond between her and the other so-called minority language users in Europe. A Hungarian friend describes how taking part in mobility programmes has helped young people overcome her country's natural shyness and an 'anxiety to talk to and meet foreigners'. Not in official terms a minority language, Hungarian, nevertheless, is not spoken by many people beyond Hungary's landlocked frontiers, and this gives a feeling of isolation which can only be dispelled through contact with other cultures. 'I think critical thinking could be a benefit for us: get to know others, other's culture, compare it to our one and realise our values'.

This same point is made by a German friend for whom 'trying to understand others may help you to rethink yourself' is the essence of mobility projects and the intercultural approach: 'It gives people an opportunity to learn to see themselves in the mirror of other people's mindsets'.

After 'being closed for 45 years', my Bulgarian friend says it is through mobility that 'we can learn real things', not just through books and television. 'And of course this helps us to feel more like others'.

Because of her country's remoteness 'at the northern border of Europe' and because her language, not unlike Hungarian, is also 'of its own kind and not spoken anywhere else in the world', a Finnish friend has no lack of motivation to take part in European projects and learn foreign languages. For her, they are 'a key skill in modern society', a lifeline to other cultures. 'Because of the cold climate, difficult language and the introvert nature of Finnish people Finland hasn't tempted many foreigners. We have led our solitary life building the welfare state we make up today'. And, it should be said, an education system which is the envy of the world!

Combating stereotypes, including the stereotype of her own country, is a particular concern of an Italian friend who told me 'we know what other people think about our lifestyle and we do our best . . . to give a different opinion'. It might surprise some non-Italians met through exchanges that 'Italian families are a bit more old-fashioned than families in other countries: the whole family sits at a same table having dinner if it is not possible having lunch too and we set the table in a different way, maybe a bit more formal than in other countries'.

Networks

The more idealistic among my friends describe the network of schools created under E-LEARNING as one big happy family and quote examples of young people and their teachers meeting in places they had only ever dreamed about through funding provided by the EU. More sceptical observers call into question the outlay of so much public money to support activities which were sometimes of doubtful educational value. They also point now to the social networks which provide a means for making contacts around the world under the control of the young people themselves and at nearly no cost. Of course what those same young people do on the social networks is also of dubious educational value, but it does show that networks can now be created without the vast outlay of time and money which was necessary in the earlier days of these programmes.

Mistakes

Learn from the mistakes of the past before launching any fresh initiative at a European level in support of schools, say my friends in France. The whole edifice is too heavy and bureaucratic – one of them compared it to the latest jumbo Airbus, another product of European partnership – which is too daunting for many schools not able to cope with the paperwork and the time involved in applying for a grant and creating a partnership.

Not homogeneous

Another error to avoid, perhaps more serious, is to consider that everybody is the same or should be. To add a European dimension to the curriculum is not to Europeanize the curriculum, making it indistinguishable from the curriculum of one's neighbours. Turning little Englanders into little Europeans does not necessarily result in the tolerance and openness needed in our schools toward the world of today and tomorrow. Although I would take issue with a number of points raised by Margaret Thatcher in her famous speech at Bruges in 1989, I agree with her when she said: 'Europe will be stronger precisely because it has France as France, Spain as Spain, Britain as Britain, each with its own customs, traditions and identity. It would be folly to try to fit them into some sort of identikit European personality'.

Top-down rigour and an insistence on form and method will remain the marks of French education and, to some extent, of Latin countries in general and the more pragmatic approach and focus on the whole individual will continue to distinguish the British and Scandinavian approaches. Through cooperation programmes of the kind previously mentioned, we can and perhaps should learn from the more rigorous approach of our Latin neighbours, and they could perhaps give more prominence to the arts in education, such as music and drama, and thereby reach more of a young person than can be measured by a mark out of twenty.

Money

The same French friends agreed with me by questioning the approach of the commission to base its support for education and training on 'giving money away'. By perpetuating this grant-giving rôle, the commission reinforces an increasingly unattractive culture in which the concept of Europe is closely bound up with money, that the European dimension is something you buy mainly with funding provided by Brussels. In a below-stairs exchange with other soldier-monks, I wrote in 1998: 'The monks in their monasteries back in the dark ages who pored over the meaning of biblical texts have been replaced by consultants who understand Euro-speak and will write your project for you on a "no success, no fee"' basis.

A far more positive view was put to me by a vocational trainer a year or so later who had benefited from a Leonardo da Vinci training grant:

> The programme conceived as a whole is utterly brilliant. What other part of the western hemisphere uses international taxes to pump-prime collaborative experiments in improving the way people learn and work? Few member states have the political continuity to plan and budget long-term for this. LEONARDO is for me one of the best illustrations of what the EU represents on the good side.

He then goes on to describe the bad side, concentrating on the commission's 'lack of robust and reliable administrative processes'. Those processes are now greatly improved and budgets have vastly increased, at least until 2013 when the current programmes will need to be renegotiated.

And that of course brings us to the crucial question of today's financial crisis. Already one hears the sound of cuts being made or considered. A Spanish friend tells me that his *autonomía* (regional authority) will no longer support a teacher wishing to go on an in-service training course abroad because of the cost of a replacement. In fact if the teacher chooses to take part, the cost is deducted from his or her salary. The British government recently considered cutting the foreign language assistants scheme but thought better of it. At a European level, unless matters improve, what will be the budget voted to support the next round of cooperation programmes to continue the Lifelong Learning Programme? One can only speculate at this stage.

Frameworks

In a worst-case scenario, we may have to return to the practices of a previous age, which were not dependent on funding from the EU Commission. The difference between now and then, however, is that thousands of schools across the EU are now part of a network or have a link of one kind or another with a school or schools abroad. Those links should continue to form the framework for joint activities, project work and in-service training opportunities, using the new technologies and, where necessary, making use of funds that may survive the cuts or, to use an old-fashioned term, by fund-raising activities in the school and local community.

In Conclusion

In the end it all comes down to the individual school and the role of the headteacher, which, of course, is where most, if not all, debates about education begin and end. If the head genuinely recognizes the need to pre-pare students for a globalized society as a future citizen of the European Union, and not just to show up well in the league tables, then the school is half way there. Long before the golden age of COMENIUS funding, a number of brave pioneering schools ensured that the international dimen-sion was firmly embedded in school policy and used their imagination and energy to create opportunities to push back the horizons of their staff and pupils, sometimes with the help of local authority but often entirely with their own resources.

The world of tomorrow, however, will certainly open up new scenarios and bring to our schools fresh challenges to face. Chinese is the fastest-growing foreign language in French schools (after English), and Spanish has far outstripped other languages (except English) in its attraction for students in Germany. Perhaps it is not too early to think about an Asian or Latin American dimension in our schools, or do we have enough on our plates with Europe? And should we not look upon this involvement in Europe as a step-ping stone to dimensions farther afield?

Just as important as the knowledge and skills acquired through mobility and an international approach to the curriculum is the impact these activities should have on the value system of the school community. Ultimately they should enrich intercultural learning within the school, tolerance toward other members of the school community, especially but not exclusively because they are of different national, religious or ethnic origins, tolerance between the sexes and between the generations. Tolerance and respect: These should be the core values at the root of a school's international policy which aims to prepare the next generation for their rôle as broad-minded and knowledge-able citizens in an increasingly globalized world.

Appendix 1

A brief overview of EU support for cooperation programmes between schools: its development over the past 40 years.

Phase one: preparing the ground (1976)

The newly established Education Committee of the European Community passed its resolution of February 1976 promoting 'the introduction of a

European dimension in schools, the strengthening of language teaching, the mobility of teachers and the exchange of information', leading to the establishment of the ARION programme of study visits for educational specialists and the Eurydice network, the 'hub' of information on education systems, with national units in each member state (1980).

Phase two: action programmes

Using articles 128 and 235 of the Treaty of Rome and following the creation of People's Europe (European Community) at the Fontainebleau summit (1985), the first major community programmes in education were created: COMETT (1986) university-enterprise cooperation, ERASMUS (1987) student mobility and university cooperation, FORCE (1987) continuing vocational training, PETRA (1988) initial vocational training and LINGUA (1989), languages in Europe, were adopted initially for periods of 3 to 5 years with budgets ranging from 80 to 200 European currency units (ECUs).

Phase three: towards a knowledge society

Following the inclusion of education in the Treaty of Maastricht (1992), and in an attempt to create coherence and encourage synergy, existing programmes were amalgamated under two overall programmes: Socrates, for school and university education, which included the action programme for schools, COMENIUS, and Leonardo da Vinci, for initial and vocational training (1994). The programmes were adopted for 5 years with budgets of 850 million ECUs for Socrates and 620 million ECUs for Leonardo da Vinci. They were extended from 2000 to 2006 with budgets increased to 1.850 million euros for Socrates and 1.150 million euros for Leonardo.

Phase four: an integrated community approach

Geared to the policy goals laid down in the Lisbon strategy, the Lifelong Learning Programme was adopted for 2007–13 bringing together all community actions into one integrated programme, including new expanded support for adult education under the GRUNDTVIG programme and support for E-LEARNING, with a budget of 13,620 million euros.

Appendix 2

Enquiries concerning the EU programmes discussed in this chapter should be addressed to the national agencies in individual member states which are listed on the EU Commission's website http://ec.europa.eu/education/lifelong-learning-programme/doc1208_en.htm. Responsibility for the overall management of the programmes is provided by the Education, Audio-Visual and Culture Executive Agency (EACEA) of the EU in Brussels. Its postal address is EACEA, avenue du Bourget 1, 1140 Brussels, Belgium; its email address is eacea-info@ec.europa.eu.

Most of the national agencies listed also coordinate E-TWINNING opportunities. Enquiries about the latter can also be directed to European Schoolnet, rue de Trèves 61, 1040 Brussels, Belgium. The website is www.europeanschoolnet.org.

Notes

1   In 1963 and 1967, British entry was vetoed by the French government led by President de Gaulle.

2   Recent predictions suggest that, as Europe declines economically, English as the world's language will also decline and be replaced by an Asian language as the lingua franca.

3   Paper for the journal *Science*, February 2004.

4   For example, 'Europeans and Their Languages', *Eurobarometer*, February 2006.

5   www.britishcouncil.org/new/folder_what-we-do/schools/

6   It is interesting to note that the EU launched a new strand of the COMENIUS programme in 2009, COMENIUS REGIO, which follows precisely the pattern established by these local authority links and provides welcome EU funding.

7   Named after Geoffrey Rippon who, as chancellor of the Duchy of Lancaster under Edward Heath and pro-Europe, was given the responsibility of negotiating Britain's entry.

8   Financed under the COMENIUS programme, they are known as COMENIUS assistants and serve for 6 months in a country whose language they are likely to teach. Some 6,400 schools now take part.

9   Article in the first edition of the European Secondary Heads Association (ESHA) Magazine, autumn 1989. ESHA was founded at a conference in Maastricht in November 1988.

10   A term used ironically to describe the seconded national experts who contributed their previous experience in a member state to the creation of programmes at a European level.

11   The Education Council is made up of ministers from each of the EU member states.

12   Under the COMENIUS programme, about 10,000 serving teachers each year receive financial assistance to attend in-service courses in another country.

13 PETRA is now covered by COMENIUS and by Leonardo da Vinci, within the EU Lifelong Learning Programme.

14 www.etwinning.net

15 In 1990 I was invited to address a conference of headteachers in one of the home counties in Great Britain and was told by the head who picked me up at the station that this would be the last conference of its kind 'because from next year we will all be in competition with each other and won't be so willing to share our ideas!'

Raising Awareness of Europe in Classroom and Community: a Scottish initiative

5

Barbara Macleod

Chapter Outline

In Scotland an interesting initiative established nearly 20 years ago has been developing nationally, especially in recent years, thanks to the work of the Scottish European Educational Trust. The principal aim is to increase awareness of Europe among young people so that they better understand the implications of the United Kingdom's membership in the EU and, as regards university students, the opportunities for them to study and work in Europe.

The history of the Trust

The Scottish European Educational Trust is a registered charity, which was set up in 1993 under the auspices of the European Movement. It promotes and encourages education about Europe to students at schools, colleges and universities throughout Scotland. It works closely with the European Commission, European Parliament, MEPs (Members of the European Parliament), the Scottish government, the Scottish Parliament, Learning Teaching Scotland (the Scottish curriculum development agency), the British Council, SCILT (a language teaching body) and the National Union of Students. The trust is completely self-financed with office costs and events being sponsored by individuals and companies. In addition, the trust has in the past successfully applied for grants for specific events from the European Parliament and the European Commission. The criteria for these awards vary from year to year, and the current 2011 criteria do not apply to work carried out by the trust.

For the first few years after its inception, the trust was of relatively small scale, its main event being a Euroquiz for primary schools in the Edinburgh area only. As this grew in popularity, local authority areas around Edinburgh – East Lothian, Midlothian and West Lothian – requested their own quizzes and the event gradually expanded until, in 2006, via David Martin MEP, Standard Life agreed to sponsor a Scotland-wide competition, with local heats and a final in Edinburgh. At that stage the trust became independent from the more politically focused European Movement. The current chairman is Gerald Wilson, C.B., former head of the Education and Industry Department at the Scottish government. The Trustees also bring a wealth of experience: Dugald Craig (West of Scotland Colleges), Alison Edwards (retired languages teacher), Christine Fitton (Lifelong Learning UK), Moira Frizzell (former deputy head, Stevenson's FE College), James Ivory (chartered accountant, treasurer), John Mulgrew (former director of education and chairman of Learning Teaching Scotland) Bob Payne (founder of Eurodesk), Stuart Rycroft (former secondary school deputy head) and Roderick Skinner (former European Commission official). There is a part-time national organizer (Barbara Macleod), and each year the trust takes on a young intern to help with the work.

Jose Manuel Barroso, president of the European Commission, attended the final of the first Scotland-wide Euroquiz in the City Chambers in Edinburgh in May 2006, while he was in the city receiving an honorary degree. He said after his visit: 'I have seen at first hand something of the excellent work of the Scottish European Educational Trust. Promoting an increased awareness of Europe among young people is a project worth supporting.'

Current activities

The activities of the trust for schools are planned to complement the Scottish government's 'Curriculum for Excellence' stipulating that pupils should be:

- confident individuals
- effective contributors

- successful learners
- responsible citizens

Euroquiz

The Euroquiz remains the main event run by the trust and continues to be sponsored by Standard Life, although 2011 is the last year of this sponsorship agreement. From an initial event attended by six schools in Edinburgh, the 2010 Euroquiz was attended by more than 400 schools in all 32 local authority areas in Scotland. The number of people touched directly and indirectly by the quiz in 2010 was approximately 37,300. This includes more than 2,000 pupils taking part in the heats, plus teachers, teaching assistants, parents and other relatives, siblings, headteachers, other schools staff (such as janitors) and spectators. The quiz is now very much part of the curriculum, and schools tend to teach Europe as a subject to their primary sixth year (P6) classes in the run-up to the heats. All of the P6 pupils in the participating schools learn about Europe, not just the four pupils taking part in the quiz. The final is web-cast to all Scottish schools, available on the parliament's website. Through the quiz, information about Europe and the European Union is therefore disseminated to a large number of people in Scotland.

It would be impossible for the trust to run the quiz without the support of the local authorities, whose international co-ordinators take on promoting the quiz in their areas, disseminating information to the schools, organizing the venue, and appointing a quizmaster. Each local authority in Scotland has an international co-ordinator, but in only two authorities (Edinburgh and Glasgow) are these full-time posts – in other areas the international co-ordinators also have many other responsibilities. The trust has relationships with the international co-ordinators, as well as with the directors of education services, the local council leaders and the Members of the Scottish Parliament. The trust provides all of the materials for the quiz: questions and answers, powerpoint presentations, scoring sheets, instructions for advance administration, programmes for the day, detailed information for the schools, certificates and draft press notices. In addition, a list of useful websites is provided for the schools, together with order sheets for materials from the European Commission and the European Parliament. The heats are often attended by council leaders, who present the trophy and the prizes. Representatives from the trust attend each heat to offer support; these include trustees, former MEPs, European Parliament and European Commission staff, and former employees of the European institutions. Local media coverage is generally very good.

Each team consists of four P6 pupils (age 9 to 10), plus one or two substitutes. Teams are normally chosen by a competition run in the class prior to the heats. There are five rounds of questions, all for teams: (1) picture round; (2) geography; (3) culture, history and languages; (4) EU affairs, multiple-choice. The final round is a combination of questions from the previous rounds. All teams take part in rounds one through four, with the top two teams going through to the final round. All of the questions for rounds one through four are on powerpoint; the quizmaster reads out the questions and the pupils write their answers on their answer sheets. Teachers mark the papers, with each teacher marking a team not from his or her own school. The final round is an oral one. If necessary, 'sudden death' tiebreakers are used. The winning team is presented with the Standard Life trophy, and each team member receives a prize (such as memory sticks). The runners-up also receive a prize, and each participant receives a certificate.

The range of knowledge tested by the questions is very wide. Some examples are:

- H&M, Zara and Lidl – from which European countries do these originate?
- Which EU member state has the highest population density?
- What are the numbers ten and 11 in French, German, Italian or Spanish?
- Which of these words – internet, robot or hotel – is of Czech origin?
- *Hasta luego* means 'see you later' in which European language?
- Can you name six of the 23 official European Union languages?
- In which year did the first European Parliament elections take place?
- What is the name of the president of the European Commission?
- Name all six Scottish MEPs.
- Which European language is officially spoken in Brazil?
- Which is the largest city in the EU?
- Which country is Rafael Nadal, winner of Wimbledon in 2010, from?
- Which three countries share a border with Luxembourg?

The final of the Euroquiz takes place in the Debating Chamber of the Scottish Parliament. Thanks to generous sponsorship, the trust is able to pay for the schools to attend the final, providing overnight accommodation when necessary. Teams from outlying areas, especially the Scottish islands, are particularly grateful for this as they are often prevented from taking part in most competitions because of the costs involved. Teams from Ireland and Germany (where Standard Life has offices) took part in Euroquiz 2009, but this proved to be difficult logistically and the limited resources available to the trust regrettably made it too expensive to repeat.

The work of organizing the final in the Parliament is time-consuming. For example, for security purposes, each pupil must provide signed consent forms for the parliament and for Standard Life, together with permission to use photographs or to broadcast images of the pupils. Any pupils who do not wish to be filmed are placed at the back of the debating chamber and the parliament's broadcasting team are asked to make sure that that area is not filmed during the web-cast. This and other administrative tasks increase the workload of the trust in advance of the final, and extra staff are often drafted in to help on a voluntary basis. Trustees are on hand on the day to distribute papers and add up the scores but happily the ever-helpful Events Team from the parliament are in charge of the room layout, registration and the seating of the pupils.

The Scottish Parliament's deputy presiding officer[1] asks the questions and the head of the European Parliament office in Scotland gives the answers. The trust has to obtain permission for this from the Corporate Body of the Scottish Parliament. This has now become a major event in the educational programme of the Scottish Parliament, and is their contribution to the Europe Day celebrations in Scotland. Some MSPs offer the teams from their constituencies tours of the parliament prior to the final taking place.

Participating pupils sit in the MSPs seats, with the spectators sitting in the visitors gallery. Spectators, who include parents, other pupils, members of the Consular Corps, MSPs and representatives from major companies and organizations, are given sheets on which to write their answers. The whole event takes just more than two hours, and is broadcast live on the Scottish Parliament website. In 2010 the event attracted more hits on the Scottish Parliament's website than any other external event run at the parliament that year.

The trust works closely with the broadcasting team at the Parliament prior to and during the event; for the powerpoint presentation of the questions and answers, broadcasting of songs and anthems displaying the scores and the filming of the event for the simultaneous broadcast. In addition, the team provide a cd rom of the quiz final, one for each participating team and one for each of the teams who will take part the following year, so that they get an idea of the format of the quiz.

Many MSPs choose to visit the school of the participating team from their constituency on the day of the quiz rather than to attend the quiz in person, in order that they can watch it live with the rest of the class. This has proved to be popular with the MSPs and with the pupils and teachers.

The format of the final is similar to that of the heats, with four rounds for all pupils and a final round between the top two teams. Buzzers are used in the final round, adding tension and a sense of excitement. The chairman of Standard Life normally presents the winners with their trophy, medals and prizes and the deputy presiding officer gives the prizes to the runners-up. The responsible minister in the Scottish government also addresses the audience and this show of support from the government is greatly appreciated. All participants receive promotional material and snacks.

The winning team for the past 2 years has been St Mary's Duntocher Primary from West Dunbartonshire, an area of relative deprivation. They have been particularly pleased to have beaten some of the top private schools in Scotland. On the back of winning the Euroquiz, St Mary's have been featured in the *Times Educational Supplement*, the *Scotsman,* in local newspapers and on local radio. The local MSP has visited the school, as has the local director of education services. The team also had a stand at the Scottish Learning Festival and their presence there attracted a deal of interest, besides providing a showcase for the trust's work. Speaking of the school's involvement in the quiz, the team's teacher, Claire Donnelly, said:

> Our school has no previous involvement in any aspect of Euroquiz and we have been most impressed with the organisation right from entering the regional heats. Holding the final in such an important venue [as the Parliament] added to the sense of occasion for them. The parents who attended to support the team were also very impressed and felt it was memorable day for both themselves and their children. The concept of the Euroquiz is an excellent tool for learning, covering a wide range of curricular areas and developing skills in talking, listening, research and just as importantly, team building, responsibility and self esteem.

As well as the support offered by the Scottish Parliament and the local authorities, the trust is also grateful for the support and advice it receives from the Education and European Divisions at the Scottish Government. Mike Russell MSP, cabinet secretary for education and lifelong learning, has said of the quiz:

> The Euroquiz is a wonderful way to learn about Europe and its rich history and culture. It opens minds to other cultures and other ways of thinking which is of huge benefit in our multicultural society. Euroquiz fits well with our Scottish Curriculum for Excellence.[2]

Comments and reactions from pupils and teachers include:

> Thank you for giving our pupils the chance to interact with children from all over the country in such a friendly and encouraging environment, for letting them meet with adults who are in the European workplace, and for the challenge to research and learn about Europe. I honestly believe that this experience will be valuable in their journey to becoming responsible citizens, effective contributors, successful learners and confident individuals. (Morag Paul, Inverkip Primary School)

> It was an experience we will never forget which afforded us the opportunity of a closer look at our parliament building. The children were delighted to meet and work in groups with other P6s from all over Scotland and, ultimately to compete in such a nationally prestigious event. The quiz threw up some ideas for the future, for example, debating teams, school and authority wide, and some curriculum development issues. (Mara Matthews, Midlothian Council)

> The most important message we can pass on to young people is that achievement and success are attainable to all irrespective of race, creed or social class. We must believe in them and encourage them to believe in themselves. This young team said 'yes, we can' and in the process gained a very respectable score in the finals of the Scottish European Educational Trust's Euroquiz. They are so proud of themselves. (Mrs Lusby, Headteacher, Rowantree Primary School, Dundee)

> I think we should have this Euroquiz in P5, P6 and P7. (Participant, West Dunbartonshire Euroquiz)

> We're the Eurochampz (sic) aboard the Euro Express we try so very hard we're aiming for success!! (Rowantree Team, Dundee)

To sum up, the Euroquiz is a tremendously popular and enjoyable event and one which has aroused interest in other parts of the United Kingdom and in other EU countries.

Speaking competition

For senior pupils the trust has run a Speaking Competition for S3 pupils (age about 14) for a number of years, which allows students from all over Scotland to compete with their peers in an arena of innovative debate. The students who take part cannot have represented their school at any external speaking or debating competitions. This allows students who have not previously had an opportunity to present their own ideas in front of their peers to do so. This is in contrast to most of the established speaking competitions and debates (such as Observer Mace and the Donald Dewar Speaking Competition) and for this reason it is popular with schools.

The 2009 Speaking Competition was sponsored by the European Parliament and the winning team was from Benbecula, Western Isles. The prize was a visit to Brussels for the two pupils and the teacher and a highlight of the trip was a day spent at one of the European Schools in Brussels, sitting in on a geography class in French for non-native speakers. They were impressed at the level of language, and both pupils vowed to continue their language learning. Since then, one of the pupils has spent a summer in Germany (organized by the Goethe-Institut via the trust) and is aiming to study languages at university. Another highlight was the visit to the European Parliament, where they were lucky enough to have a meeting with Hans-Gert Pöttering, the president of the Parliament. This was organized by the head of the European Parliament Office in Edinburgh, with whom the trustees have a close working relationship. The *Stornoway Gazette* covered this in detail, with a front-page article and photograph.

Because of lack of sponsorship, the trust was unable to take the winners of the 2010 Speaking Competition to Brussels but the event in Scotland was highly successful.

IBM agreed to sponsor the 2011 Speaking Competition, and the trust was delighted to be able to take the winners of the four regional heats, plus the top-scoring runner-up team, to Brussels at the end of March to compete in the final. This took place at Scotland House, hosted by the Scottish government and Scotland Europa.

This year pupils have been asked to give a presentation on the importance of language learning and give their ideas on how to make this more enjoyable in schools. This topic ties in with a review the Scottish government is running on the teaching of modern languages, and the pupils' ideas will be presented to the Scottish government and to the relevant committee of the Scottish Parliament.

Because of the high volume of entries for the 2011 competition, students wishing to participate were required to write an essay of no more than 200 words on why they believed learning a foreign language was important and how they believed it could be made more interesting. Members of our board of trustees then selected the six schools they felt had submitted the best essays from each of the areas (Aberdeen, Edinburgh, Greenock and Stirling), and these schools then competed with one another for a place in the final. The areas were chosen to give a wide geographical spread.

The topic of the presentations given at the heats was the same as that set for the entry essays, and in addition to presenting their ideas on language learning, the students were required to give a summary and vote of thanks in the European foreign language of their choice, which is not their mother tongue. Languages used were French, Spanish, Catalan, German, Italian and Norwegian. Although a few of the students spoke in languages they had learned from a parent or from living abroad, the vast majority were speaking the additional language they were learning in school. The level of language was very high, with some standing out from the crowd. It was inspiring to witness students bringing humour into their summaries and votes of thanks in a language they have been learning for only a few years.

At the final in Brussels, the linguistic content will be increased, with pupils also being asked to give their introduction in their chosen European language. In addition, Mark Pentleton from Radio Lingua will instruct the pupils in how to make a short video of their visit and will help them to produce the video before they return to Scotland. Radio Lingua is also providing the prizes of an i-pod for each member of the winning team, pre-loaded with a language course of their choice.

The ideas that were presented by the students throughout the four heats were varied, imaginative, well thought out and highly perceptive. When it came to the second part of the question, 'How can we make language learning more interesting?' there was a unanimous consensus among all of the students: Not only is it possible to make the way foreign languages are taught more interesting, it is vital. A flavour of the pupils' views is given here to show what an admittedly small cross section of young Scots think about language teaching. Clearly there seems to be dissatisfaction with the status quo.

The winners of our Stirling heat managed to state most succinctly what many other students had partially articulated; traditional methods of teaching are 'old fashioned' and 'boring' and therefore ineffective. These students argued that copying from the board or doing exercises from a textbook are not stimulating enough to encourage learning, and in order to improve the foreign language skills of our country as a whole, we must make language learning more active and more modern. In other words, we need to move away from the academic and towards the interactive, if we wish to improve our language skills.

Very common ideas

There were several ideas which came up repeatedly during the heats, about how language learning could be made more interesting.

One idea often raised was that if foreign exchanges were a standard component of learning any language, then students would not only become more proficient through speaking to native speakers, they would become more confident and enjoy learning languages more. Students acknowledged that not everyone was able to take advantage of exchanges, even if they were available, because of the cost; however many suggested that it should be an opportunity available to everyone and therefore perhaps paid for by an appropriate body.

Several of the students highlighted the importance of learning an 'authentic' accent, and of these students the majority stated that the best way to learn an accent was to visit the country or to communicate directly with native speakers. These students said that by using Skype, it would be possible to set up direct lines of communication, inexpensively, with students from other countries all over Europe and the world. This type of web-based chat, it was suggested, could be used alongside exchanges, in order to consolidate the relationships between partners before they met each other.

Many students said they believed that the oral part of learning a language was both highly important and inadequately catered to. Their idea was to introduce immersion days when students would only be permitted to speak in their foreign language during their language lesson. This idea ties in with the idea of having language assistants in each language class, as many students also said they thought conversing with a native speaker was most beneficial to their speaking ability.

This idea also closely mirrors the concept behind the European Commission's support for content and language integrated learning (CLIL). CLIL involves teaching a variety of school subjects in an additional language. One pair of students in the Stirling heat mentioned CLIL, stating that they believed it would be a fun and effective way to learn a language.

Fairly common ideas

The use of interactive whiteboards was both commended and condemned by a selection of the students. Some described them as a fun way to learn, a welcome alternative to textbook learning, which allowed them to play games in their additional language. However, others stated that they felt the games provided were 'babyish', inappropriate for students of their age.

Another point raised regularly was that watching foreign films, along with listening to foreign music and reading foreign literature, was a good way to familiarize oneself with a foreign language. Students from one school suggested that if films were watched with subtitles, that would allow pupils the opportunity to follow the story, improving their enjoyment of the film while still allowing them to learn from the sound of the particular foreign language being spoken.

Highly imaginative ideas

There were a few ideas which were less conventional. One of these was for students to take part in a bus trip around Europe, over the summer holidays, allowing them to come face to face with a variety of European cultures and languages. They highlighted that this experience would have the same advantages as a foreign exchange, recognizing the necessity of communicating in an additional language within the cultural setting of that language, yet such a cultural tour would provide exposure to not just one country but many. The students who put forward this idea acknowledged the impracticability of the proposal unless substantial funding could be provided,but it certainly showed that they were 'thinking big'! It also showed a recognition of the importance, which other teams acknowledged, of having an appreciation of the culture of countries in studying their language. The students also acknowledged the possibility of a 'virtual' European tour, whereby, for example, a language class could dedicate one lesson a week to exploring the culture of a particular European country in the language they are learning. The classroom could, they suggested, be arranged with objects (models of famous monuments, foreign maps, flags, even food) and the lesson could revolve around incorporating these things into conversations in the language of the country they symbolized.

In keeping with this concept of virtual travel, students from another school proposed that an entire language class be given 'virtual glasses' which when put on, transform the environment they are in into a foreign one. For example, a scene of Paris could appear, and it would be the students' task to describe, in their foreign language, the objects and scenery they can see. Another example could be that a railway station would appear, and the students would have to navigate their way to a certain destination, using the phrases they had learned in class. The technology cannot be far away for bringing this kind of virtual experience into the classroom.

Here are a few comments about and reactions to the Speaking Competition:

> The competition embraces the aims and capacities of the Curriculum for Excellence in a way that allows pupils to get a realistic and practical experience of acquiring confidence as individuals, taking their role as effective contributors and caring citizens to heart and spreading that message among their peers. I have also benefitted in my role as a Guidance Principal in gaining an insight into the workings of the various European bodies and the career opportunities that may be available to young people interested in working in Brussels or elsewhere in Europe. (Marion Morrison, teacher, Lionacleit School, Benbecula, Western Isles)

> Throughout the experience I have learned so much about Europe. The trip to Brussels opened my eyes to opportunities I never knew I had and many doors have been opened to me. (Nadine Froughi, Lionacleit School, winner 2009)

> The Speaking competition was an amazing opportunity which has widened our horizons for the future. We have gained in confidence while talking in front of audiences of many ages, and have expanded our knowledge of the European Union and our place within it. (Sarah Armes and Sinead Leach, Broughton High School, Edinburgh, Speaking Competition winners 2008)

> This is exactly the kind of thing that our pupils need to have the chance of participating in. (Hugh Fraser, director of education, culture and sport, The Highland Council)

The trust attaches importance to the encouragement of the learning of other European languages in our schools. It is a means of giving young people a real sense of awareness that they are part of a large European community and, in later life, may improve their employment opportunities in a world where workforces are becoming increasingly mobile. The language theme will continue in the Speaking Competition in the coming years.

Information days for colleges and universities

The trust also runs information days at universities, promoting European programmes such as ERASMUS, COMENIUS, Language Assistants and IAESTE.[3] These sessions are followed by talks on employment in Europe, both at EU institutions and at other organizations, and on internships and volunteering in Europe. Speakers include representatives from the European Commission and European Parliament, the British Council, Young Scot and Scottish companies which operate in continental Europe. Most importantly, young people who have already studied or worked abroad speak of their experiences and are available to chat to students informally. Following discussions with the Foreign and Commonwealth Office, particular emphasis is placed on information about the European Civil Service examinations in order to increase the number of young British people choosing a career in the European Union institutions. These events are run in conjunction with the National Union of Students.

Each year the trust arranges four or five information days in different institutions. The events are much appreciated by students and the institutions themselves. Information about opportunities to study and work in other European countries is, of course, available from the many excellent careers offices in universities and colleges, and some university departments have well-developed links with institutions in Europe. But highlighting the opportunities at a single event – particularly with young people giving a firsthand account of their experiences – has proved invaluable.

Other activities

The trust acts as a facilitator to provide educational establishments with speakers on Europe-related topics. In addition, the trust provides a conduit between the European Parliament and Commission and schools, passing on material and information about competitions and events.

Final thoughts

Reflecting on the trust's work over the years, it is worth underlining a number of points.The involvement of all local authorities in Scotland is key to the work of the trust. We have built up close relationships with the international co-ordinators and directors of education services at local authorities and are pleased that pupils from all areas, including the islands, are involved in our events. The trust has been at pains to ensure that it is not viewed as a proselytizing organization of behalf of the EU. It has made it clear that the objective is to widen horizons of young Scots, especially those from less prosperous areas, by raising their awareness of the implications and opportunities of being part of a large European community.

Working in partnership with other organizations has also been mutually beneficial and, in addition to our close links with Learning Teaching Scotland,[4] the Scottish government, the Scottish Parliament and the European institutions, the trust has run joint events with the National Union of Students, Scottish universities, the British Council and Scottish CILT (language teaching body). We were the Law Society of Scotland's partner organization for the Donald Dewar Debating Competition last year.

It is also striking that the trust's work has its impact on the wider community. Preparation for the Euroquiz involves not only the pupils themselves but also their teachers and families, not to mention other supporters of the school from the Parents' Association to the school janitor. The heats and the final are also widely reported in the local and national media and the final is web-cast. This element of the trust's work is incidental to its main role but is making a modest contribution to a better awareness of 'things European' among a wider Scottish audience.

The trust has worked hard to become the first port of call for European education in Scotland, with a good website and a constantly updated list of useful resources for schools and universities. There certainly seems to be a continuing strong demand for the kind of services which the trust provides.

Annex discussion

The SEET initiative is seen as a prime example of a voluntary non-governmental organization (NGO) taking a lead in fostering the European dimension in schools. The contribution of civil society is at last recognized in the European Union. Article 11 of the Lisbon Treaty serves as a framework to guide dealings between the EU and civil society so that these dealings are open, transparent, efficient and continuous, as in the Scottish example. However, these dealings and communications between the EU Directorates and NGOs have to be instigated and sustained.

The National Council of Voluntary Organisations (NCVO) is the umbrella body for the voluntary sector in England, with sister councils in Wales, Scotland and Northern Ireland. This council has 7,000 members and represents and supports more than half the volunteer sector in the United Kingdom. In July 2009 it was instrumental in creating the European Network of National Associations (ENNA) whose remit is to address the range of issues affecting voluntary organizations across the EU. One of these issues is the precarious relationship between civil society and the EU which was originally created for two partners only, governmental and business enterprise. ENNA is also focusing on the development of a European charter which would ensure that all voluntary sector bodies have a relationship with the EU and have recognition as partners, for instance, of special interest to us in education. This is a step toward empowering civil society where people come together to make a positive difference in their lives and the lives of others, for mutual support and to pursue shared interests and causes. ENNA's remit includes acting as a voice for the pan-European voluntary sector in this respect. Civil society is a latecomer third party, and although lamentable it is not inexplicable that the commission may have reservations about the operation of a charter.

The approach from the voluntary sector is to rebuild communities and institutions from the bottom up. This involves a great deal of networking, and technologies have been proposed as potential facilitators for this. Returning to questions of education, Barbara Macleod has offered the dream to have a Euroquiz in every country with the finals at the European Parliament. Thus the discussion comes full circle to affirm where an NGO has made a difference and could possibly expand that influence in education.

Notes

1 The presiding officer and two deputies, equivalent of the speaker and deputy in the House of Commons at Westminster, are elected by fellow MSPs.

2 The national curriculum for Scotland, see www.scotland.gov.uk/Topics/Education/Schools/curriculum/ACE.

3 IAESTE, the International Association for the Exchange of Students for Technical Experience, www.iaeste.org.uk. British Council offices are the agency in the United Kingdom.

4 The national agency for curriculum development and delivery in Scotland, ltscotland.org.uk.

6 Pedagogy, Citizenship and the EU: practitioners' perspectives on the teaching of European citizenship through modern foreign languages

Mairin Hennebry

Chapter Outline

In recent times a perceived need has emerged to re-engage citizens locally, nationally and globally in social and political activity. Between the national and the global lies the European sphere, and 'education for citizenship' is attracting much interest among new and old member states alike. Indeed there is broad agreement in the literature that, while the EU continues to exist, structures are needed for preparing students for European citizenship.

One purpose of these structures that has been identified by advocates of such an education is to address a public lack of awareness of the benefits of political and economic integration, which is leading to diminished levels of popular support and to the 'Democratic Deficit' in Europe (Ollikainen, 2000).

Citizens can be defined as 'those able to exercise their rights and responsibilities in a democratic society and in order to exercise their rights they must be familiar with them and understand the scope and the limitations of their rights.' (Starkey, 2005, p. 25). Evidently other definitions exist, but Starkey makes an important point. Equipping people with the knowledge and tools to exercise their rights and responsibilities seems almost as important as bestowing these on them in the first place. Indeed this understanding is echoed in the European Charter for Democratic Citizenship and Human Rights Education adopted in May 2010, in which the Council of Europe defines education for democratic citizenship as

> education, training, awareness raising, information, practices and activities which aim, by equipping learners with knowledge, skills and understanding and developing their attitudes and behaviour, to empower them to exercise and defend their democratic rights and responsibilities in society, to value diversity and to play an active part in democratic life, with a view to the promotion and protection of democracy and the rule of law. (p. 7)

Although this definition does not explicitly refer to European citizenship it, nevertheless, outlines the foundational principles to any form of democratic citizenship, as seen through the Council of Europe. It is to be assumed then that any expectation of education that equips young people for active European citizenship would at the very least seek to manifest and develop these traits. This charter is a recent development but understandings of democratic citizenship throughout EU policy and initiatives have always expressed similar ideas and principles.

In 1993, the member states committed to introducing a European Dimension in Education, wherein school education systems within each country would seek to enable active European citizenship (European Commission, 1993). Little empirical research has been undertaken to examine the impact of this step on classroom practice and on attitudes and perceptions of young people. Existing research seems to suggest that evidence of learning about Europe is scarce (Convery et al., 1997). Much of the literature seeks to propose ways and means of addressing education for European citizenship and, although little of it questions whether such education is or can be effective, the discussion has placed particular emphasis on the role of modern foreign language (MFL) instruction. What, then, is the rationale for this view of MFL?

In England, the House of Lords European Union Select Committee (2005) and the Nuffield Language Inquiry (2000) stressed the value of linking language learning with citizenship education, respectively that citizens may take advantage of the opportunities offered by the EU and that cultural understanding may be developed. Reflecting the literature, the European Commission continues to promote languages as key to building understanding among citizens and preparing young people to accept their responsibilities as European citizens integrated into society (2008), although again the basis is largely theoretical and hypothetical.

The arguments presented in the literature for the role of MFL are as follows: MFL departments are well placed to promote the European dimension, since the necessary use of authentic materials provides a natural pathway into the discussion of the target culture and other associated topics (Convery et al., 1997). Citizenship and language learning share the goals of addressing learners' identities and promoting and developing skills for communication and participation, making them ideal companions and collaborators (Osler et al., 2005). Furthermore, the teaching of European citizenship through MFL could be seen to be associated with motivational issues. One motivation theory purports that instrumental and integrative factors of language learning contribute to language-learning motivation (Gardner, 1985) and indeed empirical evidence suggests that some language learners can be primarily motivated by employment prospects, cultural enrichment and overseas travel (Creanza, 1997).

Much of the literature indicates that, by developing an understanding and appreciation of other ways of life, the intercultural aspect of language teaching makes an essential contribution to education for democratic citizenship (Byram, 1992; Breidbach, 2002). Supporting this, Starkey (2005) points to the need to persuade teachers and students of the practical advantages of an intercultural approach. In addition, there is research evidence to suggest that a greater focus on cultural and social aspects of language learning, for instance through exchange visits, has the potential to bring benefits to the ideals underlying European citizenship, such as developing positive intercultural attitudes and an appreciation of diversity (Fisher et al., 2000).

Given these arguments, there is an arguable case for a close association between language learning and education for European citizenship, though this would seem to apply to a particular brand of language learning and not purely vocabulary and grammar acquisition. Nonetheless, whether this is taken into account in the MFL classrooms is to be explored.

Teachers' knowledge and beliefs

Among the various belief systems that frame teaching approaches, two are recognized as being commonly found in Western educational systems (OECD, 2009). The first of these embraces direct transmission beliefs about teaching and the second a constructivist view. According to Staub et al. (2002), the first of these implies that the role of the teacher is to communicate knowledge in a structured way, to give students clear and solvable problems explaining correct solutions. The second places the student as active participant, rather than passive recipient, in the process of acquiring knowledge. A constructivist approach gives greater prominence to the development of thinking and reasoning processes than to the acquisition of specific knowledge. The belief system adopted is significant as educators' beliefs about teaching and about their role as practitioners impact heavily on the learning process (Prawat, 1992).

Given the importance that is increasingly attributed to the role of MFL in education for European ctizenship and the recognized significance of teacher agency, it is perhaps surprising that there are few studies, if any, focusing on MFL practitioners' views and attitudes toward the issue of the European dimension. Some work has been undertaken to explore teachers' attitudes and perceptions more generally across disciplines and these studies offer a useful context and starting point.

Convery et al. (1997) investigated pupils' perceptions of Europe in England, France, Germany, Italy, the Netherlands and Spain. Student secondary school teachers from across all disciplines in the United Kingdom were also interviewed. Student teachers of various subjects were positive about European citizenship. Almost all the student teachers said they would consider incorporating a European dimension occasionally in their teaching, although, because of a perceived lack of knowledge, they did not feel competent to teach it. Furthermore, the study reported an almost complete lack of in-service training for teachers on the European dimension. Nevertheless, the creativity and appropriateness of the ideas proposed by student teachers for teaching the European dimension suggested benefits of a bottom-up approach, rooted in teachers' practical experience.

Interactions between student teachers' experiences of study abroad and their understanding of European citizenship were investigated by Osler

(1998) in seven European countries. The majority of participants were highly committed to the development of intercultural awareness and understanding. However, they were unable to agree on what constituted common European values or how the school curriculum might effectively contribute to developing European citizenship. These findings reflect the dichotomy between perceived enthusiasm among teachers for European citizenship education and a recognized lack of clarity surrounding the concept and how to teach it.

Convery et al. (2005) also offer a useful consideration of practitioners' attitudes toward the teaching of European citizenship, arguing that if pupils are to be equipped to make educated choices about their role in Europe then a European dimension must be included within education and explicitly address the development of a European identity. These studies offer a helpful general understanding of teachers' own perceptions and attitudes toward issues associated with the teaching of European citizenship. Given the emphasis placed on the role of MFL to this end, it is useful then to consider the issue in more detail, qualitatively focusing on the perspectives of practitioners in this specific field.

The research

The research presented here forms part of a larger study focusing on the impact of formal MFL instruction on developing active European citizenship. The focus of the data presented here is on the perspectives of MFL practitioners on the teaching of European citizenship through MFL.

The parent study consisted of secondary school adolescents in the maintained sector in England, France, Ireland and Spain. One inner-city and one rural school in each country participated in the study. The schools were chosen through consultation with staff at university education departments in the relevant countries who were given an understanding of the aims of the project. A limitation of the study is that schools could not be randomly selected since there were necessary scheduling constraints and since there had to be a certainty that schools would be willing to cooperate with the entirety of the study. The MFL teachers of the student participants in each country were interviewed. There were six male teachers and 13 female teachers. Table 6.1 shows a summary of how the teaching experience was distributed across the schools.

Teachers were interviewed individually in their native language. Their responses were transcribed, translated and coded according to the question categories. The quotations included in this chapter were chosen in most cases for their representativeness and in some cases because they highlight a specific issue that might add detail to an understanding of the issues.

Table 6.1 Summary of Teaching Experience Distributed across Schools and Countries

Country	Inner City	Years of Teaching Experience	Rural	Years of Teaching Experience
England	Nottingham	Teacher 1–30	Oxfordshire	Teacher 1–20
		Teacher 2–15		Teacher 2–10
				Teacher 3–13
France	Paris	Teacher 1–36	Boulogne-sur-mer	Teacher 1–3
	Banlieu	Teacher 2–33		Teacher 2–32
Spain	Madrid	Teacher 1–31	near Salamanca	Teacher 1–15
		Teacher 2–2		Teacher 2–28
		Teacher 3–30		
Ireland	Cork	Teacher 1–12	County Cork	Teacher 1–10
		Teacher 2–18		Teacher 2–19
		Teacher 3–20		

The teacher profile

Overall, teachers were passionate about language teaching and language learning, with these being the most common motivations for becoming a language teacher. In one interesting case, however, language teaching was seen rather as a channel for encouraging social change in an introspective, post-Franco Spain. The majority of the teachers referred to a period of time spent abroad, which had encouraged them in their passion for learning languages and for knowing more about the target culture.

The teaching of European citizenship

There was unanimous agreement among teachers that school education has a role to play in developing European citizenship:

> Certainly it's something that would be of benefit to students. (Ireland)

> If they could see it as one big Europe and we all need to be speaking different languages, it's certainly going to make my job as a language teacher so much easier because they would see the point . . . (England)

> Without a doubt . . . that would help to overcome nationalism and narrow-mindedness and it could even provide a means of resolving conflict. I think that the European context would really help the students to see nationalist problems in relative terms. (Spain)

> In fact we're not just French, we are European, so definitely 'citizenship' should be developed and 'European citizenship'. (France)

From varying perspectives, these comments support the teaching of European citizenship. The teacher in England stood out particularly in her focus on the teacher rather than the student, perhaps motivated by the particular struggles that MFL teachers in England face. Other particularly strong emergent themes were developing student mobility and an awareness of the wider context. There was unanimous agreement that schools have a part to play in such an important issue. Several teachers felt that giving greater prominence to the issue of European citizenship would encourage students to look beyond their local confines as well as enhancing their language learning experience.

Being informed on Europe

Teachers were asked to comment on what they believed might constitute the content of European citizenship education. All teachers referred to certain attitudes or knowledge that they felt European citizens should possess:

Irish teachers

- foreign language skills
- European laws and entitlements of European citizens
- understanding of the concept of co-operation
- understanding of the issue of immigrants in the society
- current European affairs

English teachers

- foreign language skills
- Europe's common history
- current affairs

Spanish teachers

- organizational features of the EU
- the citizen's place and role within the EU
- understanding of the principle of democracy
- internal and international political issues
- Europe's common history
- the development of the EU
- what it means to be a European citizen

- the rights, responsibilities and opportunities for personal progress available through European citizenship
- the advantages and disadvantages of the EU for the nation

French teachers

- the history of other European countries
- a given level of political understanding
- foreign language skills
- learn how to travel
- common values
- understanding the goals of the EU and adopting them

(Hennebry, 2009)

There was also agreement on the need for inter-cultural understanding through knowledge of shared European history or values. In contrast to teachers in Spain and France, teachers in England and Ireland made no explicit reference to European politics and were relatively restricted in their suggestions. Spanish teachers were the most detailed in their responses and referred to a direct relation between the EU and European citizens. Irish and English teachers, in particular, saw an awareness of current affairs as helpful to combating negative attitudes.

Language teaching and citizenship

Overall, teachers were positive about addressing cultural aspects of language learning as a means of improving cross-cultural understanding:

> Knowing languages, knowing oneself, always leads you to recognise the need to know other people, other cultures, other realities . . . languages are a very important channel for getting to know reality. (Spain)

The cultural dimension of language teaching was also considered to be motivational:

> [I]f we did more culture with them I think that would have a big impact on their desire to learn. (England)

> Culture has to be part of the language that you teach . . . you're making a huge mistake by alienating it and children are fascinated . . . (Ireland)

Teachers showed a distinct bias toward the cultural rather than political aspects of language learning, although they did not specify what they meant by 'teaching culture'.

Across the four countries, teachers contextualized language learning in the wider world, considering it an important means of encouraging inter-cultural communication. They showed that preparing the pupils for real communication with other individuals and groups was, in their opinion, one of the most important aspects of language teaching:

> I always want to capture the context where a language is used so that the children could actually go into that context and use what I've taught them in a real way. (England)

Teachers also viewed language teaching as a tool for equipping pupils with positive attitudes towards other cultures:

> [T]he most important thing is that opening of the mind and when you learn a language it opens you up to knowing other cultures. (Spain)

> [T]hey hopefully also experience some of the literature of the country which will open up their perspective on the culture, . . . and then it will bring them to the whole political-social strata that will really open up their knowledge of the country, how it works and even the social fabric of the country. (Ireland)

In particular, the teacher in Ireland placed great weight on the role of MFL in developing an awareness of literature and political and social systems. The wider literature supports such an understanding of MFL teaching, proposing an association between language learning and public and political discourse (Byram, 1992; Breidbach, 2002). Teachers saw their role as broadening students' horizons, enabling them to transcend their immediate environment:

> [Y]ou're trying to say . . . it can get you out of your little box and make you see that there's something bigger out there . . . (England)

> [T]eaching languages is mostly a cultural question. . . through the means of the language one should try to get people to understand each other better and to live constructively alongside one another. (France)

The majority of teachers saw language teaching as a means of introducing learners to a new culture, equipping them with tools and skills to communicate effectively across borders.

Challenging the ideal

Despite the positive attitudes toward language learning and the enthusiasm for the idea of language teaching and the principles that underlie it, a number of challenges were referred to. In England, one of the key difficulties raised was the nature of the National Curriculum (NC):

> In practice it's very much like any other lesson . . . everybody is to a greater or lesser extent constrained to do something they don't want to do. (England)

One teacher in England felt constrained within her secondary school teaching to an approach that contradicted her own beliefs about teaching. In her work at the primary school level, however, this same teacher found she was able to be faithful to her beliefs and concluded that this approach resulted in greater learning:

> [I]n the primary school it's lovely because, they learn so much quicker and you can take things in and you can give them as it were real tasks where they really have to use the language and I'm sure that is more effective . . . (England)

She later shed further light on the nature of secondary MFL teaching:

> [I]t's become horribly tight and to do with jumping through hoops frankly. It is all about what's a subordinate clause, have I included one, have you got 3 tenses there, have you made your verbs agree, have you made your adjectives agree . . . certainly it's not about learning the culture or citizenship of countries in Europe.' (England)

This particular educator's concerns were not an isolated case among teachers in England. The NC was consistently seen as restrictive and form- rather than content-focused, leading to mechanistic and disengaging language teaching.

Another teacher in England alluded to a lack of creative flexibility in the curriculum, saying educators 'would like to do more culture but we tend to just go through the textbook'. Since textbooks used at secondary schools in England tend to be closely based on the NC, this comment reflects both on the available materials and the curriculum. In exploring this issue further, one teacher offered a particularly useful insight into what might be a key stumbling block for the teaching of culture in greater depth:

> It's almost a vicious circle, that before you can look at cultural stuff and particular authentic materials on a particular topic . . . they need to reach a certain level of German and so you're actually trying to build their language up but they're doing that out of context so contextualising is a tricky part of it but it's very important. (England)

Comments such as this call for the design of materials that present the culture at a linguistically accessible level as a matter of priority.

Views among Spanish teachers were mixed. Generally teachers were satisfied with the content and structure of the curriculum, though one teacher raised concerns:

> [T]he curriculum continues to deliver the subject as if it was a dead language, in other words texts, writing, grammar knowledge . . . there might be some more relevant topics but they don't specifically address the issue of Europe. (Spain)

Teachers in France, however, believed that their curriculum addresses cultural topics and affords professional freedom and flexibility:

> They try to insert cultural aspects but in any case the language teacher is very free. You can do a lot to deliver the target culture and more and more this is becoming a priority. (France)

Similar sentiments were echoed in Ireland. Teachers seemed satisfied with the curriculum and textbooks, believing that they address cultural topics and allow enough time for this:

> We are given the syllabus with various topics to cover and there is an emphasis on the cultural element; this must be covered . . . (Ireland)

Such comments from teachers in Ireland indicate that certain rigidity exists in the curriculum. However, unlike the curriculum in England, it was considered to cover cultural topics more satisfactorily, suggesting that curriculum guidance is not in and of itself problematic for teachers.

Overcrowding the curriculum was referred to in all four countries, though it was of particular concern to teachers in England:

> Because of the demands of the course we don't have the time to think or to look at it as much as perhaps we'd like to. (England)

[C]reativity is what's missing and with that could come more of a cultural under-standing but if you stop what you're doing so that you can do a little project on whatever it is, then when you next come to try and do it there's even less time for it and the trend is towards compressing the languages curriculum.' (England)

Another teacher in England suggested a solution for addressing European citizenship despite time constraints:

The teacher, who's a very busy person, will tend to rely on the materials that are easily to hand, so I think having that content in a course-book would be very use-ful. (England)

In other words, a more structured approach to the inclusion of European citizenship in the curriculum would offer a means of ensuring that such issues are covered in the classroom.

Distinguishing the cultural from the political

For most teachers, the scope that MFL teaching contributes to European citizenship confined itself to the cultural and social aspects, with little or no reference to the political, except when prompted. One teacher in England mentioned that the subject in its present form does not allow political discussions, because of the students' lack of linguistic competence and a basic lack of awareness of the relevant topics:

[T]heir knowledge of how this country works is fairly minimal in some cases, and their knowledge of how this country fits into Europe is almost non-existent, so the question would be where would you start teaching European citizenship. (England)

Similarly, French teachers believed such issues would be too difficult conceptually for students in the early years of secondary school and suggested careful attention needed to be given to modes of presentation. Only one teacher argued that addressing the matter of Europe was not the role of MFL:

I don't think it's the role of language teaching to address European issues. That's mostly a matter for History, Geography, Civic Education . . . (France)

It was clear through the course of the interview that this teacher believed language teaching to be about the language culture rather than Europe, which he considered politically motivated.

Another teacher in England suggested that teaching European citizenship could disengage pupils whereas the majority of teachers in Spain favoured more explicit teaching for European citizenship through MFL.

Interviews revealed a reluctance to engage with the political and legal aspects of European citizenship, stemming from a perceived lack of understanding among students, lack of time in the curriculum and a sense that these matters are addressed through other curriculum areas. Additionally, however, teachers lacked confidence in their own knowledge and awareness of the political aspects of European citizenship, although they were aware of online resources they could access in order to obtain such information. Across the four countries, however, there was agreement that a cross-curricular approach would be most effective, with subjects such as history or geography highlighted as potential contributors. While current systems already adopt this approach in theory, overall teachers were clear that the existing situation is confused and patchy to the point where the European dimension is often not thoroughly addressed in any subject. In principle, Spanish teachers gave equal importance to a political understanding of European citizenship as to the cultural. Teachers in Ireland believed there is sufficient provision for the teaching of the political aspects of European citizenship through two specific subjects: civil, social and political education and social and personal health education. Together with a fourth-year option in European studies plus certain elements in the religious education curriculum, they complete a spectrum organized for such political aspects.

The idea of a cross-curricular approach is not a new one. The European dimension was originally intended to permeate the curriculum so that all subjects would play their part (Commission of the European Communities, 1993). In dividing up the responsibility among several subject areas, however, the European dimension in some curricula seems to have been diffused so thinly and so vaguely as to render it almost invisible in schooling.

Training for developing European citizenship

MFL teachers in England and Ireland felt overall less equipped to teach European citizenship and pointed to the perpetual need for further training created by the ever-changing nature of European affairs. Teachers in England who were currently involved in teaching the citizenship curriculum were among those who did not feel properly equipped to teach the European aspect of it, perhaps because they were more aware of what such teaching might involve in terms of knowledge and awareness. Half the teachers in Spain felt it was within their capabilities to teach European citizenship provided they had access to appropriate resources. The other half would wish to be offered a short course in preparation. In France, most teachers felt able to teach European citizenship in terms of the skills required, but would welcome a training course as beneficial, requiring also guidance on the content of such teaching. Suggestions were collated as to what training might be helpful:

Table 6.2 A Summary of Suggestions of Useful Training Proposed by Teachers in the Four Countries

- discussion forum for teachers to share ideas and resources
- resources
- suggestions and teaching techniques for presenting particular topics
- clear directives from the department
- a clear explanation of what is meant by European citizenship in the educational context
- subject-specific training
- a framework from which to approach the issue

Initiatives do exist that seek to address these training needs. A particularly pertinent example is the Intercultural Studies in Teacher Education to Promote European Citizenship (ISTEPEC) partnership that brought teacher institutions together from a range of European countries for 2-week modules where participants explored ways to offer initial teacher education for the purpose of teaching European citizenship. Some of the topics included: the study of the history, geography and institutions of Europe; some insight into languages, cultures and shared values; and, more important than anything else, the curiosity and the motivation to want to learn and find out, together with some pedagogical approaches for how to engage students with these issues (Mailhos, 2007). However, such opportunities are not common and interviews with teachers in the study suggested that awareness is low of opportunities that exist, once again indicating a divide between Brussels and the classroom.

Discussion and implications

The research sought to investigate MFL practitioners' views on the teaching of European citizenship in their lessons and the contribution they felt the MFL curricula might make to this end. The importance of equipping young people with the necessary attitudes and knowledge for active European citizenship was acknowledged by teachers in the four countries. Partly because of their own firsthand experience of it, teachers believed that placing greater emphasis on the target culture has the potential to engage learners more effectively. These views not only support the theory set forward by Gardner (1985) but also the enthusiasm found among teachers in previous research, for the teaching of the European dimension findings of Convery et al. (1997). Practitioners, the literature and language learners alike (Creanza, 1997), concur that greater attention to the target culture in MFL teaching could afford students a wider, applied context, offering them a greater understanding and awareness of the world in which they live. Thus, in principle there is agreement among language learners, practitioners, the research literature and the European Commission that language teaching can play a unique role in developing European citizenship, albeit with a clear bias among MFL teachers toward cultural rather than political aspects.

Nevertheless, in contrast with student teacher participants in the Convery et al. survey (1997), levels of enthusiasm for teaching the European dimension among more experienced teachers in the present study seem tempered by a sense of realism and a more acute awareness of the challenges that come with it. It is important to note that the enthusiasm of the student teachers might have been a result of the European Commission's Green Paper on the European Dimension of Education (1993) that was published 4 years prior to Convery's survey.

This study yielded an important insight into the difficulties and challenges of teaching the European dimension in the current context. In particular, teachers in England felt that the MFL National Curriculum lacks flexibility and is essentially disengaging young learners as much as teachers, because of its lack of exciting content. These views supported Starkey's (2005) concerns at the current lack of adequate cultural content in the available teaching materials. The issue, however, was less prevalent in other countries, where the curriculum provided sufficient opportunities for developing cultural aspects or was more flexible in allowing the teacher to supplement the issues mentioned. Common to all four countries was a sense that training for the development of European citizenship would be beneficial.

Although all teachers seemed guided by the curriculum to some degree, even where a centralized curriculum is enforced, its implementation seems to vary according to the individual teacher and context. While this is inevitable and perhaps to some extent, desirable, it is essential that the unique nature of delivery and content across the member states does not result in unequal access to rights and opportunities. If the curriculum is viewed as a store into which some teachers delve deeper than others, then arguably it should address issues that are truly relevant to today's language learners, while affording teachers sufficient flexibility and ownership to make professional judgements about their teaching that are based on their familiarity with their students and their context.

Most of the teachers interviewed wished for the modification and simplification of, not an addition to, the present curriculum. New teaching ideas imposed on teachers 'from above' without consultation, provoking little visible improvement in language learning and attitudes among pupils, were generally rejected. Teachers in England expressed a lack of ownership, feeling that the current curriculum does not promote teacher autonomy and does not address the issues they consider important for their students. Across the four countries there were teachers who felt that the curriculum could do more to make the target culture more salient in the language classroom. Arguably, this would in turn contribute to the knowledge and understanding necessary for active European citizenship (Byram, 1992; Breidbach, 2002).

Teachers in all four countries preferred a cross-curricular, integrated approach to European citizenship, rather than introducing it as a distinct subject. Particularly teachers in Ireland, who already had experience of this type of approach, suggested that integrating European citizenship into a number of curriculum areas allowed for greater coverage of the subject. Nevertheless, even these teachers felt that students could be better informed, suggesting that specific planning and thorough implementation would need to be ensured within such an approach.

Returning to the belief systems of direct transmission and constructivism, it appears that teachers' experiences show them being torn between the two. Teachers seem to support a combination of the two approaches. On the one hand, they express a desire to equip their students to explore other cultures and ways of life, opening their minds to other worlds and giving them the tools with which to discover these worlds beyond the classroom. On the other hand, they ascertain that in developing a European dimension there is a body of knowledge with which students should be provided. In the case of England, particularly, though to some extent in the other countries also, the reality of the classroom, of the curriculum and of the perceived need to teach to the exam, leads teachers to express a sense of constraint to teach rule sets and vocabulary as a means of meeting the requirements set out by the

NC. Thus a set of beliefs more akin to the direct transmission approach takes pre-eminence and teachers feel compelled to adhere to teaching approaches that do not completely reflect their own beliefs about teaching. Added to this, the body of knowledge they are constrained to provide does not match the knowledge they believe would be most useful to their students. Thus teachers' self-efficacy is undermined and levels of job satisfaction are negatively impacted upon (Caprara et al., 2006).

There is a clearly expressed need for further professional training and information to address education for European citizenship. Teachers in England point to a particular set of challenges, and across the four countries there is an inconsistent approach to the European dimension in education. In order to ensure equal access to rights and opportunities for young people across Europe, this situation appears to call for collaborative efforts between professional teachers, their representative bodies, learners and the European Commission to devise an appropriate MFL curriculum in the new and established member states.

Foreign Language Assistants in Schools: making sure of the future

7

Martha Wörsching

There are more than six billion language learners in the world, of whom only a minority suffer from the disability of monolingualism.

> (Jim Coleman, 2005)

The fact that [the Language Assistants programme] has outlasted empires and survived world wars and revolutions is a testimony to the power of the appetite of human beings to seek knowledge and understanding across frontiers and cultural divides.

> (Sir David Green, director-general, British Council, in Rowles et al., 2005)

Abstract

This chapter reviews the history and role of the assistantship scheme in the context of modern language teaching and learning in Great Britain; it points to available evidence and findings related to the benefits of foreign language instruction for students and schools and its relevance to the efforts to close the 'linguistic skills gap' in Great Britain. In addition, the chapter considers the experiences of foreign language assistants as 'cultural ambassadors' for their own countries and as learners of a second language within its cultural context. Finally, the benefits and challenges of educational and cultural mobility for young people in a globalizing world dominated by the English language will be critically assessed in view of the needs and proposals for European education in the future.

Introduction

The Language Assistants Team at the British Council invited university tutors as usual to a briefing session at the beginning of the academic year of 2010 to 2011, to update us on the application process for our students aiming to go abroad as English language assistants (ELAs) in 2011/12. However, what we could not have expected then was to be told that students in England and Wales – in contrast to students in Northern Ireland and Scotland – could actually not apply for places at the moment, because, as a result of the coalition government's spending review, the application process had been put on hold. We could not believe our ears! Was this programme, which we had publicized to our students as an excellent opportunity to live and work abroad before going into their final year, now suddenly abolished? How could year-abroad tutors and administrators have information meetings for potential candidates, if we had to tell them that 'yes, it's an excellent opportunity, you really should apply, but you cannot apply yet'?

As the information sank in, colleagues in higher education as well as past and present assistants started a protest campaign targeting the Department for Education (DfE) and created a Facebook site for supporters of the protest. The on-line petition 'Save the British Council Language Assistants Programme' was set up. We wrote to our MPs and MEPs[1], encouraging them to query the situation with the DfE. In the *Independent,* on 23 October 2010, the article 'Century-old Teaching Programme Suspended after Spending Cuts' claimed that the scheme could now be in jeopardy, ending a long tradition of 'British students . . . travelling abroad to teach in foreign classrooms as language assistants', among them luminaries such as Rory Bremner, Fiona Bruce, Angus Deayton, Alastair Campbell, Reeta Chakrabarti and J. K. Rowling.

The Telegraph of 16 November 2010 ran an article by Vicky Tuck, principal of the Cheltenham Ladies' College and a past president of the Girls' Schools Association, with the heading 'Coalition Cuts Turning Languages into an Elitist Subject'. While outlining the parlous state of affairs of language learning in this country today and highlighting the particular advantages of the experience of teaching one's own language abroad (which she herself had enjoyed in her youth), the author came to this conclusion:

> If we want British students to learn foreign languages and stick with the subject to GCSE and beyond, then we need inspiring teachers with confident subject knowledge. That confidence is best acquired by the kind of linguistic exposure the teaching year abroad provides.

Two days later, on 18 November 2010, David Walker, professor of French at the University of Sheffield, wrote in a letter to *The Guardian* that it 'beggars belief that the so-called minister for education should be so blind to the scheme's benefits that officials are hesitating over funding the British Council to play its part'. He continued:

> For months the British Council has been awaiting a 'ministerial steer' as to whether it can go ahead with the language teaching assistantship exchange programme which it co-ordinates with its opposite numbers overseas. The scheme enables young people to take up language teaching posts in countries whose language they are learning.
>
> The work placement is a paid position to defray the cost of study abroad; it offers classroom experience to those considering a teaching career, engagement with workplace disciplines and immersion in a foreign language; and it enhances intercultural skills. The UK gains not only from the experience gained by British students and other young participants, but also from the reciprocal agreements whereby foreign students live and work in Britain and form lasting links with British people and institutions.

Information about the problems with the scheme also reached our students working as assistants abroad, and they sent e-mails expressing their concern. Then, after weeks of waiting for information about the fate of the scheme while at the same time talking to second-year students about their plans for the next year and regularly checking the British Council website, at last we were sent by e-mail on 24 November the latest update: 'Recruitment is now open for candidates in England and Wales.' The programme has been reprieved, at least for another year or two. But why does it matter so much, and why is its existence so important for this country and its education system? To answer these questions, one needs to look briefly, first of all, at the situation of language study in schools and higher education, before considering the value of the programme and of educational and linguistic mobility in general.

Languages in schools and higher education in Britain

During the last decade, the developments in language studies in schools and higher education have been a depressing story. Mike Kelly, professor of French at Southampton University, warned[2] in 2002 that the government's proposal to make foreign languages optional would have serious consequences. Kelly argued that, as the country depends on language skills, one cannot leave the take-up by schools either to student motivation or to national compulsion alone; as Kelly maintains, 'compulsion alone is not enough either. A more motivated student is likely to learn more effectively'. In 2004, the Labour government made languages optional after the age of 14, and consequently – as has become clear since – the steep decline in take-up in state schools has become inevitable. As Kelly predicted in 2002,

> [f]rom the point of view of higher education, *leaving the market to regulate school language learning at 14–16 will accelerate the existing decline in student applications to study language degrees. It will increase the rate at which language departments are being closed* [emphasis in original], and further reduce the numbers of UK students going into school teaching in languages. Language degrees may be confined to a handful of the more prestigious universities, and foreign language competence could become even more identified as an elite accomplishment. (ibid.)

That Kelly's predictions have become true should be of serious concern to those responsible for the future of education, and not just teachers of languages. Thus, the Dearing Report (2007), following a comprehensive review of school languages policy, produced evidence of a serious decline in take-up of the subject. Dearing recommended that all primary schools should teach languages by 2010; however, he did not support calls to reverse the decision of making languages optional beyond the age of 14. The intended mandatory teaching of languages at primary level was later abandoned by the government; the teaching of foreign languages in an age-appropriate way would have required a significant effort to train additional teachers in the subject area as well as a restructuring of the primary curriculum, while also planning for a good fit with the secondary curriculum to produce more motivated young linguists keen to continue with the subject. Since the Dearing Report, the General Certificate in Secondary Education (GCSE) results for languages have further declined. The latest available GCSE results in August 2010 are seen as evidence of 'The Language Crisis in British Schools' according to the education editor of the *Independent*:

> For the first time ever, French has slipped out of the top 10 of the most popular subjects at GCSE – the most obvious sign of the seemingly inexorable slide in languages take-up in schools, which employers say will damage British students on the international jobs market.
>
> Fewer than one in four youngsters (22.7 per cent) now sits French, with the numbers falling from 341,604 students in 2002 to 177,618. This year alone, there was a further 5.9 per cent fall. German has slumped from 130,976 to 70,619.
>
> (Richard Garner, 25.8.2010)

The article cites a number of experts who blame the policy of making languages optional. Wendy Piatt, the director general of the Russell Group of research-intensive universities, is quoted as saying that the take-up of languages today is 'inadequate to meet the needs of our universities, economy and society'.

That the situation in schools has had the effect Kelly predicted for higher education is also supported by the Worton Report (2009). The report suggests that 'there has been insufficient "joined-up" thinking about the role of foreign languages in the UK over the past decade; there remains no sense nationally or internationally that the UK is committed to multilingualism and thereby to informed cultural interactions' (Worton, 2009, p. 2). With an overall decline in student numbers, there is 'growth in Asian, Modern Middle Eastern and African and Iberian Studies. Similarly, home and overseas student numbers are declining, but EU students are up 13%' (ibid.). The report reflects that the language colleagues in university departments, whether they teach specialist or non-specialist students, feel beleaguered. However, the report also provides a number of positive recommendations, such as increased collaboration among all levels of education as well as national and international institutions and stakeholders. Worton also calls on universities to use their admissions policies to demonstrate the importance of the study of foreign languages, in the attempt to overcome the linguistic skills gap and foster intercultural understanding through institutions fit for a modern society.

With such problems in schools and universities, one may ask why there are still young native speakers of English who have embarked on studying another language and who even see it as 'one very big adventure'; this is the title of the winning article submitted for the languages, linguistics and area studies (LLAS) Student Award in 2010[3]: 'Encouraging school pupils to study languages, linguistic or area studies at university'. As the author, Daniel Finch-Race, a third-year student at the University of Edinburgh, writes:

> So let's get down to the nitty-gritty of why people often avoid languages: they're tough. Sure, starting out with a foreign language, it's easy to get lost; everything is hidden in darkness. . . . Why not try exploring a little? . . . You'll realise that there's so much out there for you to see. . . . Nobody's expecting you to be perfect, but anybody you meet will appreciate you trying to understand their culture and language. They'll go that extra mile to help, showing you the road less travelled, sharing their culture with you, and opening up the horizon. . . . What's keeping you? (Finch-Race, 2010)

Whether this article will really persuade a 14-year-old to continue with languages when he or she has many other options and pressures to contend with may be questionable, but what is clear is that this third-year student knows what he is talking about – he has travelled the road and *loved it*. Linguistic and educational mobility is indeed an adventure with rich rewards, as all of us who have experienced it can certify.

I was lucky to start while still at school working abroad during a long summer holiday, then took a gap year slaving away as an *au pair*, loved being an assistant in deepest Lancashire and, like quite a few of my colleagues, I came via the German Academic Exchange Service (DAAD) into a permanent post at a British university; for some years now I have been involved with the assistantship programme. Originally, our department was founded in 1972 as a pioneering Department of European Studies where all students studied at least one foreign language, entering with A-level qualifications, and a large part of substantive teaching was in the target language. However, this has changed over the last decade as fewer and fewer students with good language skills applied to study here. Now the renamed department teaches a wider-than-ever range of languages – from beginners to degree level – to non-specialist students on a university-wide language programme. Without the study opportunities at European partner universities supported by the ERASMUS scheme and especially without the British Council assistantship programme, we would have found it very difficult during the last decade to motivate students to take up or continue with languages and still teach up to degree level. So why is the assistantship programme so important for language learning, and what is so special about it?

Language assistants programme – more than 100 years

That the language assistants programme has a long tradition stretching back to the beginning of the twentieth century is well documented in the Centenary Brochure published by the British Council and the then Department of Education and Skills, edited by David and Valerie Rowles (Rowles et al., 2005). The editors were themselves ELAs in the same school in the Pyrenees, the father in 1959–60, with his daughter following in his footsteps 26 years later; and if this were not enough to demonstrate the personal knowledge the editors bring to their task, the reader learns that '[i]t was during David's year in the Pyrenees that he got to know Valerie's mother, and they subsequently married – after, of course, she had spent a year as an FLA in Hertfordshire in 1963–64!' (ibid., p. 33). This may be an extreme case of people falling in love with a foreign culture *and* a foreign language speaker, but it also shows – as the brochure illustrates with numerous examples – that being an LA is generally a life-changing and culturally enriching experience.

The programme goes back to the beginning of the last century, a time of a shift in language learning away from the grammar and translation approach, with the emphasis now on the spoken language. The role of the new LAs was, on the one hand, 'to expose learners to real ('authentic') language' and, on the other, 'to aid their understanding of neighbouring countries and cultures' (ibid. p. 3). The programme started in 1904 with a proposal from the French government to the English Board of Education to exchange LAs between the two countries, and 'it was swiftly agreed that the idea had merit and the following year a formal convention was concluded' (ibid., p. 4), followed shortly after by a similar arrangement with the Prussian government.

The programme originally consisted of a secondment to schools of young, part-time teachers who would conduct reading and conversation lessons while continuing their own studies. Later, students who were unqualified as teachers, joined the programme, most of them undergraduates who had completed two years' study at university.

The programme started on a modest basis. 58 English teachers (41 men and 17 women) were placed for the year 1904/05 in French schools. In that first year, there were also vacancies for six English Language Assistants in Prussia . . . (ibid., p. 4).

Quoting from a memorandum of the English Board of Education from 2 October 1905, the Centenary Brochure gives an impression of the situation these pioneers could expect: 'The English Assistants shall receive at the Institution to which they are attached a suitable room, board, lighting and heating and household, but no personal washing.' (ibid.)

Since these early days, the number of countries involved has grown, including now many more languages (Arabic, Chinese, French, German, Italian, Japanese, Russian, Spanish and Urdu), but what has remained is the principle of reciprocity between countries: there are bilateral agreements to exchange assistants (with the exception of Japan, Russia, Oman and Pakistan, who at present provide FLAs only). In Great Britain, the programme 'was administered by the Board of Education and then the Department of Education and Science until 1964, when it was taken on by the Central Bureau of Educational Visits and Exchanges (CBEVE) until 1992, when the Bureau was integrated into the British Council' (Rowles et al., 2005, p. 5). The British Council now cooperates with partner organizations in other countries, such as ministries of education, national agencies, or British Council offices overseas.

Over the years, the programme continued to grow. 'Until the 1960s, the placement abroad was only as a language assistant (and even this was discouraged at Oxbridge as diluting the intellectual content of the degree for merely practical gains)' (Coleman, 2004). At the time when Great Britain joined the Common Market in 1973, with figures of language learners at schools and universities buoyant, the number of FLAs in schools peaked at 4,578 in 1973 and 1974. On the other hand, the highest number of ELAs came in 1983 and1984, with 2,555 young people working abroad (ibid., p. 5). More recently, during the last decade, the numbers of assistants going abroad as ELAs and coming in as FLAs have shown a steady revival:

Language Assistants 2000–01 to 2010–11

Year	No. of ELAs to UK	No. of FLAs from UK
2000–1	1569	1905
2001–2	1460	2266
2002–3	1784	2671
2003–4	1752	2700
2004–5	1950	2659
2005–6	2120	2680
2006–7	2139	2649
2007–8	2150	2813
2008–9	2068	2924
2009–10	2339	2776
2010–11	2463	2481

(Source: Talin Chakmakjian, British Council Language Assistants Team, pers. comm. in email, 13 April 2011).

Of course, some country programmes are relatively small, while others are attracting large numbers of applicants. As Talin Chakmakjian wrote:

> France is our biggest programme, in terms of the number of posts offered to us by our partners, and we also receive the largest number of applications (from France). The 2nd and 3rd largest are Spain and Germany respectively. 40% of the total no. of applications received this year were for France, 27% for Spain and 13.5% for Germany (80.5% in total – UK-wide). (Talin Chakmakjian, 13 April 2011).

At this stage, it is too early to say whether the inability to open the recruitment process at the usual time in the autumn of 2010 had a negative effect on the numbers of ELAs from England and Wales for the academic year 2011/2012; and the future of the scheme depends, of course, not only on keen young people who want to apply but also on the willingness of education authorities here and abroad who have to fund it. With numbers of students taking languages declining and educational budgets under pressure, local authorities or schools may feel that they cannot justify assistantship posts, especially in times of spending cuts. Thus in Leicestershire, with 286 primary and secondary schools, the numbers of FLAs are not high: eleven were requested by schools for 2011/2012 (eight for French, one for German and two for Spanish), while in the academic years 2009/2010 and 2010/2011 there were 16 FLAs working in the county (International Links Coordinator, Leicestershire

County Council, pers. comm., 26 March 2011). Often schools share assistants, but a decline from 16 to 11 does not bode well, especially not at a time when we hear that 'languages [are] crucial to closing the gap in achievement between state and private school pupils'.[4]

Going abroad as a Language Assistant

In contrast to the programme's early years when assistants received no more than board and lodgings, they now receive a modest salary which is enough to live on. As the Centenary Brochure records, in 1956–57, the payment for FLAs was '£350 over the whole period of appointment. 2005/06 sees an annual salary for FLAs of £6,240.' (Rowles et al., 2005, p. 5). Today, according to the British Council website, assistants in EU countries receive about €800 net on average for 12 hours of teaching per week. In addition, to encourage work placements abroad among English native students, who are much less likely to study or work in a EU country than their European counterparts, since 2007 British universities have waived fees for their students on a work placement abroad. Thus, with their assistantship salary plus the ERASMUS grant available since 2008 to ELAs working in EU countries, the financial situation of assistants is secure. Working as an ELA is, therefore, an opportunity open to students from any background.

What has changed as well is that students applying for assistantships are no longer just from departments of modern languages, but there are also non-specialist language students for whom study or residence abroad is not compulsory, yet they are motivated to improve their language skills while hoping to gain useful general skills for their future career, whether this will be in teaching or not. The majority of applicants are second-year students who spend their third year abroad before coming back for the final year; as a year-abroad tutor for many years, my experience is that they usually return to apply themselves with increased energy to their studies, as they have improved 'their ability to engage critically with academic work' (Mitchell et al., 2005), while they have also gained a clearer view of what they want to do after graduation. Thus, the benefits of the time abroad are substantial for undergraduates (cf. Coleman, 1997, 2004 and 2005). In addition, there are also graduates opting for assistantship experience which can equip them with additional qualifications before applying for jobs in an increasingly competitive graduate market.

With the numbers of students studying foreign languages declining in Britain, it is nevertheless interesting to see that the numbers of applicants for assistantships have stayed relatively high. The best promoters of the scheme are former assistants. They can provide firsthand information about the everyday challenges and opportunities which come with the post, and the British Council also appoints some of these as 'Ambassadors' who can provide valuable advice to second-year students who need to be persuaded that they should venture abroad. Any motivated student can find excellent on- and off-line documentation and case studies on the British Council website. In most countries there are induction courses in specific regions for the new LAs before they start work at their school, to familiarize them with the school system and the tasks expected of them, and these induction sessions are also a good opportunity for meeting fellow assistants and setting up a network of contacts in the host country. Most returners will admit to some trepidation when first facing their new students in the classroom, and the way they are welcomed by the English teachers and integrated into the host school may not always go completely smoothly. However, most of them become aware soon that they can play a special role in the school, '. . . a living, breathing and youthful representative of another culture who helps to develop in students not only more confidence and competence in language skills, but also a greater understanding of how people from different countries think, feel and lead their lives.' (Rowles et al., 2005, p. 2)

'Engage with the exotic': language learning, teaching and residence abroad

So why is the continuation of the assistantship scheme so important for a country like Great Britain where speaking another language is not the norm, a country in 'the parlous state of foreign language teaching, . . . an island basking complacently in the warm glow of globalisation' (Guardian Leader, 5.12.2005)? To answer this questions, I would like to argue that one needs to look at the activities of language learning and teaching during the residence abroad, and do this in the context of what Jim Coleman means when he says: 'With global tourism people consume the exotic – with the Language Assistants programme they must engage with it.' (Rowles et al., 2005, p. 2).

Coleman, who worked as an LA in France in 1968 (Coleman, 2005) – as did his own mother during the Depression years in 1934 under more austere conditions (Rowles et al., 2005, pp. 8–9) – has been involved in extensive research on the role of residence abroad as part of undergraduate study. In his 2005 inaugural lecture as professor of Language Learning and Teaching at the Open University on the topic of residence abroad and university language learning, Coleman deplores the fact that, for the majority of native English speakers, it is the norm to avoid learning other languages; however, he also suggests that the psychology of foreign language learning produces serious anxieties for the learner: 'Individual identity has been created . . . through . . . learning the native language; learning a foreign language demands willingly and repeatedly and over a long period of time to abandon that security, that identity, that familiarity . . .', and this can lead necessarily to feelings of intense anxiety and insecurity (Coleman, 2005). In order to cope with such feelings, the individual has to engage actively with the language and everyday culture of the host country, and this can be experienced by the student as a major confrontation. The process of language learning is thus not without personal conflicts, while at the same time the experience of progressively getting better at communicating in the new linguistic and cultural landscape provides opportunities for intense pleasure and individual enrichment, which can be particularly rewarding for the young adults who are in the process of forming their own independent social identity. Thus, in the process of individualisation, the autonomous discovery of new ways of living and thinking in the host society can be experienced as fundamentally liberating and personally rewarding.

Similar findings are reported by Brenda Johnston et al. (2005), who draw on research evidence arising from an ESRC-funded project on the development of criticality in undergraduates. The authors maintain that during the year abroad, 'the self undergoes considerable changes . . . in terms of personal qualities and abilities to relate to wider experiences and conceptual frameworks than hitherto' (ibid., p. 1). The authors identify three major changes:

> Firstly, the students face quite considerable problems, of one type or another, . . .
> They are required to develop extensive problem-solving skills and to draw on personal resources. In surviving this process, students tend to develop enhanced confidence in their ability to survive difficulties, to be more willing to take risks. These

are characteristics required in criticality, especially at the higher levels. Secondly, . . . the students are exposed to a different culture which challenges their existing view of the world. Sometimes these challenges are difficult and uncomfortable. Capacity to challenge existing formulations and to be aware of, understand and evaluate alternative viewpoints is required at higher levels of criticality. Thirdly, the students' language improves. This is more than a technical skill, given (a) the close relationship between language and cultural awareness; (b) the links between language and the ability to access and process information; and (c) the role of language in mediating experience. The enhanced language facility enables the students to engage more meaningfully with a wider range of issues in their final year at university. They may acquire the ability to use linguistic concepts from an unfamiliar culture in ways which enable them to think in new ways in terms of that culture. Language can also be viewed as a basic knowledge resource. (ibid.)

In his summary of research on residence abroad as part of a university degree, Coleman also refers to the linguistic progress of students, underlining that 'interacting with native speakers is more productive than simply attending classes: this may be why work placements appear more beneficial than university exchanges' to the students themselves (Coleman, 2004). This 'interaction with native speakers' is arguably demanded much more of students in work placements such as assistantships, while students studying at partner universities abroad, often living in residence halls with other 'foreigners', may share most of their time with the typical ERASMUS university crowd, young people from all corners of the EU, keen to practise their English with our students. In addition, an increasing number of universities in the EU are offering lectures in English, thus our students cannot escape the increasing Englishization of European higher education deplored by Coleman (2005). The fluency of their fellow students in two or three languages, therefore, may contribute even more to our own students' feelings of linguistic inferiority and does not motivate them to use and thus improve their language skills, which had been one of the major objectives of their going abroad in the first place.

In contrast to university students, the LAs cannot so easily escape into Anglophone company; they usually live with native families, in shared accommodations with natives. They have to shop and cook for themselves, deal with colleagues and students in and out of the classroom and cannot avoid using the target language in many everyday situations. However, probably the greatest advantage for them in terms of cultural and intercultural awareness, compared to the experience of others on work and university placements, is having to teach their own language. This means that they also have to engage with the exotic. The process of teaching their own language and culture while learning another language in an 'alien' cultural context forces them to reflect increasingly on their own cultural identity and see its relativity. If learning another language has the effect of 'denaturalising the native language and culture' (British Academy, 2011), then teaching one's own language opens also the chance of seeing it as 'exotic', and this in turn needs increased engagement and reflexivity. I can still remember the first day of my assistantship when I greeted a class of sixth-formers with *Grüß Gott*, to which they responded with mild hilarity, having been taught before by teachers exposed to different regional forms of German. Little did we know then that, in less than a year, a sizeable group of these students would celebrate their A-levels mountaineering with their teachers and me in the Bavarian and Austrian Alps, providing us all with intense intercultural, linguistic and personal experiences. As Coleman says when listing his six objectives of the residence abroad (academic, cultural, intercultural, linguistic, personal and professional), intercultural competence is gained through the 'awareness of [the] relativity of cultures – including one's own' and it is achieved through 'cognitive *and* affective learning' (Coleman, 2004). Thus, it may not be surprising that, through their intensive engagement with the language as teachers as well as students, 'the experiential learning during a year abroad is more highly valued than the cognitive, content learning of three years in the UK university' (Coleman, 2004).

What is undoubtedly 'a life-changing experience for most students' (Johnston et al., 2005) needs to be prepared and supported properly by the home institutions (Coleman, 2004, 2005), but what is essential is that it is a time when students can experience autonomous learning as never before. To support this, in times of electronic communication, the role of the tutor at the sending institution can be to give feedback and regular reports on their progress, which in turn encourages the students to become aware of their actual learning progress and so enhance it. Proper accreditation of the time abroad as well as thorough debriefing after their return can help students value and build on their own learning strategies and the new skills they have acquired. All this can best take place in the context of the returners acting as 'ambassadors' for the scheme, thus allowing them to share their experiences – positive and negative – with the next generation of students going abroad. In collaboration with a number of universities and the Centre for Recording Achievement, the British Council has also developed a Personal Development Portfolio (PDP) 'to recognize the transferable skills and experience acquired during the language assistantship in a more formal way' (Hoggan, 2007). The portfolio can be customized by sending institutions in accordance with their own forms of accreditation. Generally, assessment and accreditation encourage students to become more fully aware of the many forms of formal and informal learning taking place during their assistantship, confirmed by a student who maintains that it forced her to 'actually realise how much . . . [she'd] accomplished. Once you realise this, it gives you even more impetus to go even further' (Hoggan, 2007).

Conclusion: linguistic, educational and professional mobility in the future Europe

The impetus which individual students gain from working as assistants goes far beyond their own personal benefits. Indeed, linguists, educationalists and economists have provided ample evidence of the importance of international educational mobility in a globalizing world (Altbach et al., 2007; Becker et al., 2009; Bhandari et al., 2009; Brooks et al., 2009, 2010; Coleman, 2004, 2005; Drummond Bone, 2009; HEFCE, 2009; King et al., 2004, 2010; Parey et al., 2010), and it seems quite obvious that, without the century-old assistantship scheme, the outward international mobility of British students, already low compared to other European countries (King et al., 2004), would be even more problematic. The literature shows that one of the major barriers to greater student mobility is the lack of a foreign language (cf. Brooks et al., 2010; King et al., 2004). As a major political project of the EU, the ERASMUS programme was created in 1987 to forge a common European identity, while the signing of the Bologna Declaration in 2002 demonstrates 'an explicit commitment to creating a European higher education space and to furthering it among teachers, researchers and administrative staff, as well as students' (Brooks et al., 2010, p. 86). However, as King et al. (2004) report, data on European exchanges show that the flow of incoming students from EU countries is twice the outward flow: 'The institutional surveys confirmed the key role of language in both channelling mobility and acting as a barrier' (ibid., p. 13). Thus, the creation of a common European identity and an increased intercultural awareness cannot be achieved. As Brooks et al. highlight, the 'exposure to cultural difference may be limited' for many outgoing students, 'due to the dominance of North America as a destination country' (2010, p. 98).

In contrast to this, students who go to teach English in other European countries not only form that part of outgoing students who themselves gain substantially in terms of linguistic, cultural and intercultural benefits, but as role models of geographic, educational and linguistic mobility, they also contribute actively to the linguistic, cultural and intercultural learning of school children in European as well as non-European countries. The reciprocity of the scheme should also guarantee that young Europeans come to this country as LAs to help native English speakers at primary and secondary levels understand the value and pleasure of learning another language and to motivate them to venture abroad for their own education. As the autumn 2010 petition to the DfE put it:

> This programme has a very significant impact on the education of pupils in primary and secondary education both in the UK and across Europe. For many school pupils, the assistantships represent the only opportunity to meet and learn from a native speaker of the foreign language they are studying. Language assistants – often quite close in age to the pupils they teach – become vital role models and a source of inspiration.

LAs, therefore, are not only important for today's schools in Great Britain to help overcome the linguistic skills gap and inspire native English speakers to become competent speakers of other languages, but they are even more important for schools in the future Europe, where speaking only one language will not be enough or where only an elite can speak multiple languages (cf. British Academy, 2011, Kelly, 2002, Worton, 2010[5]). To provide all young people in Britain with life-chances in the Europe of the future, they need to have the capacity to realize their entitlement to learning languages, and realistically, this can only be achieved through a change in policy, namely through making language learning compulsory again and funding this new policy adequately. The decline in language learning over the last decades is in its own way a stark reflection of the increasing educational inequality in this country and in turn evidence of a social inequality that is more pervasive than in most other EU countries. If a child's language learning, like taking music lessons, has come to depend more and more on parental income and the postcode, then demanding languages for all students up to the age of 16 is not a defence of the status quo (Beadle, 2011[6]) but should be seen as a critique of the scandal of unequal educational provision and the socio-cultural deprivation of many of our schoolchildren. My experience as an LA many years ago teaching in both grammar schools and secondary modern schools certainly showed that 'boys from northern council estates' did not find it 'pointless' then to learn languages, and many did it with real enthusiasm. We are not doing young people a service if we do not demand that this society owes it to all of them to be educated for the future wider world and that it would be in the interest of a future, united Europe to prepare them all to study and work abroad. To close the 'gap of achievement between state and private school pupils', as Kathryn Board, the Centre for Information on Language Teaching's (CILT)[7] chief executive demands, '[C]hildren in state schools have to have the opportunity to learn a language, and understand the benefit of learning a language, for social mobility, for employment as well as for leisure'[8].

To achieve this, the assistantship scheme is an important part of proactive policies of language education which need appropriate funding now, as we need LAs now and for the future. The LAs as young mobile learners and speakers of other languages must be seen as a precious resource from which the future teachers of modern languages here and in other parts of Europe can be recruited. Not all of them will go into teaching, but wherever they will work, they will be advocates of cultural exchanges in the future Europe, and they will also be the future parents of children who think that speaking just English is not enough. With their active experience of different styles of pedagogy and an understanding of different educational systems and cultural traditions, they will act as role models and inspire the next generation of language learners, who will know and care more about Europe than most young people in Great Britain do today.

Notes

1   Colleagues had suggested writing to MEPs, as they were thought to understand that the axing of the programme would not be conducive to increasing the woefully low number of native English speakers with foreign language skills and not aid or strengthen Great Britain's presence in the EU. There were some positive replies, but I also received the following from an MEP who shall remain nameless: 'I am uncertain what you expect me to do about it, if anything. I have no expertise in language training. As an MEP, I get by very well in English.'

2   Kelly, M. (2002), 'Excusez-Moi, Êtes-Vous un Terroriste?' *Times Higher Education Supplement*, 29 March 2002: 22–3.

3   Finch-Race, D. (2010), 'One Very Big Adventure', Subject Centre for Languages, Linguistics and Area Studies, www.llas.ac.uk/resources/paper/6174.

4 Shepherd, J. (2011), 'Dumping Languages Stunts Life Chances, Schools Are Told', *The Guardian*, 27 January 2011.

5 Worton, M. (2010), 'We Need to Put the Case for Languages, and Universities Should Lead the Way', *Times Higher Education*, 21 October 2010.

6 Beadle, P. (2011). 'The English Bac and the Status Quo', *The Guardian*, 26 April 2011.

7 CILT, previously a government agency, merged on 7 April 2011 with the Centre for British Teachers, Reading.

8 Quoted in 'Languages Plea to State Schools', *London Evening Standard*, 27 January 2011.

Models of Bilingual Schooling

Lynn Erler, Jackie Holderness, Marc Wolstencroft,
Judith Woodfield and Gabriela Meier

8

Chapter Outline

There has been no better time before now to consider the future of bilingual schooling in Europe. This is because linguistic and practice-based research findings in bilingualism have been crossing over into European policies providing guidance documents that have clear conceptual underpinnings. Bilingual schooling is distinguished here from bilingual education only insofar as the former focuses primarily on the school-based conceptualization and realization of bilingual or plurilingual teaching and learning. Bilingual schooling is itself, however, no simple topic because it does not merely involve teaching linguistic aspects of two (or more) languages. It involves bi-cultural and multicultural knowledge and an understanding of the complex cross-connectedness of the languages which is integral to being bilingual, including the roles each language plays in the learner's and the school's life, from innermost personal levels to issues of power in the immediate and wider communities. There are many different approaches to creating bilingual education. More and more school programmes are being developed in Europe, some researched and reported on, only a few evaluated. In this chapter, we first establish a preferred ideology for bilingual education and then propose a framework identifying the influences on its realization in a school. There then follows a selection of working models of bilingual schooling, presented and described in their own words by key people engaged in them.

What are not included in this chapter are arguments for and discussions about the advantages of bilingualism and bilingual education. These are assumed and can be found in the literature on bilingualism that has appeared over the last half century. It is clear from studies in applied linguistics, psycho- and cognitive linguistics, neuro-science, literacy and education, as well as reports from the chalk face and from bilinguals themselves, that being bilingual is of benefit to all concerned.

Bilingualism

What is 'bilingual'? For the sake of expediency here, it is the ability to handle at least two languages in some way along an imaginary continuum that includes being able to 'get along' in a conversation to possessing native-like capacities, including literacy, in the languages. In addition, the term 'bilingual' carries with it deeper layers of knowledge and understanding of languages and cultures.

The purpose of this chapter is not to offer detailed consideration of the vast literature on bilingualism. Colin Baker's (1988) reviews of the research and theories about bilingualism, which had appeared up through the 1980s, dispelled misconceptions that bilingualism was somehow detrimental to the child and that bilingual schooling would impede rather than, as it clearly does, promote cognitive development. He advocated the effectiveness found in certain immersion programmes and above all the valuing of languages equally regardless of their status in the socio-political realm. He set the tone for later studies, influencing European policies[1]. A review by Suzanne Romaine (1995, 2nd edn) of the growing applied linguistic literature on bilingualism included further details surrounding definitions of bilingualism, the 'bilingual brain' and types of bilingual children as well as attitudes toward bilingualism at local and higher political levels. Most recently, Ofelia García (2009) has brought together the many issues which have emerged from what she terms the 'translanguaging' between languages and cultures that occurs with bilingualism to focus on what constitutes types, models and directions in bilingual education. She includes chapters on socio-political and geo-political attitudes and official policies to give a global perspective. At a different end of the spectrum of studies, in a clear view of what bilingualism and bilingual development can mean at the personal and familial levels, Edith Esch-Harding and Philip Riley (2003) provide valuable support for parents and for schools as well when dealing with children and families. There is still much to be learned about the social, political and linguistic dimensions of bilingualism, the bilingual brain and the processing and development of bilingualism, with many questions which researchers continue to engage in.

Language ideologies in schools

What has clearly come out of the literature is a distinction between two fundamental ideological approaches to bilingual schooling identified by John Edwards (1984) and refined by García (2009). One conceptualization provides language programmes where the ultimate aim is fluency in a majority language. Any support given to another, possibly minority, possibly mother tongue (MT) language is viewed by the school as an interim measure on the road to full competency in the majority language. A manifestation of this includes foreign language teaching where language is simply a subject in the school curriculum. Such aims in education fall under García's (2009, p. 7) umbrella expression 'monoglossic', used to describe the pedagogical approach to different languages as if they were unrelated autonomous systems, where there is no acknowledgement in the schooling of the complexity and richness of knowing and using two or more languages in real contexts for pertinent reasons. Monoglossic ideology is evident, for instance, in the separation of languages in most secondary schools in England into two distinct departments, English and modern foreign languages (MFL), with no cross-fertilization or cross-referencing between them.

   In contrast to monoglossia, Edwards' (1984) promotion of language maintenance or enrichment for bilingual education is taken up and expanded to 'heteroglossia' by García (2009, p. 7) which is a more complex concept than

Edwards' description. A heteroglossic view sees a bilingual's languages as 'multiple voices. A heteroglossic ideology of bilingualism considers [the bilingual's] multiple language practices in interrelationship', acknowledging 'the complex social realities of multilingualism' (p. 9) lived by bilinguals and which ought to be integral to bilingual schooling. Creating bilingual programmes within such an ideological framework is not at all straightforward, as García (2009) and other much earlier authors (such as Spolsky et al. eds., 1977) have pointed out. There are numerous players, forces and local and more distantly situated variables that exert an influence on the conceptualization and development of a bilingual schooling model. Consequently every school will have a different programme, specific to the school's and the learners' circumstances and to the decisions made by those in power. These circumstances include, inevitably if not immediately, the political aims of the nation–state in which the school is located.

Heteroglossic models of bilingual education at school level validate a child's two (or more) languages, aiming to develop them including biliteracy as equally as possible. In addition to curriculum structure, the ideologies, aims, motives and commitment of the principal players or influences, described metaphorically below as the linked, integrated sides of a triangular framework, are ingredients for the success of a bilingual programme. The aims, motives and commitment may well be multifaceted; they are certainly multilayered and will include rationales based on any number and combination of personal, societal, economic and political factors. What is important is the theoretical and in-practice egalitarian status of the languages in the school, encompassing as well an attitude of recognition, validation and development toward the child's mother tongue.

European guidance

Recognizing the multilingual, multicultural heritage of Europe and wishing to facilitate the mobility of people and ideas, the Council of Europe has produced many pieces of guidance and recommendation, partly as the result of research in council-supported projects for language policy development and the democratization of language in schooling. Driving concepts behind these language education policies have been clearly distilled in the Council of Europe review document, 'Plurilingual Education in Europe—50 Years of International Cooperation':

Plurilingualism: All are entitled to develop a degree of communicative ability in a number of languages over their first one in accordance with their needs.

Linguistic Diversity: Europe is multilingual and all its languages are equally valuable modes of communication and expressions of identity. The right to use and to learn one's language(s) is protected in Council of Europe Conventions.

Mutual Understanding: The opportunity to learn other languages is an essential condition for intercultural communication and acceptance of cultural differences.

Democratic Citizenship: Participation in democratic and social processes in multi-lingual societies is facilitated by the plurilingual competence of individuals.

Social Cohesion: Equality of opportunity for personal development, education, employment, mobility, access to information and cultural enrichment depends on access to language learning throughout life.

(Council of Europe, 2006, p. 4)

We see here an emphasis on socio-political aspects of languages reflecting the desire to construct a future Europe that is not only economically dynamic but diametrically different from the last 2,000 years of almost continuous warfare among its peoples. At the specific language teaching level, however, there is in this same document guidance support for the development of language awareness and cross-linguistic understandings, the recognition and development of transferable skills across languages, and cultural awareness alongside reciprocal respect for others. These are complex topics which require expert training in them (Carder, 2007).

Influences and attitudes

Distilled from the vast research into bilingualism and from EU, EC and especially Council of Europe documentation, a model framework of maintenance or enrichment heteroglossic bilingual education in schools for the future Europe is proposed here as a three-sided structure, drawn with deceptively simple labels. Each side of the triangle has actually many layers to it that include political, social and cultural aspects, and the sides are interlinked in ways not shown in a two-dimensional drawing[2]. Nevertheless it aims to present the matrix of influences which exert greater or lesser impact on decisions and practices. Attitudes toward languages permeate from all sides of the triangle.

A conundrum in the EU and certainly in England is that politicians are aware of many languages being spoken across Europe and within their own country[3] yet in many EU schools monolingual and monoglossic attitudes

Policy –
legislation, guidelines,
recommendations from
authorities, institutions,
research, training at pan-,
national and local levels

bilingual
schooling

School –
ethos, structures, leadership,
teachers, curriculum, activities,
professional development

Child –
linguistic and cultural background,
family, identity, personality, future prospects

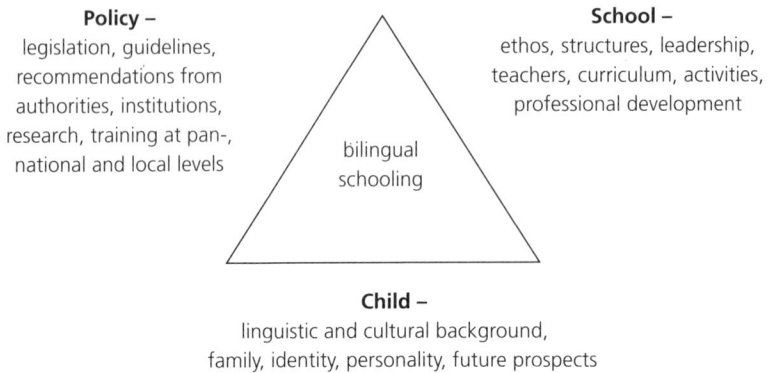

Figure 1 Matrix of Influences on Bilingual Schooling

prevail, as if other languages were at most academic and not part of the reality of students' lives and their society. There is often no recognition of an obligation of schooling to enable the student to develop the best possible results from his or her linguistic abilities.

In England the attitude toward bilingualism has been one of neglect, if not denial. Since the 1980s there has been some recognition of children who enter secondary school bilingual in ex-colonial languages such as Gujarati and Urdu, usually referred to as 'community languages'. This has led to General Certificate of Secondary Education (GCSE) exams being developed for young people who, if given the opportunity by the school to do so, can choose to follow such a GCSE course. This move forward in mother tongue education at secondary level has not implied or instigated maintenance or development of the language at primary level. Ready access to a higher certificate (A-level) in the language is rarely available, and there are to date few university courses where a student can pursue his or her community language at university level. In short, the maintenance and possible enrichment of a few MTs has been treated as an optional school subject, not as a policy for validating balanced bilingualism. Recently a government-funded research project attempted to find out just how many community language teaching centres there are in England, but post-election governmental decisions have altered the focus of the research group and the answer is still not known.

By contrast, certain other European countries have subscribed to EU and Council of Europe recommendations, notably those which have begun to adhere to the Treaty of Maastricht (1992) with its point on education in mother tongue as well as two additional foreign languages. Gabriela Meier (2010a, p. 40) notes an influence that has spread from this: '[R]egional minority languages, which were not official European state languages, gradually came to be included in the 1+2 formula, thus promoting a more diverse idea of European multilingualism'[4]. Follow-on agreements since Maastricht, however, do not represent binding legislation and hence cannot be widely enforced. In addition, the difficulty of providing for MT education is manifest in the numerous immigrant languages that exist throughout Europe, today many that are not languages of European origin. Nevertheless the aspirations of the recommendations that have emerged from the EU, prodded by the European Parliament, and from Strasbourg's Council of Europe can be and sometimes have proved in practice to be inspirational.

Four models of bilingual schooling

Four examples of bilingual schooling were presented at the English Trust for European Education (ETEE) conference on 'Schools for the Future Europe' in June 2010 in Oxford. These examples appear below in the words of the respective practitioner or researcher who has personal experience with the particular model. In two cases, they portray what they have themselves decided, devised and developed for their individual school context. All involve one or two-way immersion programmes and content and language integrated learning, or CLIL. One-way immersion is characterized by CLIL where selected subjects are taught in a foreign language. CLIL has been promoted by the Council of Europe as an extension to simple foreign language lessons, with the potential for greater engagement in the foreign language (FL) and more rapid learning. In one-way immersion, the learners may or may not be a linguistically homogeneous group. In two-way immersion, classes consist of speakers with two different MTs, and the two languages of instruction are used to teach all subjects.

The first model is that of the European Schools, specifically the only one in the UK, situated in Culham, Oxfordshire, described here by a teacher at the school. Over 55 years ago the first European School was set up in Luxembourg[5] and in total 14 European Schools were established for the families of employees at EU projects and institutions in eight different countries.

Jackie Holderness, primary teacher, European School, Culham

The European Schools' model of multilingual education

The EU's language policies promote multilingualism and aim for a situation in which every EU citizen is competent in at least two foreign languages in addition to his or her mother tongue. This goal is reflected in the curriculum of the European Schools (ES), where children start their second language at 6 years of age and their third language at 13 years.

The European Schools and their aims

The aims of the European Schools were expressed in words attributed to Jean Monnet which have been written on parchment and sealed into the foundation stones of all the European Schools:

> Educated side by side, untroubled from infancy by divisive prejudices, acquainted with all that is great and good in the different cultures, it will be borne in upon them as they mature that they belong together. Without ceasing to look to their own lands with love and pride, they will become in mind Europeans, schooled and ready to complete and consolidate the work of their fathers before them, to bring into being a united and thriving Europe.[6]

These words point to the unique identity of the European Schools, with their potential to create inter-cultural understanding by uniting different cultures, languages and pedagogies.

The ES curriculum and language teaching

Each of the 14 European Schools is organized into distinct language sections. The school intake, how many children speak which languages, determines which language sections are created. There is not only a linguistic mix but also a pedagogical mix of teaching styles and cultural traditions, brought by native speaker teachers who are seconded from their home country system. For example, a French child learns most subjects in French from a French-speaking teacher who has been recruited from France. That teacher will be in contact with and also teach French to children from other language sections for their second (L2) or their third (L3) language.

Pupils follow the specially designed curriculum framework of the European Schools, common to all 14 schools and centrally controlled by the Board of Inspectors and the Board of Governors co-ordinated in Brussels. However, details of content and pedagogy are left to teachers and the school to determine locally. Each school draws up a local plan, or syllabus summary, which takes into account local and contextual factors. Through curriculum 'harmonisation' teachers across the language sections are encouraged to use similar instructional strategies and assessment formats. Teachers are prompted to coordinate learning objectives so that they are complementary across language sections.

Primary-aged children learn all subjects in their MT; they have L2 every day and for European Hours, a weekly lesson, taught across the language sections. At the secondary level, a German teacher, for instance, could teach dance and drama to children from all the language sections because they have elected that particular option. The teacher may, in fact, choose to do so in any language he or she knows. It is a good opportunity to learn alongside pupils from different sections about European culture, music and art.

The secondary model

The following subjects are compulsory for years one through seven of the secondary school (equivalent to years seven to 13 in England):

- first language (MT)
- language 2 (one of English, Spanish, French or German)
- mathematics (taught in MT)
- science (taught in MT): Science is taught as an integrated course in years one to three and as three separate subjects in years four to five. A science subject— biology, chemistry or physics—is compulsory in years six and seven.
- history (in L2 from year three onward)
- geography (in L2 from year three onward)
- ethics/religion (taught in MT)
- physical education (taught in MT and L2)
- art and music (compulsory in years one and two)
- a third language (L3) is compulsory in years two to five
- philosophy is compulsory in years six and seven
- in year three, pupils choose to study Latin, music or art
- there is a small range of options for years four and five, including economics and another language (L4) with a greater range of choices in years six and seven

European Schools and bilingualism

In the European Schools, pupils are fortunate to be able to develop a balanced and elite[7] form of bilingualism. In general, they come from a socially privileged group and speak high-status languages. It is also accepted that children can secure bilingual competence via a range of routes. In simultaneous bilingualism, a child learns two languages from birth, usually because each parent decides to speak his or her mother tongue to the child. However, many children become bilingual in a sequential way, where L2 is learned after L1 is established. The European Schools subscribe to a sequential model, introducing the L2 at age 6 but only for one lesson per day. Literacy is established in L1 through the nursery and into year one. Reading and writing in L2 are not formally introduced until year three.

The model of bilingual education followed by the European Schools where history and geography are taught exclusively in the L2 in order to aim for balanced biliteracy is the approach known as CLIL which is also used for the topic-based European Hours programme, which each child follows throughout primary. At secondary level, the CLIL programme includes electives or options.

There are some resemblances to a two-way immersion (TWI) process, in as much as subject or cross-curricular content is taught through the second language. However, though students receive 1,100 hours of L2 instruction over their 12 years of schooling, immersion in L2 is only partial because only a fraction of each day is devoted to teaching L2. Importantly, lessons are shared with pupils from other language sections. This encourages the pupils to use the language they are learning as a means of crossing the communication barrier between them and pupils with other languages. Because the goal is primarily oral competence, as a necessary foundation for literacy later on, the European Schools' approach is also highly 'communicative', with pair and group work and a focus on poetry, literature and song.

The success of the European system has been partially ascribed by Hugo Baetens Beardsmore (1993) to the fact that L2 lessons continue to focus upon competence in the language, even when the L2 has become the medium of instruction for secondary subjects.

As the Center for Applied Linguistics in the United States acknowledges, 'Achieving a high level of co-ordination across languages is challenging for teachers' working in a CLIL model (Howard, et al. 2006, p. 5). In reality, while European School L2 teachers liaise effectively within their own language section, they are rarely given the time or opportunity to work with other L2 teachers from different sections. Shared visits and activities across year groups enable teachers to work together across language sections and enable children to get to know teachers and students from other language groups.

Certainly, the development of bi- or multilingualism and bi- or multiliteracy is a key goal of European education, which culminates in the European Baccalaureate (EB). This challenging exam is very broad and requires students to write humanities essays in L2 and reach a specified standard in L3 as well.

European Schools were set up to enable pupils to reintegrate into their home education system, either when their family returns home or when the student chooses a university. European School graduates can choose a university which is either in their home or host country. For example, a French child schooled at ES Culham may choose to study in Italy or Germany. European School graduates are educated to be able to move confidently between countries, cultures and languages. Through uniquely European experiences, such as the Model European Parliament, exchange programmes, Intersport competitions and the annual Euro parties, they meet other European students and learn to appreciate that a European education is more than the achievement of the EB. It is the forging of a European identity, which transcends nationality or language.

* * *

A model of bilingual education that is in some ways similar to that of the European Schools and TWI has been developed independently in a British primary school by the school's co-headteachers. Rather than being a creation of the European Union, here the superstructure consists of two single nation–states operating together at a local level: France through the Agence pour l'Enseignement Français à l'Étranger (L'AEFE) with its curriculum for teaching French in schools abroad; and, a local education authority (LEA) in London following the English National Curriculum. The programme is described by the English school leader, or headteacher below.

Marc Wolstencroft, Headteacher of Wix Primary School, Wandsworth

Wix is an imposing four-storey Edwardian building that towers like a cathedral over its south London neighbours. In its time, it had been a popular community school, but over the years changing demographics led to a smaller and more socially deprived intake (more than 50 per cent on free school meals[8] in 2004). This, coupled with inconsistent management, progressively weakened the school to the point that it was under threat of closure, as I discovered shortly after being appointed to the post of headteacher in September 2004.

The reason why Wix could avoid being turned into bijou flats was because in September 1993, the Lycée Charles de Gaulle, a high-performing and popular French state (albeit fee-based) school located in London, started leasing empty space at Wix for its primary feeder classes. The leaser was the LEA of Wandsworth, where it was hoped that the co-existence of the two schools within the one building might lead to positive developments, but when I arrived, the two schools had little sympathy for each other.

Strategically the only way forward was to create something that the two schools could share in and the idea of a jointly owned bilingual stream fitted the bill perfectly. My hunch was that, given the status of the lycée, this would raise the aspirations and change the image of Wix in the local community and give us a dynamic by which we could start to integrate the two schools, as we have subsequently started to do. I was fortunate that my French headteacher counterpart, Gerald Martinez, the French authorities and the LEA supported the idea. After much preparation, the first bilingual reception class of 28 pupils began in September 2006, drawing 14 students from a local Wandsworth selected intake and 14 from lycée applicants who are fee paying. This was in addition to our normal 'classic' English reception[9] class recruitment, so that there were now three parallel teaching groups: one English, one French and one bilingual.

Our idea was to try to combine the best elements of both educational systems, by means of teaching half the week in English, the other half in French, a total of 2.5 days a week in each language in separate rooms. Establishing a bilingual stream necessitates creating an entirely new educational ecosystem. The French and English educational systems are very different and everything needed to be negotiated, from classroom furniture and holiday dates to the age at which phonics is taught.

The launch of our first reception class was a journey into an uncharted territory, and our first term was very rocky, as we found our fair share of unknowns.

Ultimately the reason why the bilingual stream works is that we have retained the strong support of a group of parents who early on recognized the significance of what was being offered, not the least because language education has increasingly become the preserve of private education in England. The reputation of the bilingual classes has grown as it has taken in the dimensions of a school within a school; we are massively oversubscribed as a result.

In summer 2010 we tested the oldest bilingual class, age 7 or year three, in the French national CE1[10] assessments and the English optional SATS[11]. The pupils performed at the same level as an average class in France and significantly better than an average English class. Notably impressive respective results were achieved in half the normal teaching time and by the means of a condensed and restructured curriculum reflecting the compromises necessary to harmonize the two countries' approaches. For example, we delay the teaching of English phonics to year one, while in the French system they start at a slower pace.

Wix Primary has benefited enormously from the injection of a group of generally professionally skilled and motivated parents, who have helped rebalance the school intake and increase its social diversity and resources, both physical and human. While the social intake of what we term the 'classic' English classes, those who do not follow the French or the bilingual programme, has remained much the same, some parents, irrespective of their circumstances, continue to be ambitious for their children, but also at the same time a substantial and contrasting minority of parents still fail to engage effectively with their children's education. The bilingual class parents are a self-selected group who apply through Wandsworth Council, as do all parents, indicating their preference for the bilingual class. By all measures, these parents are much more engaged with their children's education. Standards in the English classic classes have risen significantly, but they vary from year to year (as one might expect from small sample sizes); raising them permanently still remains one of the major challenges in the school as it is for many schools across the country.

The Wix bilingual project has demanded an immense degree of commitment, collaboration and self-belief. It demonstrates the crucial importance of a highly committed and supportive group of parents, a close-knit team of passionate, skilled teachers who are receptive to different ways of teaching and to the importance still of taking calculated risks. The children in the bilingual classes are happy, self-confident, verbal and work orientated; both we and our French partners are proud of what we have achieved. The Wix project has gained a national and international profile and is cited by others as being inspirational. Some groups under the British government 'free school' legislation are hoping to emulate our work using languages other than French.

*   *   *

Accounts of two other immersion models follow below: one strictly within the British context as an exemplification of CLIL in a state secondary school, the other describes a heteroglossic model from a study of two-way immersion in Berlin, Germany.

Content and language integrated learning has developed in part as a solution to the challenges involved in creating heteroglossic curricula. In contrast to learning a language as a school subject, learning subject matter through a language, for example, in a CLIL programme, can create the conditions for broadening and deepening thinking and conceptualizing in and about that language. The bilingual's experience of knowing and using a second language both receptively (comprehension when listening and or reading) and productively (speaking and writing) is difficult to capture and describe. Children speak of seeing or understanding the world from others' points of view (Esch-Harding et al., 2001). Teachers speak of learners' broadened conceptual thinking and of multiple approaches taken to accomplishing tasks. It is evident from neuro-science that the bilingual brain is more active than the mono-lingual brain when problem solving. CLIL is thought to support and extend the learning of another language and has appeared within European guidance on bilingual education as an area of teaching where recently 'the greatest number of practical initiatives have been seen' (Goullier, 2010).

A framework for CLIL in an English secondary school includes fitting it to the National Curriculum for Modern Foreign Languages where learning in a foreign language is measured against attainment targets (AT) at levels one to eight, roughly corresponding to the Common European Framework (CEFR)[12] levels of language competence. Learners' successful progress through the AT levels can support success in exams. A school's standing locally and nationally is determined by its national exam results. There have been years of struggle in English schools to encourage students to study a foreign language beyond the required age of 14, and if they do so to achieve grades between C and A* on their national General Certificate of Secondary Education (GCSE) language exams. Bringing CLIL into a state secondary school entails developing learners' foreign language skills while also challenging the learners to engage, using the foreign language, in subject concepts and ethical issues. There is a strong element of choice in the Chenderit programme with parents being well informed about its structure and content and students choosing whether they wish to continue it after their first year. There is also support from outside the school from both the local education agency (LEA) and from university-based research and guidance.

Judith Woodfield, Deputy Headteacher and CLIL programme leader, Chenderit School

CLIL at Chenderit School

CLIL was introduced as an entitlement for all year seven students at Chenderit School in 2008. All students follow one hour of CLIL geography each week in either French or German. In addition to this, students have an hour of CLIL delivered through ICT[13], PSHE[14], or tutorial time. At the end of year seven students choose whether they wish to opt for CLIL. In 2009, 70 per cent of the students opted to continue and have followed progression routes through PSHE and tutorial time. This figure of 70 per cent represents the students who, according to research that we have conducted with the University of Aberdeen[15] also see languages as an important part of their future. Chenderit is presented as a case study in the national CLIL guidelines (2009): www.all-nsc.org.uk/nsc/?q=node/94

Transferable learning and study skills are important with 66 per cent of the CLIL students saying that they have strategies to help them learn. Eighty-two per cent say that learning language skills are important to them; 96 per cent say that it is normal to make mistakes, having a go is what matters, and 78 per cent say that you do not have to be clever to use languages. There is now a culture of risk taking and creativity in language learning which establishes students as effective, independent, international learners. This points to positive developments in student attitudes and motivation for learning a foreign language, stemming from their CLIL experiences.

Comparing student achievement in languages in 2008 before CLIL was introduced with results for the CLIL years it is evident that the number of students moving beyond target level four in their foreign language is increasing year on year as the CLIL programme becomes more established. So achievement levels in MFL continue to rise. The cohort attainment on entry based on average SATS scores and CATS[16] scores has not increased in this time, rather it has decreased. The 2010 cohorts who have achieved the highest results in their foreign languages are those with the lowest average SATs attainment upon entry (27.7)

Percentages of year seven students achieving at level four and higher in the foreign language rose after one year of CLIL. Before CLIL in 2008 only 45 per cent of French and 34 per cent of German students achieved a level four ranking. As the project has been introduced, the results have risen considerably as shown by the figures below, so that by 2010 the number of students of German achieving a level four and higher had doubled and the French students had increased by 14 per cent:

(before CLIL)   2008 French: 45 per cent   German: 34 per cent

2009 French: 52 per cent   German: 40 per cent

2010 French: 59 per cent   German: 68 per cent

Tracking of students into year eight has shown further upward trends in relation to achievement.

Not surprisingly, the larger the number of lessons a student is taught using the CLIL approach, the higher the achievement of the student. The gains in achievement are highest, moreover, with lower ability students. By year eight they are a whole attainment target level higher in their foreign language skills than those students who have not followed CLIL.

The programme was controversial when first introduced, with some departments in the school reluctant to engage. This fear is understandable as the host subjects worry about retention in their subject and falling attainment. However, achievement is always in line with targets set in the host subjects, and the motivation for the subject is not affected. At Tile Hill Wood School, where the programme leader once taught, a longitudinal survey by Nottingham University showed that year eleven students could remember exactly what was learned in their geography CLIL lessons in year seven but could only recall the name of their (non-CLIL) science teacher. CLIL at Chenderit has placed the school in a confident position to embrace the 'Ebacc' or English Baccalaureate proposal by the British government in the white paper of November 2010. The Ebacc encourages students to gain GCSEs at grade C and higher in English, science, maths, MFL and either geography or history. The key to success in languages is motivation, risk taking, creativity and success at the microlevel. The CLIL students at Chenderit have developed all of these and are more likely to choose languages as an important part of their future.

*   *   *

The model of bilingual schooling which follows demonstrates an unambiguous attempt to fulfil the Maastricht (Barcelona) programme of MT plus two foreign languages with a specific socio-cultural agenda in mind.

Gabriela Meier, researcher at the University of Bath

Staatliche Europa-Schule Berlin

It is relatively well known that there are a number of two-way immersion programmes in the United States and, as outlined above, there are a few bilingual experiments under way in England. However, Meier (2010a) points out that there have also been a number of programmes in Germany since the 1960s, a movement that gained momentum in the 1990s. While there are programmes in Hamburg, Cologne, Wolfsburg and Hagen, to name a few, I will present here the one at the Staatliche Europa-Schule Berlin (SESB), which must be the largest bilingual or TWI programme in Europe. SESB started as a state-funded school trial in 1992, and in 2010 nearly 6,000 students were enrolled (SENBJS, 2008), and it is still growing. Currently, there are 18 primary and 14 secondary streams, ending with a bilingual German Abitur, the school leaving certificate and requirement for university access. The SESB streams are incorporated in mainstream schools dotted around Berlin uniting nine language combinations: German with English, French, Greek, Italian, Polish, Portuguese, Russian, Spanish and Turkish. Each SESB stream uses German and one of these locally spoken languages as means of instruction, and each stream recruits children from two linguistic communities. Thus children are educated in two languages and learn the two languages from and with one another, based on the two-way immersion model.

Strictly speaking, it is a trilingual programme, since in addition to German and a locally spoken language, all students study English as a foreign language from year five, apart from those in the German-English stream who study French. Children are selected on the basis of having one strong language at mother tongue level, and passive knowledge of the other language, aiming for a even balance of native German speakers and native speakers of the other language. In this model, children are separated for their mother tongue and partner language lessons for the first 8 years, while other subjects are taught in mixed groups. Thus, in the first year, children start to write in their mother tongue, while the partner language is developed verbally only. In the second year, writing starts also in the partner language. From year nine, there are no more separated language classes, since all students are assumed to have developed bilingual competences that allow them to participate in all educational activities in either language. More information on SESB can be found in Michael Göhlich (1998), Inge Sukopp (2005), Wolfgang Zydatiß (1998) and Gabriela Meier (2010b). In the following, I summarize linguistic and socio-cultural benefits, as well as the challenges associated with the SESB programme, and argue that SESB could serve as a model for Europe.

As far as linguistic benefits are concerned, Christiane Fäcke observed in a German-French SESB stream that 'after a few months of immersion education, the partner-language model leads to basic language competence in both languages that goes way beyond achievable and envisaged aims of foreign language tuition' (Fäcke, 2007, p. 253, author's translation). Larger primary-school studies in various language combinations by Peter Doyé (1998) and in a German-Italian stream by Sigrid Gräfe-Bentzien (2001) found that this model benefits listening skills, and Bernd Kielhöfer (2004) observed in a German-French stream that, at the end of 6 years of TWI education, all children achieved basic inter-personal communication skills (BICS) and 95 per cent achieved cognitive academic language proficiency (CALP), as outlined by Jim Cummins (1979, 2000)[17].

To date, only Meier (2010a) has examined socio-cultural benefits related to SESB. This was a quantitative study in which she compared 272 SESB students with 329 mainstream students of the same age (14–18 years) who attended the same schools. Her study, which took place in seven schools comprising seven language combinations, revealed a consistently positive effect in terms of a number of socio-cultural factors, of which the most important ones will be discussed here. Based on sophisticated statistical methods and cautious interpretation, she argues that SESB classrooms tended to be more socially cohesive and that SESB students had greater conflict-resolution skills compared to their mainstream peers. Particularly students with bilingual backgrounds felt a greater sense of belonging to their class group than mainstream students with bilingual backgrounds. Furthermore, those SESB students with a non-German background were more interested in learning more about peaceful conflict resolution and they perceived less frequent violence compared to their mainstream peers with the same background. Not surprising perhaps, but nevertheless important, is the fact that teachers reported that in SESB there were fewer communication problems with non-German parents than in mainstream schools. This is due to the fact that one of the teachers is a native speaker of the students' family language, which facilitates parental access linguistically and culturally.

Challenges identified by Meier's study concern, first of all, the recruitment of children at school entry. Only 21 per cent of SESB students in the sample had a German background, and some teachers found that this means that in some streams there were not enough German-language role models in the class, which was reported to hamper development of linguistic skills and tolerance between groups. In fact, Kathryn J. Lindholm-Leary (2001, p. 316) suggests a 50-50 balance as ideal, and Elizabeth R. Howard and Donna Christian's (2002) TWI implementation guidelines recommend at least one-third in each group if there are bilingual speakers. Another weakness was that teachers were unclear for which children the TWI model was suitable. This may be related to the advice they give to parents and affect consequent recruitment. In terms of school integration, some teachers felt that SESB and mainstream groups should be better integrated to avoid reciprocal stereotyping, but others felt that SESB had a positive motivational and aspirational influence on the mainstream sector.

In sum, Meier's study confirms findings from the United States (Freeman, 1998; Lindholm-Leary, 2001) and Israel/Palestine (Bekerman et al., 2004) which indicate that relationships within the TWI school classes are generally more cohesive. Previous research also observed that TWI education improved home–school relations in the case of migrant families (Collier et al. 2004; Lindholm-Leary, 2001; Torres-Guzmán, 2002). Thus, Meier's findings combined with previous studies lend strength to the argument that well-implemented and balanced TWI programmes develop high-level language skills and have a potentially positive effect on social integration. In Berlin, German children learn an immigrant language and thus respect and value the cultural backgrounds of their international peers and vice versa. This leads to the view that SESB students and teachers potentially provide bridges among cultures in the classroom, in the school, in the family and, in all likelihood, in the wider society. This responds to the idea that linguistic and social integration is a task for the whole society and not just for immigrant groups (Maalouf, 2008). Schools can play an important role in this. Thus, TWI education could form part of a wider language planning and social integration strategy in multilingual centres in Europe.

*   *   *

Across Europe and the world there are other models of bilingual schooling, variations of immersion and of CLIL. There is a great deal of research being carried out and that still needs to be done to understand fully bilingualism, bilingual development, the support and the optimal approaches needed for bilingual education and the many variables that impact on bilingual schooling. In the classroom and on the playground, it is ultimately the self-aware, heteroglossic teacher, supported by pervading school ethos and school practices and by parents' interest and engagement, that will be able to promote and sustain successful bilingualism.

Evaluating bilingual schooling

Creation of the CEFR was an attempt to provide a framework for tracking progress in foreign language learning, presented as a list of 'thresholds' describing aspects of the language learned. Measuring progress in language learning could thus be deemed homologous regardless of language, country, school, learners or context. Bilingual language learning cannot, however, be reduced to threshold lists, descriptors or indicators. Particularly the 'translanguaging' of bilingualism, the deep linguistic and cultural knowledge and capacities that result from drawing on all the languages one knows, cannot be captured in such reductive lists. CEFR has not been universally embraced by teachers, even in England where for two decades educators have been required to categorize and track learning by using AT descriptors. The European Languages Portfolio (ELP) has been mooted as a tool for valuing learners' languages (Goullier, 2010, p. 7). It requires the learner to self-assess competencies including in their MT; however, all is in relation to CEFR descriptors and it is not clear if there is a way forward for ELP.

In the last 10 years and particularly with the powerful OECD statistical comparisons of school learners' achievement such as PISA[18], some perceptions of education have been thinned down to indicator criteria, manipulated such that questionnaire results can produce statistical findings. It is worrying that some educationalists have allowed, much less approved, such an approach to education and policy. Results for 'country profiles' have had far-reaching effects, prompting national reactions: excessive pride in Finland; in England a retreat into own statistics without taking a needed look at the problematic heritage of the National Curriculum; convulsions of self-doubt in Germany without looking where ideas for solutions may be found in-land eastwards. Quite clearly such actions and reactions are of little use to evaluating bilingual programmes.

Bernard Mackey (in Spolsky et al. (eds), 1977) pointed out decades ago that the evaluation of a bilingual education programme must be integrally linked to the expressed aims of that programme. Evaluation is thus dictated by many variables including student intake, the role and position of MTs, the setting and the goals in relationship to the matrix of influences, which themselves must be overtly identified to understand the context. Ideally, principles addressed in this chapter should be present: the valuing of all languages equally, the aim for balanced language competency, support for MT competence and literacy and explicit inclusion of cultural awareness for understandings at deeper conceptual levels. A programme or model for bilingual schooling should include an appropriate framework for self-evaluation. If a research-based evaluation is to be carried out, the parameters of that research programme need to be co-determined by both researchers and the subjects, taking into account the context and aims of the school.

Conclusion

García (2009, p. 113) stated that '[b]ilingual education in the twenty-first century needs to do more than simply shift or maintain minority languages or add languages of power; it needs to be attentive to the dynamics of bilingualism itself.' This is not a simple recipe, but one key ingredient, urgently advised by Carder (2007) and appearing in Council of Europe documentation (e.g. Goullier, 2010), is for all school staff to be informed about and skilled in understanding these dynamics at the personal and school level. European education is *in* languages and their cultures and comprises knowledge *of* languages and cultures. Creating schools with ethos and curricula that provide these will afford the children of Europe a future of freedom of choice, movement, lifestyle and personal expression.

Notes

1 Specifically the European Charter for Regional or Minority Languages, adopted as a European Treaty by the Council of Europe in 1992. Weaknesses include: It is not legally binding, signatories specify which minority or non-official language(s) they will protect and foster and recent immigrant languages are excluded. Great Britain ratified it in 2000 to protect only Welsh in Wales and Irish in Northern Ireland. France has not ratified it and Spain only for its several autonomous regions.

2   See for instance, S. Grek et al. (2009) for a critical analysis of the struggles between Europe and national policy makers over the governance of education.

3   An EU survey, the 'Eurobarometer' in 2006 reported that 56 per cent of Europeans speak more than one language and 28 per cent speak two foreign languages. The most multilingual EU citizens are the Luxembourgers, where 99 per cent know at least one other foreign language, followed by Slovaks (97 per cent) and Latvians (95 per cent), http://ec.europa.eu/education/languages/languages-of-europe/doc137_en.htm.

4   The European Bureau for Lesser-Used Languages was founded in 1984 to promote recognition of and education in minority languages, but the bureau has no real power to pressure or enforce national or local attitudes and policies. See note 1 on the Council of Europe's European Charter for Regional or Minority Languages.

5   Luxembourg opened in 1953, with formal recognition in 1957, the European Baccalaureate was first awarded in 1959; see Part 3 of this volume.

6   There has been some disagreement about who created this inspirational statement. See G Pinck at www.eursc.eu/fichiers/contenu_fichiers1/1522/Panorama_2005_1.pdf pp. 14–15.

7   De Mejia (2002) has identified a range of status categories for bilingualism:

    ● Subtractive: L1 [MT] has a lower status than L2 [majority language]
    ● Additive: bilingualism is seen as a positive outcome, even if the languages enjoy different social status
    ● Balanced: fluent and literate in 2 languages
    ● Elite: both languages enjoy high international status

8   In England, the percentage of children in a school who qualify for free school meals (FSM) is used as a measure of the socio-economic status of the school intake.

9   'Reception' is the name given to the first year of formal schooling in England, starting at age 4 or 4½.

10 *Cours Élémentaire 1.*

11 Standard assessment tests, periodic national tests for all state schools in England.

12 'Developed through a process of scientific research and wide consultation, this document provides a practical tool for setting clear standards to be attained at successive stages of learning and for evaluating outcomes in an internationally comparable manner. It is the result of extensive research and ongoing work on communicative objectives, as exemplified by the popular "threshold level" concept'. A European Union Council Resolution (November 2001) recommended the use of this Council of Europe instrument in setting up systems of validation of language competences': www.coe.int/t/dg4/linguistic/cadre_en.asp.

13 Information and communication technology.

14 Personal, social and health education.

15 A report is in progress by Professor Do Coyle of Aberdeen University.

16 Cognitive ability tests are administered to children when they enter secondary education in England.

17 BICS and CALP were categories defined by Cummins based on their differences in register, lexis, language structures and skills: Basic interpersonal communication (BICS) is the language that is

used meaningfully at a personal level, for instance, in the family or between children on the playground; cognitive academic language proficiency (CALP) involves higher-order thinking developed through school education, for instance, evaluating, drawing conclusions, hypothesizing and predicting. BICS and CALP are not separate from each other, and the one is not superior to the other but both should 'develop jointly within a matrix of social interaction' (García, 2009, p. 38). The thrust to develop these two different sets of language competences at school has been part of the rationale behind immersion programmes.

18   www.pisa.oecd.org/pages/0,2987,en_32252351_32235731_1_1_1_1_1,00.html.

Teacher Education and Development for Bilingual Education

Shirley Lawes

Introduction

There is a great variability across Europe in initial teacher training practices and in ideas of what preparing to teach should mean. Continuing professional development also takes many forms, too numerous to discuss in detail. This chapter will explore some of the principles underpinning a possible model of European initial teacher education (ITE) that both take account of and transcend particular contexts and systems. We will draw in part on recent research on ITE and continuing professional development (CPD) to consider the potential of establishing a common framework for ITE and CPD in order to facilitate greater teacher mobility, to enrich the individual's professional learning experience and to create more openness in national education systems.

Arguing for a move toward a harmonized approach to teacher education in Europe is not straightforward, however. Prevailing views, particularly within English language teaching communities at the present time, emphasize the importance of context and 'the local' that celebrate social and cultural divisions as 'difference' and social isolation as 'identity'. But are there principles that rise above cultural identities and parochial concerns? One would not deny that across the continent of Europe important local issues and contexts exist, as well as national systems that represent different traditions. Within such diversity, it is nevertheless possible to find common principles and practices that transcend narrow national confines, that seek to make education a unifying rather than divisive force in the world. This chapter will argue that initial teacher education is at the cutting edge of developments in education and that ITE for those specializing in foreign languages is in a privileged position to break down some of the barriers that exist among European nations in terms of professional qualifications and training. The ongoing development of teachers will be discussed in terms of what common principles might be established by drawing on examples from a European project that brought together teachers, teacher educators and academics across Europe and other examples of collaborative, research-focused CPD. Let us first consider ITE.

What do various European systems have in common?

This chapter will not present specific, detailed comparison of the initial teacher education programmes offered in individual countries[1] but, rather, will try to identify what, to a greater or lesser extent, they have in common both in principle and practice. There has also been a shift in the last decade or so to practice-oriented preparation for teaching, which does not necessarily involve higher education to any great extent (see for example recent developments in England and France). At the same time, perhaps paradoxically, the levels of scholarship and professional knowledge required of student teachers in a number of countries are moving toward or are already at master's level. University-based teacher trainers, to a greater or lesser extent, have been seen as the mediators of theory and practice, and there is broad consensus that learning to become a teacher must involve elements of practical experience in the classroom supported by an appropriate practitioner. The value of the school-based mentor is more widely recognized and the role is developing more formally, in some countries seen as an essential source of guidance and support for student teachers during their practical teaching experience. Higher education (HE) has been seen to have an important role in both conducting research into teaching and learning in order to inform classroom practice and in sharing that knowledge with the teaching profession. The knowledge that underpins our understanding of language teaching and learning, as well as the foundational disciplines of the philosophy, psychology, sociology and, to some extent, the history of education, is disseminated beyond national boundaries through European research projects, conferences and publications. Where we might see some commonality of purpose in the academic world of education, schooling itself is perhaps more susceptible to the vagaries of political policy and the needs of national economies. Perhaps, then, we need to return to more fundamental questions about what it means to be a teacher.

What do foreign languages teachers need to know?

If we ask the question, 'What do teachers need to know?' we are asking one such fundamental question. It is most likely that answers will include subject knowledge (in this case a foreign language or languages), practical skills and underpinning theoretical and professional knowledge. So we might already lay claim to some consensus. But what is variable is the emphasis placed on each of these areas of knowledge and expertise, depending on perceptions of what it means to be a teacher. There are differences from country to country, for example, in teachers' roles and responsibilities, their status in society, the way school systems work, and these need to be taken into account. But context is only part of the picture and perhaps the least important. If we are concerned with looking at what is essential to teaching in a universal sense, then we can identify a number of commonalities. Indeed, a 'European Profile for Language Teacher Education' (Grenfell et al., 2004) already exists. This extensive document, the result of a project funded by the European Commission, provides an extensive framework for the knowledge and expertise required by a language teacher training to instruct in a European setting, covering guidance for the structure of programmes, the knowledge and understanding student teachers need to acquire, the pedagogical strategies and skills into which they should be inducted and the values deemed important to teachers. The framework is based on a wide-ranging survey and analysis carried out in 32 countries in Europe. While the writers claim not to be prescriptive, the framework nevertheless is detailed and manifesto-like in the way it sets out the common values, attributes and competencies desirable for student teachers of languages to acquire across Europe. The European profile focuses on descriptors of professional knowledge and good practice. We examine here what constitutes a common conception of the academic, theoretical and professional knowledge of a European language teacher.

Subject knowledge

Within Europe, the United Kingdom and England, in particular, is exceptional in its policy toward language teaching in schools. Foreign language learning is only compulsory between the ages of 11 and 14, although it is also an 'entitlement' in the primary phase. Government policy in the United Kingdom, whatever its rhetoric, has not valued foreign language learning as an essential part of all young people's education. When language learning is promoted largely for its instrumental use, it is hardly surprising that the majority of young people in English schools opt out at the first opportunity in favour of an easier or more 'useful' subject. They already speak the lingua franca, why should they bother with another? Elsewhere in Europe, English is indeed the foreign language most favoured across the continent, although the educational value of learning other languages is still recognized and language learning within the school curriculum is more prominent.

However, at least at the level of European policy, the ground has shifted considerably as to what constitutes knowing a foreign language. The traditional model of near native fluency as the ultimate aspiration of the foreign language learner has been called into question because it is unachievable for most learners and is, therefore, supposedly de-motivating (Council of Europe, 2001). Has this affected what level of knowledge we expect of language teachers? It would seem that there is now a far greater degree of variation in foreign language learning experience in degree programmes across Europe and, therefore, the subject expertise that might traditionally be seen as the corpus of subject knowledge that was the assumed prerequisite for the individual seeking to become a foreign language teacher has also changed. Nevertheless, we might assume that there is still likely to be some sort of consensus as to what constitutes the body of foreign language knowledge that can be seen as leading to the mastery that is deemed a desirable, even necessary, basis for admission to the teaching profession. As a minimum, a high degree of written and oral fluency in the target language, a firm grasp of the grammar of the language and some experience and knowledge of the culture or cultures, in the ethnographic sense, where the language is spoken would seem essential. Of course we are also seeing a greater number of native speakers of languages training to teach their own language in other European countries. Their mastery is assumed, but learning to teach one's own language in another country offers different challenges, which will be discussed later in this chapter. At the heart of mastery is the opening up to other cultures, indeed to human culture in all its forms, that is, to the best that is thought and known as it is expressed through the literature, arts and history of the country or countries where the foreign language is spoken. This is an essential part of the subject knowledge we should expect of all our language teachers.

Professional and theoretical knowledge

Educational theory and national systems develop largely out of a particular view of the role and purpose of education in society, the cultural norms and traditions of that society and, of course, out of government policy. Theory and practice in education, therefore, might be seen as 'culture bound', tied to and applicable only to one country. This view denies the possibility that there might be universal principles common to all theories of education and national systems and that to try to bridge the cultural gap between interpretations of principles in different countries is a thoroughly laudable goal.

There are four main areas of professional knowledge that are essential to developing practical classroom skills. First, the teacher should have a knowledge and understanding of the context within which they are teaching. An understanding of a national education system requires historical knowledge as well as a critical purchase on present structures and the policies that shape them. Ideally, this would involve knowledge of more than one country to enable critical comparisons to be made and a more objective view to be developed. Following from that, the content and structure of the subject curriculum to be taught would seem imperative. Language curricula are distinctive and context-dependent with differing emphases placed on communicative competence, cultural knowledge or grammatical understanding, for example, and teachers have greater or lesser freedom to decide on the content of their courses. Thirdly, knowing how to plan for successful learning in the short and medium term and to ensure progression and challenge is an essential part of a teacher's professional knowledge and relates closely to the fourth area: an understanding of the principles of good behaviour management and classroom discipline. Of course these broad areas can be broken down into more defined categories, but the point here is to identify overarching aspects of professional knowledge that can be applied and adapted to national contexts.

How do teachers in training acquire this professional knowledge? Some would argue that this knowledge is best learned in school. However, professional knowledge is underpinned by a body of theory, which is often developed through research. It is likely that experience in school initiates new teachers into the practical application of professional knowledge but fails to provide the opportunity to examine critically the theory behind the practice. Does that matter? It does if we see teaching as more than a craft and learning to teach as more than the mechanical process of becoming a competent practitioner in a particular setting. In order to transform our personal practical experience into a more generalized universal understanding of teaching and learning we need theory. Higher education has a distinctive contribution to make to the education of teachers both in introducing student teachers to the principles that guide their practice and in encouraging them to explore the dialectical relationship between theory and practice.

The findings of a study of the role of theory in secondary, modern foreign language teacher education programmes in England and France (Lawes, 2004) provided several insights into the strengths and shortcomings of the two systems in relation to both general educational theory and the applied theory of language teaching and learning in modern foreign languages. The research concluded that the scientific study of language – that is, an understanding of the nature of language and language learning, of language learning theories as propositional knowledge along with the study of education through its foundational disciplines of educational philosophy, sociology, psychology and history – far from being relics from the past, are what would enable student teachers to have a critical grasp of pedagogical and policy issues and to become 'educational thinkers'. The preoccupation with preparing student teachers to perform in the classroom is to some extent legitimate, but it is narrow and limited in aspiration. This restricted view of teacher professionalism is not only reflected in the narrowing of aspirations of teacher trainers but is also transmitted to student teachers.

The expectations and aspirations of student teachers are formed in a number of ways, and it is natural that they have considerable concern about learning the 'craft' of teaching. But at the beginning of their initiation to teaching, instrumental and functional expectations are susceptible to challenge and change. Teacher trainers who have a theoretical framework are able to put aside a technicist approach. If their expectations and aspirations are of developing educational thinkers who have a sound knowledge of educational theory and subject pedagogy, their student teachers will also become competent practitioners and principled professionals who will rise to the challenge. Nevertheless, educational thinkers still need to be competent practitioners, and preparation to teach must involve a significant amount of well-supported practical experience.

The role of practical teaching experience

While one may not consider teaching to be a practical occupation, involving simply a range of skills and competences to be learned in school, nevertheless it is practice-based, and school experience is a necessary, if not sufficient, component of ITE programmes everywhere. In some countries, an extended period of practical experience is the norm. This has important implications for the way that student teachers perceive the professionalization process (Lawes, 2004). The nature of school experience within initial teacher education in different countries is of interest in that it highlights the contrast between professional development seen as a process of training, or as an educative experience. The underpinning principles and approach that inform the initial teacher training systems shape the professional development of new teachers differentially. When student teachers undergo an initial training course that is largely practice-based, this influences negatively their attitudes to theoretical perspectives and their understanding of what theory is. The underlying assumption of a model of initial teacher training that is centrally focused on school experience is that effective practice is mainly developed through practice and that academic and theoretical considerations are secondary (Lawes, 2004).

Student teachers seem to gain most from their school experience when there are links between higher education and schools and there is a strong sense of partnership and collaboration between the two especially where mentors are supported and developed by HE colleagues. Higher education, therefore, by virtue of its distance from everyday classroom events, can have a distinctive and pivotal role in shaping student teacher development both in relation to student teachers and their school-based mentors. Effective practical teaching experience in school results from a shared discourse between higher education and school and when the relationship between the two aspects of ITE is made explicit (Lawes, 2004). How this is achieved with language teachers across Europe will be considered later in this chapter through examples of collaborative transnational partnerships in the broader context of teacher development.

Successful school experience is characterized by a systematic and progressive training programme led by experienced teachers who are trained to mentor student teachers. A developmental programme of observation, collaborative teaching building up to whole-class teaching over a sustained period is a model that has been adopted in a number of countries. The importance of well-trained mentors in schools with a designated role to advise, guide and assess student teachers should not be under-estimated. Models of mentoring include what we might call an apprenticeship model where the student teachers learn classroom skills from observing and then replicating their mentor's practice. While elements of this approach still remain in some contexts, it is widely seen as a limiting and limited approach. A mentoring model that has been much favoured in the United Kingdom in recent years is a competency model, where mentors refer to a framework of prescribed teacher competency to advise, guide and assess student teachers. A third model is a reflective model, where the role of the mentor is to help the student teachers develop their self-awareness of their strengths and weaknesses through questioning and discussion of their planning, observed lessons and other aspects of classroom practice in order to develop reflective practice. In truth, there is much overlap between these models, depending on specific circumstances; good mentoring practice is complex and highly individualized. The reflective model is arguably the approach most likely to promote autonomy as well as the acquisition of effective classroom skills and has become more broadly the underpinning ethos of teacher development more generally across Europe as a number of recent publications testify (see, for example, Baillat et al. (eds), 2010).

Reflective practice: reconciling the theory/practice divide?

A consideration of reflective practice is important in any discussion of initial teacher education and development in Europe, because it is now seen by many teacher educators and academics as *the* medium through which theory (as represented by HE) and practice (as experienced in school) could be reconciled. The notion of reflection as key to effective professional development now underpins both policy and practice in education and particularly teacher training in a number of countries in Europe.

It was Donald Schön who first popularized reflection as a professional activity in his 1983 book, *The Reflective Practitioner: How Professionals Think in Action*. He claimed to offer 'a new epistemology of practice' more appropriate to professional life than the traditional approach to knowledge that is essentially subjective in nature. For teacher educators and educational academics seeking a more experientially based professional development for teachers in the 1980s, reflective practice was seen to offer a radical approach to synthesizing theory and practice. This is now also the case in other European countries, for example in France, although the ideas have been much slower to be taken up seriously within teacher training. Léopold Paquay and Régine Sirota (2001) regard reflective practice as an 'epistemological breakthrough'[2]. Through reflective practice, often referred to as *analyse des pratiques* ('analysis of practice'), practitioners are able to 'deliberate on their own practices, objectify them, share them, improve them and to introduce changes to improve their efficacy' (2001, p. 5)[3]. Marguerite Altet (1994) places considerable confidence in reflective practice to transform teacher training and the teacher's work. Some *Sciences de l'Éducation* academics take a highly psychologically based view that shifts reflective practice more into the realms of self-analysis (Fumat, 1996, Étienne et al. 1997, Vermersch, 2001).

These interpretations illustrate the essential nature of the process of reflection as a psychological phenomenon that is necessarily subjective, placing the responsibility to improve professional practice firmly on the individual. As such, reflective practice may discourage a broader critical understanding of issues and signal a shift in the way theory is understood. Is theory now seen as process and reflection seen as an alternative to propositional knowledge (McIntyre, 1993)? Michael Grenfell, in his book *Training Teachers in Practice* offers a strong critique of reflective practice:

Reflection and the reflective practitioner are powerful metaphors; certainly ones which ring true to many involved in professional training. But do they exist in reality? Is reflection anything more than a romantic notion? We all reflect in a manner. We do not walk down the street without setting in place a whole set of explicit and implicit know-how and knowledge bases. We learn from experience, we anticipate, we act with intent and adjust accordingly as we go along. In other words, human beings are by nature reflective creatures. Is the 'reflective practitioner' therefore anything more than a truism, the product of previously simplistic models to link instruction and practice? Does it have sufficient weight to base an entire system of teacher training on it, as appears to be the case in England?

(Grenfell, 1998, p. 15)

He points out that reflection is not always effective, because '[r]eflection on a practical issue such as methodology may not be formative at all, but simply lead to a rejection or unquestioning acceptance of current pedagogic approaches' (ibid.). He notes, too, that reflection is dependent upon individuals, adding that some trainees are better at it than others, and that some can be overly self-critical. Within the confines of the classroom, the ability to reflect critically on one's professional practice is important in teacher education and development, and a part of a teacher's expertise. But the limits of 'reflective practice' must be recognized. While it is sometimes argued that reflective practice does not preclude knowledge of theoretical perspectives, nevertheless, the underpinning ethos of reflective practice points to a re-definition of theory in education, that practice has become theory (Lawes, 2004). The extent to which reflective practice should be a fundamental part of language teacher education and development across Europe is a matter for further discussion, and the issue is raised here to suggest that it should not be adopted uncritically.

Trans-national collaboration

There have been a large number of collaborative projects and initiatives, funded by one arm or another of the European Union, that show that, by working together across national boundaries, a common understanding of and approach to teacher education might be achieved. One notable example within the domain of language teacher education is the previously described *European Profile for Language Teacher Education* (2003). This is an excellent example of collaboration among education professionals across Europe to provide a framework for areas of competence. The profile is available online to teacher educators across the continent. The earlier MENDEVAL project, which looked at the mentoring of student teachers, similarly produced some excellent materials for mentor training and a comprehensive summary of models of mentoring across Europe. The European Centre for Modern Languages (ECML), based in Graz and created by the Council of Europe, has carried out a great deal of pioneering work in all aspects of language teaching and learning and teacher training. One of its current projects, ForLang, offers short, intensive training courses on a European approach to language teacher training at the Centre International des Etudes Pédagogiques (CIEP) in Paris. The European Portfolio for Student Teachers of Languages (EPOSTL), now in its second phase of development, is the product of another transnational collaboration that encourages student teachers to reflect on the didactic knowledge and skills required to teach languages and assess their own competencies in teaching. ECML also funds a wealth of transnational research and resource development projects for languages, and their website is a veritable Aladdin's cave for language teachers and trainers. These are but a few examples of transnational projects and initiatives in the teacher education and development field that are funded by the European Union. There is also the Council of Europe's Pestalozzi Programme[4] which organizes and devises workshops, seminars and modules for trainees and trainers, aiming to place human rights, democracy, and the rule of law at the common heart of education. Yet many of the initiatives and programmes remain unknown to the vast majority of language teachers and trainers. Is this a purely Anglocentric perception? It is true that elsewhere in Europe documents such as the 'European Framework of Reference for Languages' are in fairly common use, while in the United Kingdom it remains relatively obscure? Is it the case that other valuable projects, such as those previously mentioned, are widely known and referred to in the European languages community and that the United Kingdom is entirely exceptional in its greater preoccupation with national standards and guidelines to the exclusion of wider Europe? Is the problem simply part of a broader 'exceptionalism' in the attitude to Europe that seems to prevail in the United Kingdom? If so, how can we ensure that the rich fruits of European projects are disseminated effectively throughout the EU and that national governments and policy makers recognize their value? It is beyond the scope of this chapter to do more than raise these questions to promote thought and discussion, but the following example of a successful European research project may shed some light on the problems of collaborative working, on moving toward a common European-wide understanding of issues and imbedding innovative practices in education.

Éduquer par la diversité en Europe (educating through diversity in Europe): continuing professional development through a European research project

This 2-year research project funded by the Socrates 6.1.2 and 6.2 programmes, was led by the Fédération des Associations Régionales de Oeuvres Éducatives et de Vacances de l'Éducation Nationale (FOEVEN), a French organization responsible for promoting informal education and the training of youth workers. The project ran from December 2006 to December 2008 and involved teachers, teacher trainers, youth workers and university academics from eight European countries: Bulgaria, Finland, France, Hungary, Italy, Portugal, Romania and the United Kingdom. The aim of the project was to deepen our understanding of the notion of diversity across Europe, to explore diversity as a lived experience, recognizing the changing world that we live in with regard to the movement of people acknowledging multiplicity and seeing diversity as a resource rather than a problem. The idea was to experiment with different interventions in different countries to promote approaches to learning through diversity and to introduce creative learning activities in both formal and non-formal education settings that would address young people's attitudes to and experience of diversity. Another primary goal was to develop a network of education professionals from a range of domains – university, school, youth work – to share their experiences, contextual knowledge and perceptions of diversity.

It was an ambitious project, not least because of the diversity of the countries involved and the bringing together of professionals from different education sectors. In fact, this turned out to be a great strength of the project. The first challenge was to achieve a common cross-cultural understanding through the presentation of national concerns. This led to discussion and debate before arriving at a notion of diversity as multiplicity and the idea of diversity as a resource was ongoing throughout the project. This cross-cultural understanding proved to be an essential contribution to the success of the project. We were able to develop a collaborative framework with national case studies involving interventions with children and young people, developed by each country to meet local needs. For example, in Hungary a group of teachers adapted short films and used drama to explore a range of issues of prejudice. In France, one focus was diversity training of youth workers, drawing on the Hungarian films, and the other involved university researchers working with teachers in an *école Freinet*[5] looking at how approaches to diversity could be incorporated into the primary curriculum. Italian colleagues took school trips to investigate how issues of difference could be explored with secondary pupils. Colleagues in Finland ran a multicultural week in two primary schools, and in Portugal out-of-school activities involved parents around the theme of Club Caleidoscopio, which drew its inspiration from Paulo Freire and the idea of conscientization. The London project was about autobiographical writing. As an example of a Europe-wide continuing professional development project for education professionals in all sectors, the project was hugely successful.

We could identify a number of commonalities, good practices and excellent teaching materials that were transferable and that in principle transcended national contexts and were based on cross-cultural understanding. The project generated much enthusiasm among participants to continue the work through a further project focusing on teacher development in the area, and a proposal was submitted for European funding but was regrettably unsuccessful. This was unfortunate in that, while the knowledge and experience gained was published, the potential to disseminate and develop the work further with a much larger cohort of teachers across Europe was lost. How often must this be the case when the essential driver of professional collaboration is seen to be funding? How can projects be sustained and developed beyond the life of their funded period?

A case study of cross-cultural initial teacher education: the PGCE/Maîtrise FLE joint programme

In the mid 1990s, a group of English universities established a partnership with a slightly larger group of French universities to run a dual-certification programme for prospective languages teachers, the PGCE/Maîtrise FLE (*français langue étrangère*). The project was funded by the EU for a limited period and student teachers were recruited from participating universities in both countries and within a 12-month period they gained qualified teacher status (QTS) in England, through the postgraduate certificate in education, and a Maîtrise in the teaching of French as a foreign language. They spent half the year at a French university and the other half in an English higher education institution as well as in schools. The project had both principled and practical aims some of which were to increase the theoretical content of initial teacher education programmes in the United Kingdom, to improve employment prospects in France, to increase language teacher mobility and to address an increasing shortage of language teachers in the British system. Developing that particular joint programme for teacher training across national borders posed some interesting, sometimes difficult, challenges that involved addressing fundamental issues in relation to European teacher education. The experiment necessarily explored how the demands of differing national education systems could be drawn on to develop a teacher education programme that transcended national boundaries, and engaged with the questions raised at the beginning of this chapter. The joint programme was founded on a commitment to and a belief that cultural and national barriers could be broken down at most levels. However, that is not to say that to try to synthesize theory and practice across national boundaries does not present certain difficulties. The British PGCE is a rigid training programme with government-imposed standards that every student must meet in order to achieve qualified teacher status. The Maîtrise FLE, while still a vocationally orientated higher degree, nevertheless was an academic course rather than a training programme. Moreover, the English national curriculum is highly prescriptive, and PGCE student teachers are required to focus much of their attention on developing professional knowledge and teaching expertise geared to the English system. The Maîtrise FLE, on the other hand, was broadly based, more concerned with the general principles of teaching and learning French as a foreign language in a variety of contexts anywhere in the world.

A focus on intercultural dimensions enabled tutors to understand more fully not only the needs of students but the context in which they were working. Inter-cultural issues that emerged in the early years of the joint programme could be summarized as follows:

From the students' perspective:

- issues concerned with being a student in France – different styles of organisation and teaching, academic freedom and rigour, expectations, institutional norms

- issues concerned with training to teach in the United Kingdom – motivation, previous educational experiences, institutional norms, process of training, terminology
- issues concerned with becoming a teacher in the United Kingdom – notions of professionalism, building a career, cultural identity

From the tutors' perspective:

- seeking complementarity and common goals – developing points of contact, knowing one another's institutions
- harmonizing theoretical and practical approaches – sharing teaching, writing and researching, political correctness
- institutional and national barriers – entry requirements, procedures, other colleagues
- collaboration on writing and research – differing professional pressures and expectations, terminology

(Lawes, 2004)

The term 'inter-cultural' was not intended as a label to attach to any problem or difference, nor were cultural comparisons seen as an elevation of differences. On the contrary, the aim was not to elevate differences but to create a more rich and universal approach to teacher education. After all, it is only through working across barriers of culture and language that we can expand our own horizons and become more universal in outlook. From the point of view of the student teacher, this meant that they were able to present a much broader spectrum of knowledge and experience to their pupils. From the point of view of the university tutor, transnational collaboration and research offered a much greater potential for pushing forward the boundaries of knowledge and critical thought.

The important point to make about the PGCE/Maîtrise FLE joint programme was that the provision continued beyond the life of the funding and although it has been eclipsed by other developments in some of the participating universities, two programmes continue still and have embraced changes in both countries' postgraduate and teacher education accreditation systems. While not a perfect model, the PGCE/Maîtrise FLE joint programme is a useful case study. There is much to learn from this initiative, in terms of what it is that sustains trans-national collaborative work and in identifying how local demands and issues can be met while at the same time espousing a broader vision of the European languages teacher.

The way ahead for teacher education in Europe?

As the previous examples suggest, foundations have already been laid for establishing common teacher education and development programmes across Europe in terms of programmes that recognize local contexts and needs but are underpinned by common principles and agreed practices. Opportunities for transnational collaborative work, in sharing practice, research and knowledge among educational professionals across Europe should be made easier and bureaucratic procedures should be eliminated. A step in this direction would be to expand the Pestalozzi Programme with a liaison officer in every teacher education institution or consortium of institutions, rather than the single national liaison officer we have now. We need to build on what has already been achieved in a coherent and consistent way at all levels, and to create new links and initiatives. The drive to make these things happen, however, has to come from policy makers who are ready to make bold political decisions, because the way ahead is fundamentally a political and not an educational problem. The idea of a European language teacher can only be realized if there is a standard, recognized qualification across the continent, or at the very least the abandonment of national protectionist policies that restrict the free movement of teachers throughout Europe. In a general sense, national education systems can benefit greatly from greater diversity of linguistic, ethnic and cultural backgrounds within their teaching workforce and language teachers as a group, by virtue of their particular area of knowledge and expertise, are able to make a unique contribution to challenging narrow national educational aspirations and concerns and promoting the essential universality of education.

Notes

1   See, for example, Grenfell, Kelly and Jones (2003) for such comparisons.

2   'Une brèche épistémologique'.

3   'Délibérer sur leurs propres pratiques, de les objectiver, de les partager, de les améliorer et d'introduire des innovations susceptibles d'accroître leur efficacité'.

4   www.coe.int/t/dg4/education/pestalozzi/default_en.asp.

5   Schools which embrace the pedagogy of Célestin Freinet, an early twentieth-century French school teacher whose innovative approaches to democratic, cooperative and enquiry- and experiential-based school learning led to the Mouvement de l'École Moderne (Modern School Movement).

The European Schools and Enlargement

Renée Christmann

European Education – a concept with a promising future

No one will dispute the fact that education underpins the construction of any developed democratic society. With the enlargement of Europe and the increasing mobility of its citizens, it is clear that there is a real need to develop a strong European dimension in the education systems of the member states of the European Union. In that respect, the development of European education is a high-stakes issue, of major importance in a Europe which was initially built on economic foundations, the limits and weaknesses of which are now unfortunately being measured, and where the member states always wished to retain their sovereignty when it comes to the regulation of education.

It is certainly true that bilateral cooperation among member states has been established for many years, most frequently in the form of bilingual classes, sometimes leading to common school leaving certificates. But what we would like to develop is something more and something different, based on a unique experiment which started 58 years ago: the European Schools. Although the political and social context has evolved considerably since the establishment of the first European School at the instigation of visionary politicians, the educational model devised by them, which was innovative at the time, is more relevant than ever in an increasingly open Europe, where a high standard of basic education and training is essential for each and every citizen, both professionally and socially.

The European Schools

I would like to focus on the unique experiment in educational cooperation among the member states of the European Union. This is represented by the European Schools, the first statute of which was signed in 1957 by the European Coal and Steel Community's six founding countries, to provide schooling for the children of the officials assigned to that organization. The 1957 statute[1] was superseded in 1994 by a convention, to which all the member states gradually acceded upon their accession to the European Union. The Board of Governors of the European Schools is composed of representatives of the ministers of education and/or of foreign affairs of the 27 member states, together with a representative of the European Commission and the European Patent Organisation (EPO), which finances the Munich School, not forgetting the parents' representatives and the representatives of the staff of the European Schools.

Article 1 of the convention defining the statute of the European Schools stipulates that '[t]he purpose of the Schools is to educate together children of the staff of the European Communities. Besides the children covered by the Agreements provided for in Articles 28 and 29, other children may attend the Schools within the limits set by the Board of Governors.' Right from the outset, therefore, the European Schools catered, as a matter of priority for children of the staff of the European institutions, but also other children, as far as places were available, in accordance with the directives of the Board of Governors.

The main objective clearly expressed by the founders of these schools, namely to educate children of different nationalities together in order to turn them into European citizens retaining their own specific cultural identity, took concrete shape in an original, indeed revolutionary curriculum at the time, that is to say immediately after World War II, leading to a unique certificate, the European Baccalaureate, recognized by all the member states which had acceded to the statute of the European Schools and, as such, participate, through their representation on the pedagogical organs constituted by the Boards of Inspectors, in the design, delivery and quality control of the education provided and of the certificate awarded.

Although the focus is on language teaching as from primary year one, so as to promote and encourage understanding and exchanges among people, the European Schools offer a wide range of compulsory and optional academic subjects, scientific ones in particular – without, however, neglecting the literary, artistic and sporting subjects – enabling pupils to be given a thorough grounding so that they can access higher education. The teaching of languages through the medium of Language 2 (first foreign language or L2) to groups of pupils coming from different language sections along with the common activities engaged in create a context which is conducive to cooperation and communication based on the values of tolerance and mutual respect of other people's cultures, in an overall perspective of personal development.

The number of European Schools has gradually increased over the years, in line with the development of the European institutions (there are now 14 schools, with 22,778 pupils on roll, in seven countries), but the system has long remained a separate world, isolated from the rest of the educational world beyond. This situation, which is attributable largely to the primary purpose of the European Schools at the time they were established, went as far as presenting a paradox: because of their inter-governmental status, the European Schools were for a long time unable even to participate in the programmes of the European Commission's Directorate-General for Education and Culture (DG EAC). Even today, the participation possibilities are very limited.

Opening up of the system – accredited schools

Fortunately, with the resolutions which it adopted in 2002 and 2005, the European Parliament made a dent in the situation, so to speak, by recommending the system's opening up, through the wider availability of the European Baccalaureate, so that it could be taken by students other than those attending the European Schools. In response to the resolutions adopted by the European Parliament recommending the wider availability of the European Baccalaureate to include students outside the European Schools, the Board of Governors initiated a discussion process on the opening up of the European Schools system, one outcome of which was the definition and approval of criteria for European schooling in April 2005 and, in October of the same year, of the different stages of the procedure for accreditation of national schools.

At the same time, the setting up of European agencies or organizations in several countries following EU enlargement created a demand for European schooling for a number of Category I pupils, albeit insufficiently large to justify the setting up in turn of a European School on the traditional model. The combination of political will and demand from the staff of the agencies led to the devising of a new model, namely that of accredited schools, as a new type of institution providing European schooling leading to the European Baccalaureate. An accredited school is a nationally recognized school, in the state (public) or private sector, located in the territory of a member state. At the end of the accreditation procedure laid down by the Board of Governors, an accreditation and cooperation agreement is signed for each school by the authorities legally responsible for it and by the secretary-general on behalf of the Board of Governors. Pursuant to this agreement, which currently has to be renewed every 3 years following an audit of the school by inspectors of the European Schools, the accredited school is authorized to provide European schooling. Scuola per l'Europa in Parma and the Centre for European Schooling in Dunshaughlin pioneered this opening-up process.

Their highly diverse features – ranging from the closest possible mirroring of the European School model, in the former case, to the integration of pupils into the national education system, supplemented by specific tuition, notably mother tongue and foreign language tuition, in the latter – were taken into consideration for the development of the criteria for European schooling adopted at Mondorf, which provides for greater organizational flexibility while defining a compulsory educational framework which must be in place in order to be granted accreditation by the Board of Governors. The schools which subsequently applied for accreditation did so within the fairly broad confines of this framework, at least at nursery and primary levels and up to secondary year five (S5), secondary years six and seven provision being required to conform strictly to the curricula in force in the European Schools, with a view to recognizing the European Baccalaureate. An accreditation agreement in addition to the agreement mentioned above has to be signed to validate accreditation of the final 2 years of secondary education and the awarding of the certificate.

Since the establishment and adoption of European School criteria for European schooling and education by the Board of Governors at its April 2005 meeting at Mondorf (details are available in document 2005-D-342-en-4, published on the website www.eursc.eu), significant advances have been made. With a view to the system's opening up, the Board of Governors has, in particular, established a classification of the schools into:

Type I schools

These are the European Schools set up by the Board of Governors in accordance with the provisions of the convention defining the statute of the European Schools (see above).

Type II schools

These schools are opened at the instigation of the member states concerned in order to facilitate the schooling of children of the employees of a European agency or institution whose numbers are too small to justify the setting up of a Type I European School. A Type II school is associated, therefore, with the presence of a European agency or institution in the territory of the country in which the school is located, and the school is under an obligation to give priority to the enrolment of these children, called Category I pupils. The management and funding of such schools are the responsibility of the relevant authorities in the school's host country. The European Commission has started to provide the schools with a *pro rata* financial contribution based on the proportion of Category I pupils enrolled in each such school.

The Type II schools already accredited are:

- Scuola per l'Europa, Parma, Italy. Agency: European Food Safety Authority (EFSA)
- Centre for European Schooling, Dunshaughlin, Ireland. Agency: European Food and Veterinary Office (EFVO)
- School of European Education, Heraklion, Greece. Agency: European Network and Information Security Agency (ENISA)
- European Schooling, Helsinki, Finland. Agency: European Chemicals Agency (ECHA)

- European School Type II, Strasbourg, France. European institutions: European Parliament and European Ombudsman. Other international organizations present: Council of Europe and European Court of Human Rights
- European schooling at the International School, Manosque, France. ITER Programme

One Type II school is in the process of accreditation:

- European Schooling, The Hague, Netherlands, owing to the presence of EU agencies (Europol, Eurojust) and European organizations (EPO, ESA)

Type III schools

Type III schools are being set up as part of a pilot project. They are not necessarily associated with the presence of European institutions or agencies. The request to participate in the pilot project must come from a member state, which must present a school offering European schooling and education corresponding to the criteria defined by the Board of Governors in 2005. To date, one country has embarked upon the procedure seeking to be granted accreditation as a Type III school (Germany, at Bad Vilbel in Hesse). That school will open in September 2012.

Culham European Academy project in the United Kingdom

At its meeting in April 2007, the Board of Governors decided that the European School Culham should, over a period of 7 years commencing in September 2010, be phased out as a Type I European School. It also took note of the United Kingdom's proposal to transform the Culham School into an academy (coming under the English education system) and encouraged all steps likely to enable European schooling to be put in place after 2017. Chapter 12 examines the difficulties which led to this project's withdrawal at the last minute, following protracted negotiations, and the avenues now being pursued to find an alternative, building on the experience gained from this project, which all the parties involved had hoped would succeed.

Fact sheets on Type II and III schools (ref. 2010-D-35-en-1) are available on the European Schools' website, www.eursc.eu (Accredited Types II and III schools/Introduction). Those sheets include most of the facts and figures on each school and are regularly updated.

The European Baccalaureate in accredited schools

The European Baccalaureate, in its present form, can be offered in an accredited school after the signing of an additional agreement to the accreditation agreement recognizing the education provided in secondary years six and seven, which must conform to the curriculum taught in Type I European Schools. The same accreditation procedure as for the previous years must be followed.

At present, only Scuola per l'Europa in Parma has secondary years six and seven leading to the European Baccalaureate. In 2009, it entered 12 candidates for the European Baccalaureate for the first time, under the auspices of the European School, Varese, which awarded the certificate to the successful candidates. In 2010, four candidates sat the examinations and were awarded the European Baccalaureate. Following the decision taken by the Board of Governors in December 2010 regarding the centralized awarding of the certificate as of 2012, accredited schools will no longer need to be linked to a European School to register their candidates for the examination.

What is the future for an open European education system?

Deciding on and delivering the opening up of the system has been a gradual, sometimes staggered, process spurred on by the political will of the European Parliament and very real educational needs, albeit stalled at times by legal, educational, organizational or financial concerns, mostly relating to the very cornerstone of the opening up process: the provision of the European Baccalaureate. After 5 years of opening up the European Schools system, a review of the results so far was undertaken, as a basis for the future of this new open system, comprising schools with different structures and management but offering the same European education leading to the same European Baccalaureate, whose validity and recognition must remain an absolute priority and which must represent a high-value asset.

What, therefore, is the future for these schools? I will not venture to give definitive answers, for two main reasons. First, there are institutional reasons: In December 2010, the review of the results of 5 years of the opening up of the system was the subject of initial consideration by the Board of Governors of the European Schools, the supreme organ, which gives political and strategic policy guidelines. The principle of the system's opening up was clearly confirmed and the secretary-general of the European Schools was mandated to put forward proposals for possible amendments to the procedures in force. My second reason is that reflection is still in progress on a reform of the European Baccalaureate, which will constitute the hard core, the common objective of the European education system which we wish to develop. This reflection is based on the analysis and the conclusions of the external audit conducted by University of Cambridge International Examinations (University of Cambridge, 2009) and on the recommendations made by the successive chairmen of the European Baccalaureate Examining Board, and more particularly by Professor Mats Ekholm, the Swedish chairman of the 2009 Baccalaureate. This subject is addressed in greater depth in the next chapter.

In the document presented in December, a few questions designed to open up avenues for reflection were raised with, in prospect, the setting up of a coherent and reliable system offering a certificate whose recognition cannot be called into question. To ensure the future of such a system, what legal, pedagogical, organizational and financial framework and what procedures should be put in place? And who will be charged with the implementation and evaluation of the results?

The legal framework

The legal aspects are of upmost importance to ensuring the validity and recognition of the schooling and of the certificate awarded on completion of studies. At the meeting of the Board of Governors in April 2011, a new version of the accreditation agreement was submitted, taking into account the necessary modifications to be made to the text in order to draw up a legal framework which is more 'fit for purpose'. In view of the diversity of the legal status of the schools in the host countries, this is a matter still subject to possible changes according to needs.

The pedagogical framework

Given the diversity of the 'containers' (the types of schools), it is of prime importance to ensure that the 'contents', for example the curriculum, are clearly identified and that a reliable quality control system is put in place.

Some questions are still under review, and proposals will be submitted to the Board of Inspectors at its October 2011 meeting for an opinion, before being presented to the Board of Governors in December.

Is the European Schools' curriculum transposable as it stands to accredited schools, with a view to wider-ranging enlargement of European schooling? Should the Mondorf criteria be reviewed or defined more precisely? Will it be possible for the current control system, involving audits conducted by inspectors of the European Schools, to continue as it is implemented now? Should the number of accredited schools increase significantly? Should the national inspectorate not be involved, agreeing on precise evaluation criteria for that purpose? Furthermore, the decisions of the Board of Governors concerning the reform of the Baccalaureate are essential for the development of the system's opening up.

The organizational and financial framework

At present, the secretary-general of the European Schools ensures that the different organs of the European Schools are kept informed throughout the process and that they express an opinion for the benefit of the Board of Governors. Some points were discussed at the Board of Governors' April meeting. The different stages in the accreditation procedure were clarified and the financial aspects discussed further in December 2011, on the basis of a detailed review of the costs, particularly for the general secretariat but also for the European Schools, which provide de facto information and support for accredited schools.

The European Curriculum

It is to be questioned whether the content of the European Schools' curriculum perfectly matches what might be expected of a European Curriculum which would give greater importance to the European dimension itself. The six points annexed below (Annex 1) from the 2006 report of the European Parliament's Committee on Culture and Education clearly point the way forward. In another connection, the Lisbon criteria open up dimensions in terms of the provision of more comprehensive education and training for people, which it is also important to take into account, in order not to focus education too exclusively on knowledge acquisition. The next chapter gives a more detailed overview of the issues to be resolved. The Cambridge audit report on the Baccalaureate and the report of the chairman of the 2009 Baccalaureate clearly focused on that aspect and their recommendations have been considered by the Baccalaureate Working Group in formulating its proposals for reform, with a view to their implementation for the 2013 Baccalaureate. The objectives following from the aim of the reform of the Baccalaureate, referred to in this document and which have guided the work of the European Baccalaureate Working Group, can be summarized as follows:

(1) propose simpler organizational arrangements for the examination
(2) reduce the cost without, however, jeopardizing the Baccalaureate's quality
(3) revise the content and organization of the examination so that it meets the present-day requirements of universities
(4) make arrangements to publicize the certificate more widely and make it more easily accessible

In any event, it is important for the European Curriculum which will be taught in the schools concerned (European Schools and accredited schools) to be compatible with the national curricula, to allow recognition of the equivalence of years of study in accredited schools, as is the case for the European Schools under the 1994 Convention.

Relationships across different European School types

At present, there is no institutional framework governing relationships among the different types of schools providing a European education. Only a short article in the accreditation agreement stipulates that the staff of accredited schools may attend the in-service training courses organized for the teachers of the European Schools, with the caveat that this should not entail costs for the European Schools. Moreover, the provisional solution for the Baccalaureate at the Parma School necessarily implies a close relationship with the Varese School, which was made official in 2009 by means of an agreement signed by the two directors and the delegation of powers with respect to questions of the organization of the examinations in the accredited school. However, this obligatory link will disappear in 2012.

In reality, there are de facto relationships at different levels: special partnerships between an accredited school and a European School, which provides it with the information and support requested, particularly during the period when the accredited school is being set up and put in place. The directors and deputy directors are invited to certain meetings of the directors and deputy directors of the European Schools. Moreover, pupil exchanges have started to be put in place, to a limited extent and on an individual basis so far, as has participation in inter-European Schools events. I can certainly subscribe to most of the objectives formulated for the 2010 conference of the English Trust for European Education, as set out in Annex 2 below, and would recommend that priorities for their implementation be established, taking particular account of their possible financial implications.

Conclusion

The aim of this first review was to take stock of the progress to date with the opening up of the European Schools system and to draw attention to some issues that have arisen in the course of enforcing the measures taken over the last 5 years, to allow the staged implementation of the most significant reform ever decided in the European Schools. While still modest and closely related to the presence of EU agencies or institutions, the current opening up process is extremely important, in that it ultimately impacts on the delivery of the European Baccalaureate, a qualification whose status as a school-leaving certificate recognized by all member states and beyond must be preserved.

In this context, the decisions which will be taken regarding the reform of the Baccalaureate are essential and must be taken in timely fashion, while bearing in mind the students enrolled in schools which are already accredited and who will be taking the examination for the first time in 2013. Irrespective of the questions still to be addressed and the answers that will be found, only strong political will in the different Member States and the involvement of the directorate general for education and culture in publicizing the concept of European education will enable it to take on the scale which it deserves, going beyond the current experiment, which is restricted to a few accredited Type II and III schools.

Annex 1

European Parliament Committee on Culture and Education Report of 2006 (2006/2041(INI)

- whereas the information about Europe that is conveyed to pupils, teachers and students varies widely from country to country and whereas efforts must be made to agree on a common understanding of history and a definition of European values,

- whereas the main obstacles include the still limited scale of cross-border initiatives and programmes, a lack of coordination between initiatives, a lack of visibility and accessibility, as well as inadequate or unsuitable tools for carrying out these tasks,
- whereas there are many obstacles and difficulties which currently face teachers in order to implement the European dimension in their lessons including the lack of up-to-date, high-quality informational and educational material on the European Union available in all EU languages, and whereas the European Union should assist them in this endeavour,

{The European Parliament}

(1) Considers that all education systems should ensure that their pupils have by the end of their secondary education the knowledge and competences they need, as defined by their respective educational authorities, to prepare them for their roles as future citizens and members of the European Union;

(2) Stresses the importance of finding a clearer and uniform definition across the Member States of the meaning, substance and scope of the 'European dimension';

(3) Urges the European Council and the Ministers of Education to update the above-mentioned resolution passed on 24 May 1988, on enhancing the European dimension in education, in particular taking into account the enlargements to the EU, which have occurred since then;

(4) Urges the Council to recognize the two different aspects of the European dimension – first access to information about the EU: its institutions, methods, practices, initiatives, and secondly knowledge of Europe's shared history and cultural heritage, the development of linguistic skills, and a grasp of European current events, all of which may supplement national curricula;

(5) Stresses the importance of using multi-media and Internet educational resources as modern teaching methods for introducing the European dimension into school curricula; with this in view, recommends for instance the setting up of a multilingual Internet service that will present best practice, provide educational assistance and serve as a platform for the exchange of experience;

(6) Insists on the need for continued improvement in the provision of language teaching, for example within the COMENIUS section of the lifelong learning programme; recognizes furthermore that it is difficult, in some Member States, in particular for those whose mother tongue is English, to maintain sufficient interest and motivation in becoming proficient in other European languages, thus underpinning the level of mutual understanding and empathy across Europe; in this connection learning the languages of neighbouring peoples is especially important.

Annex 2

Type II and Type III European School heads, parents and teachers invited to the 2009 and 2010 Oxford conferences of the English Trust for European Education, and now planning to establish an organized network, have determined its objectives as follows:

(1) to maintain and make available up-to-date information on European School Type II/III institutions and developments, and to promote communication across them;

(2) to represent European School Type II/III institutions and projects on common issues and relate, liaise or negotiate with the ES Board of Governors and other bodies as may be appropriate;

(3) to exchange good practice in reconciling national and European Baccalaureate criteria and expectations;

(4) to contribute to future European Baccalaureate development and relationship with kindred examinations;

(5) to offer support as needed for European School Type II/III parent and interest groups, and to relate to Interparents as may be mutually acceptable;

(6) to promote staff development for European School Type II/III teachers;

(7) to facilitate teacher-exchange, inter-visitation and conferencing across all types of European School;

(8) to facilitate/share expertise on teacher recruitment and advise on teacher appointments to Type II/III European Schools;

(9) to promote European inter-school activities across all types of European School;

(10) to develop communication, including pupils transfer records (given that curricula will be related but not be identical);

(11) to promote pupil exchange and inter-school activity across all types of European School;

(12) to promote, develop and publish good practice in European schooling.

Note

1   For the 1957 Statute, 1994 Convention, and all documents for the legal basis of the European Schools, see www.eursc.eu/index.php?id=96#70.

The Future of the European Baccalaureate: recognition and reform

John Sayer

Introduction

Suddenly, after half a century, the European Baccalaureate (EB) is in the news: first, because the European Parliament has demanded that it should not be exclusive to the European Schools; secondly, because the European School at Culham, the only school in Great Britain accredited to offer the EB, has been trying to become part of the English system, bringing the EB with it. Until now, few, outside the European Schools and university admissions officers, had ever heard of the EB.

Secondary education in Great Britain has been ill served by its leaving examinations. Over the past century, in the various manifestations of local examinations, the leaving examinations have passed through phases of control by universities, by the Schools Council and by franchise from government-controlled agencies, and now the widely discredited GCE A-level examination, most recently castigated by the Royal Society for its lack of breadth (2011), looks set to return to supervision by the universities. In all these phases, reform has been little more than external and structural. Despite the mantra of a broad general education, examinations have been pick-and-mix single-subject hoops, the culmination of increasing specialization from the age of 13 or 14 and resulting in a uniquely narrow approach to lifelong learning. Only the Welsh Baccalaureate has shown recognition of the problem.

Choice, diversity, and individualization are no doubt excellent watchwords, but in schools they have also become part of a throwaway society. Focus on chosen interests should never have led to jettisoning the rest. Educationally, and in terms of lifelong learning, the very least would be to maintain and refresh all parts of the curriculum. This disease of discarding subjects is peculiarly British and especially English, exacerbated by over-examination. Post-war attempts were made to counter the tendency, by including a variety of general studies in sixth forms, but these failed to survive the examination-driven system and became an examined additive.[1] Other countries in Europe have introduced an element of choice in secondary education, but most without abandoning the broad education across arts and sciences, languages and mathematics (Eckstein et al., 1989). The Lisbon Convention[2] of 1997 underlined the need for equivalence and recognition of qualifications not only at university level but in qualifications giving access to higher education. Since then, more progress has been made toward convergence in central and eastern European countries than elsewhere (West et al., 1999).

The European Baccalaureate owes its origins to the establishment of the European Schools (see Chapter 10), requiring a qualification equivalent to those of the first nations involved in the Treaty of Rome, so that the families of personnel displaced by involvement in European projects would not be educationally disadvantaged upon their return to the home country, would follow a curriculum recognized by all as equivalent and would leave school with a qualification recognized for higher education in any of the member states. As the European Union has grown, the EB and the curriculum leading to it have been recognized by all 27 current EU members and are indeed controlled and modified by them jointly. Far from being a lowest common denominator, the EB is accepted because it has just about everything which 27 national curricula require and so much more besides. So it is well worth looking at, not because we want more standardization, far from it, and not because it is perfect, for it is also in need of constant review, but because it has unique features worth promoting.

What is special about the European Baccalaureate?

The EB is the school certificate of education awarded at the end of the 7th class of the European Schools secondary cycle, the culmination of a curriculum from the first class of primary school. The certificate is fully recognized in all the countries of the European Union as well as other countries. In the UK, the then Department of Children, Schools and Families has produced its very positive publication on the European Schools and European Baccalaureate (DCSF, 2009), as a guidance for universities and schools, without however pursuing its potential further.

To obtain the EB, a minimum of 60 per cent is required. Currently, 40 per cent of the Baccalaureate award derives from the assessment of performance and course work in the subjects taught in the sixth and seventh classes (ages 16–18), and the final exam currently consists of: 1) written examinations in five subjects, which represent 36 per cent of the marks, of which mother tongue, first foreign language and mathematics are compulsory for all candidates; and 2) four oral examinations, which count for 24 per cent of the marks, of which mother tongue and the first foreign language are compulsory, as well as history or geography (examined in the first foreign language) if the candidate has not already taken a written examination in these subjects.

The Examining Board, which oversees the examinations in all language sections of the European Schools, is chaired by a university professor and is composed of examiners from each country of the EU. Those awarded the EB certificate have the same rights and benefits as holders of other school-leaving certificates in their countries, including the same right as nationals with equivalent qualifications to seek admission to any university or institution of higher education in the EU.

The EB covers and requires an exceptionally broad curriculum, a multi-disciplinary 'package' which avoids the British school habit of throwing away previous learning. Mother tongue and foreign languages are not just subjects themselves but vehicles for other subjects. History and geography, for example, are taught and examined in the pupil's first foreign language, called the working language. The study of a first foreign language (English, French or German as the working languages of the European Union) has been compulsory throughout the school from the first primary class. A second foreign language is started in the second year of the secondary cycle, and a third language may be chosen in the fourth year. Language classes are of mixed nationality and usually taught by native speakers. Art, music, physical education and games are pursued in groups of mixed nationality, as are extra-curricular activities. Schools are accredited for the EB only if the EB inspectorate is satisfied that they offer such a curriculum and environment, where communication in two or more languages is normal, natural and necessary.

In Great Britain, it is frequently observed that the decline in language learning is the result of the predominance of English as the lingua franca, giving young people the false impression that they can make their way in the world without another language. The recent debate in the House of Lords (Hansard, 2010) is one of many to have discounted that. For the EB, the school itself is an environment in which a command of other languages is normal, natural and necessary for survival. It is not just a multilingual environment but a multicultural European experience with cross-cultural socialization as an aim and a reality.

Many other schools, particularly in the major conurbations, bring together pupils with a wide variety of mother tongues, and some do their best to create a multicultural environment, but this is despite and outside the curriculum, not because of it, and is often haphazard. The European Baccalaureate and the curriculum leading to it are deliberately designed to enable professionally mobile families to return to their own country without educational disadvantage, having followed a curriculum recognized in every EU country as at least equivalent to its own. With this in mind, mother tongue teaching is offered wherever possible, even in the less pervasive European languages.

So the perceived strengths of the European Baccalaureate and the curriculum leading to it are that they are the summation of a multilingual, multicultural European environment offering cross-cultural socialization at the same time as recognized compatibility with national curricula. They also reflect the emphasis on the European dimension of education, yet by promoting mother tongue teaching not only in the three EU working languages but in other languages wherever possible, it enables pupils of mobile families to adjust back into their national systems. The EB curriculum is not simply strong on European language teaching but has the objective of multiliteracy;

it offers an exceptionally broad multidisciplinary curriculum, harmonized by the involvement of national inspectors to maintain links with national systems. It is also recognized by universities in all member states and well beyond. One should add from a British perspective the system's unique ability to award the Baccalaureate on the day after concluding oral examinations, in a proclamation ceremony before the school year is concluded, as compared to the nail-biting tedium of weeks of anxiety experienced in the national systems before young people know whether they have achieved the grades required to pursue their chosen higher education studies.

The EB's distinctive weaknesses are that it has been, until now, confined to the 14 (Type 1) European Schools and therefore brings a relatively small number of candidates to universities, and although recognized, it is unfamiliar to many admissions officers. In addition, it has an unwieldy central administration even for the present small number of schools, and one which would need considerable reform to cope with wider access. Another weakness is that its policy is governed by the unanimous decisions of a governing body consisting of 27 member states and has been slow to adapt to modern requirements, notably to information technology. Finally, it is expensive and would have to reduce time costs in order to be competitive in an examination market.

Comparison with other school-leaving examinations

In 2007 the Board of Governors of the European Schools agreed to commission an external evaluation of the European Baccalaureate. The contract was awarded to the University of Cambridge, and its evaluation, carried out during 2008, culminated in an impressive and finely detailed report (Cambridge, 2009), running to 153 pages, with subject-specific annexes covering 216 pages, which cannot be adequately summarized or discussed here. Among the questions addressed were those very much in the minds of parents and young people: comparisons with alternative examinations, in particular with the International Baccalaureate and the British GCE A-level. The conclusion for the study of French, for example, is summed up in its report annex.

The specific aims of the EB Language II programme are introduced by a statement that Language 2 studies are vital in providing the student with the means of accessing European culture in its diversity, and, in a European

School context, of being able to follow human sciences courses being taught in Language 2. The stated aims are then to develop the ability of students to communicate effectively in both the spoken and written language and to understand 'messages' (both spoken and written) of all kinds, including literary and cultural. When it comes to the specific objectives for years six and seven (the relevant years for this report), however, the only objectives mentioned are to *maîtriser la pratique de l'argumentation, développer une réflexion abstraite, critique et ouverte aux cultures européennes*, and *développer un commentaire qui prenne en compte les spécificités littéraires* ('master the practice of argumentation' and 'develop a commentary which takes account of specific literary concepts'). In this sense, the EB course aims to accomplish very different goals from the other two (which share a good deal of common ground), which makes any comparative evaluation open to the criticism of not comparing like with like (Annex 1.9.1).

The report concludes that the emphases are so different that there is no merit in speculating as to how the IB or A-level candidates for French would have fared on it, or of how the EB students would have fared on a course much more obviously orientated toward language acquisition. However, this is precisely what parents and candidates have to judge. The study of first degree outcomes (Kelly et al., 2009), based on a sample of 502 former European School pupils, compared the performances in final examinations of first degree honours courses at British and Irish universities of students who had taken the European Baccalaureate with the performances of a similar number of students who had studied A-levels. This showed that, in terms of the probability of getting a good degree, a European Baccalaureate score of 80 or more was roughly equivalent to 360 UCAS points awarded for A-levels (3 A grades AAA); an EB score of 70 to 79 was equivalent to a UCAS score of 320 to 340 (ABB to AAB); and an EB score of 60 to 69 was equivalent to 280 to 300 UCAS points (BBC, BBB). The conversion table in the 2009 Department for Children, Schools and Families guidance (DCSF 2009), which has also compared EB entry and final degree scores, is similar at the upper end but much less generous to the EB for lower scores. Comparisons may be invidious, but they have to be made.

So we have to go back to the question of objectives. The case for the European Baccalaureate is an educational one and, at the same time, a question, in the widest sense, of political policy. Are the EB objectives the ones wanted for the future in Europe, that is to say for the future of our children in Europe? If the answer is affirmative, what is missing?

The Cambridge evaluation of the EB addressed the three questions asked of it: to determine to what extent the European Baccalaureate is fit for purpose; to obtain recommendations regarding the measures to be taken to guarantee the quality of the European Baccalaureate and its recognition by the member states; to identify the questions to be taken into consideration and the actions to be undertaken, in order to be able to offer the European Baccalaureate to more students outside the European Schools.

These were questions from within the existing European Schools Board of Governors. Fit for what purpose? The study included comparisons with British, Irish, French, German and Swedish school-leaving examinations and the International Baccalaureate, which is considered to be broadly compatible with these and also essentially monolingual. But Europe, even the limited Europe of the EU, has 27 member states, and the Council of Europe has 47. It would be a nightmare to attempt comparisons among all of these, but the comparison made in the Cambridge Report over five subject areas with six western European school-leaving examinations can certainly serve as an illustration of the questions which might be addressed across a more representative cross-section of the EU or Europe as a whole. The main differences identified related to differing purposes.

The recommendations made in the report are comprehensive, across curriculum, organization, teacher training and publicity. Three models for expansion are formulated, the first being adoption of the existing curriculum in its entirety, the second targeting the 2 years leading to the final examination, and the third establishing a 'core' curriculum which would allow more expansion and links with, for example, the European Common Framework for Languages (Council of Europe, 2001) or the *option internationale* of the French Baccalaureate.

Matching European education policy

What the EB has in common with all the other school-leaving examinations is that it is not designed or revised to match the declared educational objectives of the European Union, which came later. It does, however, come nearer than its national alternatives and at least is addressing the issue.

One strong point of the EB administration is that it is chaired each year by an independent education expert, who can look at the system from outside and bring a wider perspective, as well as share the experience of actually operating the system. In his challenging report[3] for his presidential year

2009, Mats Ekholm, professor of education at Karlstad University in Sweden, paid tribute to the efficiency of the existing system, but asked whether the EB meets the policy criteria agreed by the European Parliament and Council of Ministers, concluding that it falls short. Here at least the question is asked. If it were asked of other school-leaving examinations, which national systems have still to do, the answer would no doubt be even more negative.

The Ekholm report was based on his experiences of the European Baccalaureate, including visits to all the European Schools during the examination period in June and July, as well as through studies of examination tasks and analysis of the examination outcomes. It concluded that the EB has an efficient organization that fulfils the demands made upon it. It is a well-organized system for the examination of the students on its existing criteria, and it works well.

However, Ekholm's critical review of the content of the examination, looked at through the lens of the EU's reference framework of the Lisbon strategy (EU 2006), concludes that the eight core ambitions of this strategy are touched on by an astonishingly small portion of the examination. The use of the first language and of a second language is covered to some degree, which is also the case for parts of the competencies that the students have in mathematics and in natural sciences. Digital competence, a sense of initiative and entrepreneurship, cultural awareness and expression and learning to learn are examples of ambition areas that have disappeared in the examinations. In mathematics and the natural sciences, little effort was given to test the competence of the students to take a stand on issues. In these subjects, a dominant part of the written examination deals with the competencies that the students have acquired to use the tools of the disciplines. The examination items used in geography, history and philosophy show a broader coverage of the knowledge that the students have acquired. The optional examination tasks that are presented to the students during the examination create variations that lead to conclusions that students are not passing the same Baccalaureate.

The use of the term 'external' for the second examiners is questioned. A fair amount of second examiners are selected from earlier teachers and school leaders of European Schools and do not represent a true external perspective when acting during the examinations. The inspectors are not an external force as they are deeply involved in the management of the system. The European Baccalaureate is perceived as less external than it wants to be with a lower degree of uniformity than might be assumed, and is seen as using old-fashioned examining techniques.

Based on this critical review of the European Baccalaureate, several proposals were made by Ekholm for future use. A more comprehensive approach toward the examination procedures is recommended so that the European Baccalaureate will mean the same thing in the future. The examinations need to be based on the reference framework of the Lisbon Strategy for the EU. Some kind of template for the content of school subjects is recommended, to be used when constructing tasks for examination. The use of digital technique and other means that are used in realistic situations needs to become common. The European Schools are asked to adjust examination routines to answer the need to cover broad aspects of student knowledge. Assessments need to be made in adjustment to the kind of knowledge that the students develop and should not be restricted to ritualized examination periods. A recommendation is made that the European School system should trust school directors, educational advisers and teachers to conduct the European Baccalaureate, with only random sample controls. The European Schools are recommended to simplify examination dispensations for students with special needs to a simple article specifying adjustment to the needs of the student.

The Ekholm Report is challenging, needs to be addressed by the European Schools Board of Governors, and is now part of ongoing deliberations. It expresses an informed individual perception, which can itself be challenged. Some of the objectives not perceived in the formal examination may have been better achieved by the required environment of learning. Nor should we necessarily accept the Lisbon accord as the 'be all and end all' of European education policy; it is, after all, conditioned by an EU which many members see as having a primarily economic purpose. But its questions are important and legitimate and would be even more so for most national or international alternatives.

The European Baccalaureate and European policy for education

Could the EB and should the EB reform take account of European policy recommendations as agreed in the Lisbon accord? Here they are in summary form, expressed as competence outcomes.

Key competences for lifelong learning

Key competences for lifelong learning are a combination of knowledge, skills and attitudes appropriate to the context. They are particularly necessary for personal fulfilment and development, social inclusion, active citizenship and employment.

- Key competences are essential in a knowledge society and guarantee more flexibility in the labour force, allowing it to adapt more quickly to constant changes in an increasingly interconnected world.
- They are also a major factor in innovation, productivity and competitiveness, and they contribute to the motivation and satisfaction of workers and the quality of work.
- Key competences should be acquired by: young people at the end of their compulsory education and training equipping them for adult life, particularly for working life, while forming a basis for further learning; adults throughout their lives through a process of developing and updating skills.
- The acquisition of key competences fits in with the principles of equality and access for all. This reference framework also applies, in particular, to disadvantaged groups whose educational potential requires support. Examples of such groups include people with low basic skills, early school leavers, the long-term unemployed, people with disabilities and immigrants.

Eight key competences

This framework defines eight key competences and describes the essential knowledge, skills and attitudes related to each of these. These key competences are:

Communication in the mother tongue is the ability to express and interpret concepts, thoughts, feelings, facts and opinions in both oral and written form (through listening, speaking, reading and writing), and to interact linguistically in an appropriate and creative way in a full range of societal and cultural contexts.

Communication in foreign languages involves, in addition to the main skill dimensions of communication in the mother tongue, mediation and inter-cultural understanding. The level of proficiency depends on several factors and the capacity for listening, speaking, reading and writing.

Mathematical competence and basic competences in science and technology: Mathematical competence is the ability to develop and apply mathematical thinking in order to solve a range of problems in everyday situations, with the emphasis being placed on process, activity and knowledge. Basic competences in science and technology refer to the mastery, use and application of knowledge and methodologies which explain the natural world. These involve an understanding of the changes caused by human activity and the responsibility of each individual as a citizen.

Digital competence involves the confident and critical use of information society technology (IST) and thus basic skills in information and communication technology (ICT).

Learning to learn centres on the ability to pursue and organize one's own learning, either individually or in groups, in accordance with one's own needs, with an awareness of methods and opportunities.

Social and civic competences: Social competence refers to personal, inter-personal and inter-cultural competence and all forms of behaviour that equip individuals to participate in an effective and constructive way in social and working life. It is linked to personal and social well-being. An understanding of codes of conduct and customs in the different environments in which individuals operate is essential. Civic competence, and particularly knowledge of social and political concepts and structures (democracy, justice, equality, citizenship and civil rights), equips individuals to engage in active and democratic participation.

Sense of initiative and entrepreneurship is the ability to turn ideas into action. It involves creativity, innovation and risk taking, as well as the ability to plan and manage projects in order to achieve objectives. The individual is aware of the context of his or her work and is able to seize opportunities which arise. It is the foundation for acquiring more specific skills and knowledge needed by those establishing or contributing to social or commercial activity. This should include awareness of ethical values and promote good governance.

Cultural awareness and expression involves appreciation of the importance of the creative expression of ideas, experiences and emotions in a range of media (including music, performing arts, literature and the visual arts).

These key competences are all interdependent, and the emphasis in each case is on critical thinking, creativity, initiative, problem solving, risk assessment, decision making and constructive management of feelings.

(EU 2006, pp. 13–18)

Current reform proposals for the European Baccalaureate

As outlined by the secretary-general for the European Schools Board of Governors, the working party for EB reform now has a specific brief,[4] informed from inside the system.

In April 2008, the Board of Governors approved the amendments to the Regulations for the European Baccalaureate (the so-called 1984 Agreement) allowing schools accredited by the Board of Governors to provide the European Baccalaureate.

The working group is proceeding with its work on the basis of both the external evaluation ordered by the Board of Governors from Cambridge University and the reports of the Presidents of the Baccalaureate, notably covering the last three years.

The working group is to bear in mind that the original aim of the reform pursuant to the Resolutions of the European Parliament, was precisely to make the Baccalaureate available to pupils not enrolled in (Type I) European Schools.

In addition to the educational and organisational aspects of the European Baccalaureate, the issue of its cost for accredited schools should be considered. Indeed, the present cost per pupil of the European Baccalaureate within the system is too high. Measures already taken and those submitted to the Board of Governors within the framework of the reform of the Baccalaureate should make it possible to arrive at a more reasonable amount.

The emphasis is on ensuring an example of quality. As with the Cambridge report, there is no explicit brief to relate the curriculum or examination to the Lisbon recommendations.

Le but de la réforme

L'exemplarité de l'éducation offerte par les Ecoles européennes peut constituer une voie de qualité pour les élèves scolarisés dans des milieux multiculturels et multilingues en Europe.

Si l'on souhaite que l'ouverture du système devienne possible, des dispositions doivent être prises en vue de simplifier l'organisation actuelle et réduire les coûts sans pour autant compromettre la qualité du Diplôme. La réforme du Baccalauréat pourrait contribuer à la révision de son contenu et de son organisation, afin que celui-ci réponde aux exigences actuelles des Universités et/ou d'autres établissements d'enseignement supérieur et également à faciliter le processus visant à le rendre plus largement disponible.[5]

(Schola Europaea, 2010, p. 2)

Conclusion

The working party set up to make recommendations is due to report its findings, in time for implementation for the Baccalaureate examination of 2013, though no doubt this will become an ongoing review process. Quite properly, the review is within the existing framework, in which the curriculum, the examination, accreditation and inspection are all under the auspices of a directorate general for general services, which provides a service to EC personnel. This may be extendable to a few more schools (Type II and III) on the fringes of a system conducted essentially for Type I, but it would be inadequate for a real opening up of the kind no doubt envisaged by the European Parliament, such as the objective proposed in a 2009 debate for at least one European School in each EU country. There are many possible scenarios, one of them as now which would require minor adjustments and answers to questions such as those raised from within, for example, who is to provide the funding for accrediting, inspecting and examining. This could continue to function, but is already coming under increasing criticism as a perk for the elite, and could lead to the discrediting, undermining and ultimate dismantling of the European Schools.

In the present scheme of things, the best that could be hoped for in, say, the next 5 years, would be a honing of the present curriculum and procedures, to ensure the maintenance of quality and clear criteria for the accreditation of schools applying to enter the system. It would be optimistic but not unrealistic to hope that in the next 10 years there could be one or two accredited schools (Type II, III) from each member state. They would need to organize themselves as a network to develop those activities which are at present provided for Type I schools through the joint Board of Governors and inspectorate, under legislation which would not allow for funding to these accredited schools. There is already broad agreement that such activities would be, as set out in the preceding chapter. It is encouraging to see that five existing Type II schools are already applying COMENIUS funding to promote the exchange of pupils.

Once something of that order has been achieved, as a strengthening of what the Cambridge review presented as a Model A, and once there is confidence that modest extension can be achieved without the diminution of quality or reputation, it may be possible to envisage moves toward Model C. This would enable such national developments as the French *option internationale*, the Abi-Bac, or even the accredited Europa-Schulen of several German *Länder* to join a European Baccalaureate framework. Model C would also enable the European Baccalaureate to encompass vocational or professional options which it has previously declined. It is an irony that the French baccalaureate, which half a century ago was one of the models for the EB, has since developed such options in addition to the international variant. French pupils can elect to take a general baccalaureate or specialist technical or professional baccalaureates, which are more vocational. The general one comes in three guises: Baccalaureate L, which focuses on literature; Baccalaureate ES with an economic and social sciences emphasis; and Baccalaureate S, a science-focused version. Crucially, however, this does not mean dropping subjects as the English do. Regardless of the specific Baccalaureate course they are undertaking, all pupils continue to study French, history, geography, a foreign language, philosophy, maths and science, with marks weighted toward their specialist areas.

Let us go further. The present EB system is inadequate for any European School because it is under the control of a directorate which has no relevance to education (being concerned with questions of services to employees and the ES as an employment incentive), with a Board of Governors so constituted that change and development are difficult to achieve. For any significant extension of the system within the EU, the curriculum and examination should come within the ambit of a reformed Directorate for Education and Culture, perhaps as a freestanding agency with close links with the Council of Europe's education team. Accreditation of schools might also be from there, and inspection should be nationally conducted under franchise and principles determined through the Directorate for Education and Culture (or agency), no doubt with external visitors. The curriculum and examination and school grant functions of the Board of Governors should transfer to be serviced by the appropriate directorate, leaving the General Services Directorate to determine what support is given to its employees, no doubt with their representation in some form, as would be the case for any major private employer supporting the schooling of personnel families.

It would then be clear that the expense of inspection should be borne by national or local funding. The Directorate for Education and Culture would have charge of a budget for its activities and to support institutional, professional and curriculum development in addition to inter-school activities across European Schools of all three types. European education would surface. This is obviously a long-term perspective, but one which should be projected, in the terms of the preamble, as *'l'avenir du modele éducatif des Écoles européennes'* ('the future educational model of the European Schools'; Schola Europaea, 2010, p. 1).

On Europe Day 1960, to celebrate the 1959 opening of the first European School in Luxembourg, a commemorative stamp was issued[6] bearing the joyful image of six children joining hands before their school building, and with the Latin tag: *Ex Foedere Sex Nationum* ('from the federation of six nations'). Today an EU stamp would show 27 children, soon no doubt to become 30, and the image has to change. Many of the school-leaving examinations of recently acceding EU countries are of much longer standing, and some, like the Romanian Matura, have changed little over eight decades. There is a strong case, in terms of social cohesion, for working toward reforms which will wed these backgrounds to a common future. For extension beyond the European Union, something wider than an EU directorate should be envisaged. There is a case for examining in this context, as in others, the relationship between the European Union's approach to education and that of the Council of Europe and the desirability of an independent trans-European advisory body to help shape the future.

Notes

1 General studies, for example, as a single subject for GCSE, GCE AS and A-level examinations, normally taken by pupils aged 16 to 18.

2 Lisbon Recognition Convention (1997) applied to all member states of the Council of Europe and of the European Cultural Convention. Strasbourg/Paris, Council of Europe/ UNESCO.

3 Ekholm, M. (2009), Report of the Chairman of the 2009 European Baccalaureate Examining Board, Schola Europaea website ref. 2009-D-609-en-1.

4 Schola Europaea (2009), Reform of the European Schools System. 2009-D-353-en-4, 17/24. European Schools Secretariat, Brussels.

5 Schola Europaea (2010), Réforme du Baccalauréat Européen, 2010-D-289-fr-3, European Schools Secretariat, Brussels.
The aim of reform: The exemplary education offered by the European Schools can constitute a quality route for school pupils in multicultural and multilingual environments in Europe. If the wish is to make it possible to open up the system, measures must be taken to simplify the present organization and reduce the costs without thereby compromising the certificate's quality. Reform of the Baccalaureate could contribute to the revision of its content and organization, so that the former meets current requirements of university and other higher education institutions, and equally to facilitate the process aiming to make the Baccalaureate more widely available. (Author's translation).

6 Michel (2004/5), Europa-Katalog-Band 1-West, Luxemburg No. 621. München: Schwanenberger Verlag.

12 Learning from Culham as a Case Study

John Sayer

Chapter Outline

Background

This is a story of a school 30 years untouched, happy and successful in its own terms, then caught in a painful choice of closure or change; a school set up under European Commission regulations as described in Chapter 10, primarily to serve the employees seconded to a large joint European project, but becoming predominantly one for other families of bilingual background within reach in the area, and then facing a future of joining the national system or disappearing; a school out of reach of local league tables or SATs [1] or the vagaries of national curriculum; a school neither maintained nor private, both free and partly fee-paying, a school in no man's land.

No man's land was ideal for the new Joint European Torus (JET) nuclear fusion project[2], out of harm's way, but within a belt of growing new research-, science- and technology-based industries, not least Harwell, the British atomic energy research centre. Great Britain had just been allowed into the EU, Ted Heath was looking to attract large European investment, and a key attraction would be an adjacent site for a European School.

And there it was: the Church of England College of Teacher Education, forced into closure in the early 1970s as part of the rationalization of initial teacher training, standing empty, unpurchased and perhaps unsaleable because of charity law confining it to educational purposes. It had been set up in the mid-nineteenth century, seminary-like, residential, away from the distractions and temptations of townships, in the middle of nowhere, and was no longer the scene for future teachers to connect with a changing society. It was purchased by the Estates Agency of the Crown, at a price reduced to take account of years of over-payment for student per capita grants, and became, uniquely at the time, a central government-owned site for a school. Leased to the European Commission without charge, it passed into the hands of the European Schools Board of Governors, and became in 1978 the one and only European School on British soil, its site minimally maintained still by tender from London but its management and new development funded from Brussels. The first head to be appointed had a respected background in Oxfordshire and Berkshire schools; thereafter, senior appointments went the rounds of member countries, rather like the rotating EC presidency. Staffing was mostly by secondment from national systems, with local appointments confined largely to part-time *chargés de cours*, and the headteacher otherwise on the receiving end of staff to be inducted. Salaries, particularly for teachers of the secondary age range, are out of this world, a mixture of enhancement above national scales, displacement allowances and tax concessions, with appointments guaranteed for 9 years and security of status, tenure and pension rights when returning to the seconding country or transferring to another European School. Teachers were of course also granted free priority access to the school for their children.

René Christmann's chapter sets out the formal system common to the European Schools. In each country, there will be contrasts with local customs. So at Culham, it is the parents who organize, finance and advise on transport, whether by coach or shared car; it is the parents who organize extra-curricular activities and remunerate one of their number to co-ordinate them; it is the parents who bring the school to life outside the formal curriculum, and who notify the government's contractor of repairs and maintenance needs. It is a school receptionist who puts on school plays, while school meals are contracted out. The parents' association, CESPA,[3] is a recognized part of the administrative system and has its place on the local administrative board, which has the task of complying with central decisions and can recommend to the central Board of Governors for all 14 European Schools. On the other hand, the local parent body does not share decisions on policy, curriculum, staffing or management, there being no governing body for the school itself.

The children of European agency employees have priority access, free of charge. They are termed Category 1 children. Other major European employers with plants nearby, such as BMW or NPower, may pay a full fee for children of their staff, as they might in a private school. These are Category 2 pupils. But that still leaves room for other families who wish their children to have a bilingual European education. They pay a contribution calculated not as a fee but as an estimate of the extra cost of including them in classes which would have to run anyway in the different language strands or sections of the school. This contribution may amount to about a quarter of a full-cost fee. So there are three categories of children in the school, the third being by far the most numerous.

The buildings are a mixture of the original gaunt mid-nineteenth-century stone chapel and residential college round an attractive quadrangle, and twentieth-century additions to the college, such as the less attractive gymnasium or hall, dining annexe and kitchens. To these have been added, since the opening of the school, a charming new area for the primary age range, a residue of temporary hutments become permanent, a brutal tower of minimal standard classrooms, and a sports hall. Over the road, further meadows were leased to form additional sports fields, later with a connecting bridge. At the time of purchase, the county architect's office estimated the site could accommodate just over 1,000 children; after the building for school use, central government estimated nearer to 1,500. Both took little account of the size of rooms, 80 teaching spaces many of which would be too small for a locally funded school, but easier to work with in the European School sections, some having diminutive teaching groups. Specialist areas such as laboratories remained unimpressive. The oil heating system creaks wastefully. But it is a lovable place to work and play in, with a pleasant library and staff room in the secondary area. Numbers in the all-age school, 4–18, rose to about 950, then declined somewhat to more than 800 on the transfer of responsibility for the JET project, which was the reason for threatened closure of the school, talked of for many years and finally proposed in 2006 after a funded review (the Van Dijk report)[4] and confirmed in 2007 as a phased closure from 2010 to 2017.

Under threat of closure

Attempts had been made over the years by the parents' association, CESPA, to resist the closure either of language sections or of the whole school, and approaches had been made to the British government with no success. CESPA, as part of the European Schools system, had its hands tied, having no mandate for change or development. The suggestion that a parallel charity should be set up with a free hand to seek solutions was eventually adopted in 2006, and in December of that year the English Trust for European Education (ETEE)[5] was initiated, with trustees composed of former and current parents, a former European School teacher now active in local politics, and a university educator formerly a leading schools head, the initial priority being to secure a future for European education at Culham.

The possibility of establishing a private school with similar aims to the existing European School had been explored by the CESPA Futures group as apparently the only feasible option, although a majority of parents, especially those used to strong state schooling in their own countries, had indicated preference for inclusion in the maintained sector. What appeared to be a chink of light appeared in 2006. The Labour government had, rightly or wrongly, inherited a programme of nationally funded schools to replace failing local authority schools in inner-city areas. Initially described as city technology colleges and then as city academies, they received priority funding and were to have a measure of independence, being under the direction of sponsors who would bring additional private funding. Anxious that academies should not be exclusively identified with remedies for inner-city failure, the prime minister, who had come to power with the watchwords 'education, education, education', was in 2006 readily persuaded to add a dimension of academies bringing 'choice and diversity' to the system: rural academies under the wing of a prestigious school or as a chain across a sparsely populated area; small independent schools, some formerly direct grant, encouraged by wealthy sponsors to extend to less privileged communities; alternative schools such as the Steiner school in Herefordshire.[6] ETEE trustees could not leave the opportunity unexplored, however unlikely, and made an immediate approach to the then school minister, Andrew Adonis, took advice from the Specialist Schools and Academies Trust,[7] made a short exploratory proposal early in 2007 in keeping with the academies scheme, and suggested a joint meeting with the Office of the Schools Commissioner (OSC), the government section charged with developing the academies programme, and the Joint International Unit (JIU) which held the European Schools file. It was not only the trustees' first meeting with the OSC but also the first time the two sections of government had ever met or conferred.

European Academy approach (February 2007)

This positive first encounter led in March 2007 to a formal proposal[8] from ETEE to the British government, after consultation with CESPA and Culham staff. Here is the executive summary, with the timelines as originally proposed in February 2007.

> The European School Culham is the only UK example of the network of European Schools in the European Communities. All European Schools are inter-governmental bodies, providing a curriculum that leads to the European Baccalaureate – an academic qualification fully recognised by all EU governments. The infrastructure of the European School Culham belongs to the British Government, which also supplies English-speaking teachers, as well as funding the maintenance of the site and all existing buildings.

> Although the school is highly successful in terms of parental demand and academic qualifications achieved by its pupils, the governing body of European Schools has determined that the Culham school no longer meets the sole purpose for which it was founded (i.e. the provision of education to employees of the European Commissions), and is seeking either its closure or transformation. The English Trust for European Education (ETEE) has therefore devised a proposal to transform the school into a state funded European Academy, serving a wider sector of the local population.

> The newly formed European Academy will be a unique all-age inclusive, multilingual, mixed sex school following the European Baccalaureate (EB) curriculum. The Academy will form part of a family of schools both in the local area and with other bilingual specialist language Academies and Schools in England and Wales and within the European Communities (through the growing network of the other European Schools and other schools following the EB curriculum).

> Links will also be forged with the local scientific institutions that have already expressed an interest in the school. We expect the synergies of these links to turn the Academy into a centre for innovation and support for other schools in the County, particularly those schools that may be in need of assistance.

> The ETEE envisages that in virtue of the Academy's premier position at the forefront of bilingual education and language teaching, a resource centre for the in-service

development of language teachers could also be created, in co-operation with other existing training institutions in the region.

The transformation of the existing school into an Academy would see the creation of an all-age institution gradually growing from the current ca 900 pupils to around 1,200 pupils. This growth is in line with the expected demographics expansion of the area. In addition only modest infrastructural development costs would be required in the initial stages.

Timelines

2007.	Board of Governors to defer & encourage transformation proposal to Type 3 Outline proposal developed. DfES and OCC to encourage expression of interest as European Academy Business plan compiled for presentation to potential sponsors.
2008.	Sponsorship interest Brokering phase. Expression of Interest, compiled by EoI consultant for agreement.
2009.	Feasibility phase: funding agreement, set up Academy Trust, deed of gift. Design group work on Academy building improvements.
2009–10.	Implementation phase. Preparation for opening Academy, curricular programme, Director-Designate, staffing appointments. Transition arrangements from 2011 agreed with BoG. Start-up grant and revenue budget agreed by DfES.
2011.	Formal opening. Building programme starts.
2012.	Completion of Phase I building programme. Opening of weekly boarding facility, ICT and technology facilities etc.
2018.	Phasing completed, first Academy cohort through EB.

This proposal was well received and led to the assignment of an OSC consultant to help take it through the first stage ('brokerage') of the procedures for establishing an academy. Two brief meetings, the second joined by the officer responsible for British involvement in the European Schools, led to the proposal being submitted also to the European Schools Board of Governors in April and to be received at its September meeting as an alternative or variant to the phased closure of ES Culham as already announced. The headteacher, who had encouraged the ETEE initiative, had unfortunately been relocated in February 2007 at short notice to set up the new European School Brussels IV, but the bursar and acting head had been helpful in providing necessary information, and there had been meetings with parents and staff at the school. By

April, ETEE could confirm that there was general support for taking the proposal forward, though with the weekly boarding proposal prudently deferred to a second phase for consideration of the future governing body.

ETEE had from the start emphasized that this proposal was not only for negotiation between the national and EU authorities, but was about a school transition, which had to be centre stage. Its detailed proposals as annexed, therefore, showed three main strands of development, the school being in the centre: academy recognition by the national government; a Culham Type III[9] school organization; and for Board of Governors – funded support and protection for the residual or legacy phasing out Type I years. An indicative calculation was made in the summer of 2007 by ETEE of the costs for phasing out, and this was taken up for the European Commission to refine and confirm. Meanwhile, in April 2007, the ES Board of Governors had minuted its encouragement to the British government to come forward with its proposal for a seamless transition as an alternative to phased closure.

> That the UK delegation and the management of the school explore the possibility of transforming the European School of Culham into an associate, Type III school and report to the Board of Governors proposing deadlines for the identification of the partners and authorities willing to take political, administrative and financial responsibility for the school and indicating the steps which need to be taken to finalize the transformation.[10]

The proposal was now in the hands of the competent authorities, in terms of national and EC procedures. ETEE had meanwhile focused on the local scene: encouraging preliminary negotiations with Oxfordshire County Council, including day nursery proposals (the age range for European Schools not being the same as local demarcations) and, in particular, with local interest groups and stakeholders. These included those large employers supporting staff families wishing to use the European School, whether in the long term or in order to return to their home country systems without disadvantage. They included, still, the JET project and several firms such as BMW, which had taken over the Cowley plant producing mini cars, and N Power, which had taken over the local power station at Didcot.

The academy proposal required a sponsor, with a commitment not only to set up an academy trust and be responsible for the project but also not least to contribute or raise up-front and longer-term enhanced funding. The rubric for setting up academies presented five stages: brokerage (to agree on a sponsor), expression of interest (the sponsor's proposal, worked out with government support), feasibility (to set up a funded preparation plan), implementation and opening. Pending the identification of an appropriate sponsor, ETEE had begun to build a list of supportive stakeholder organizations. The obvious first call was to firms currently paying the fees of Category 2 pupils, who under the academy scheme would no longer have to pay a penny. In October 2007 BMW convened a meeting of such employers, the DfES, ETEE and CESPA, and ETEE presented a proposal which would involve the transfer or partial transfer of fees saved into the sponsorship fund for the academy. Employers were invited at the suggestion of the DfES to make a provisional and non-binding indication of interest, and 15 did so between 2007 and 2008. There was confidence, moreover, that those parents who had been making financial contributions to their children's education would support a scheme by making voluntary donations for the proposed academy, which would release them from any fee paying. Early in 2008 ETEE set up with stakeholders, including CESPA (now more free to work on development, having the ES Board of Governors support), a sponsorship sub-committee with the immediate aim of building financial support for the academy trust to be established. The question was raised whether the project could not be supported within an EU education development programme, but this was ruled out, since the European Schools are outside the orbit of the commission's Directorate for Education and Culture, which had the funding for such proposals.

The DfES brokerage consultant had in December 2007 offered to help find a suitable sponsor; there was speculation that an approach might be made to an Anglican agency such as the National Society, already active in the area. This might have caused controversy across the different national backgrounds of parents and staff, and it was a relief when Lord Jay of Ewelme, who had recently agreed to become patron of ETEE, went further and agreed with Lord Adonis to form a new sponsor company, bringing together the great and the good, names which would represent interests in European affairs, languages and sciences (the academy scheme requiring one or two specialist subject areas) and be familiar to potential financial supporters.

The proposal taken forward

All this had been achieved within a year of the initial ETEE approach, and there was much local optimism. The school continued to run largely unaffected, the acting headship having been extended to July 2008. However, the Joint International Unit had taken two initiatives. First, it had offered to provide secondment funding for the next head of the European School, with a brief from September 2008 to continue to administer the school but at the same time to collaborate in a possible transition to become an academy. Secondly, it had allocated from reserve funding for a consultant to respond quickly to the ES Board of Governors invitation to come up with a costed and dated proposal. The result of the first initiative was the appointment of a new head with good experience as director of the languages 'college' of a comprehensive school; for the second, an ex-local authority chief education officer, whose very generous proposal[11] was presented by the DCSF[12] to the Board of Governors in September 2008, but then withdrawn when it became clear that there had been misunderstandings with the commission on financial matters.

Meanwhile, the local stakeholders were waiting for progress. In April 2008, the option was offered to the intending sponsor to take over an existing charitable company which had worked closely with ETEE, rather than go through the processes of securing recognition for a new one. This would have enabled a much earlier submission of an expression of interest from the legally recognized body, in keeping with the timetable of the original proposal. However, the DCSF advice seems to have been to create a new body, and it was another year before the sponsor body[13] even existed in law. ETEE and CESPA continued to share discussions with the intended sponsor, but it was now for the two systems of national government academy procedures, on the one hand, and the European Commission and European Schools Board of Governors, on the other, to continue with the intending sponsor and with the newly appointed head the progress that had been made, and for the sponsor to take over and build on the initial fundraising negotiations. ETEE and CESPA would continue to support, suggest, comment and cajole, but by November 2008 the moment was reached for formal hand-over of responsibility, when ETEE organized with JET a conference[14] of the score of supporting organizations it had kept together, to introduce the sponsor and now renamed DCSF representatives. The sponsor's business plan for fundraising could be expected shortly. In the event, the setting up of the new sponsoring company as a charity was even more protracted than expected, and meanwhile, the sponsor had accepted the offer of NPower, with its organization already geared to appeals for charity, to give a lead on fundraising. The offer was further confused by the government's modification of the financial requirement. This weakened progress, even though it had become clear that the new European Academy would need massive support beyond national funding, whether the government required it or not. No doubt NPower then awaited the formation of the sponsoring body, and of the academy trust, which would hold the endowment fund. The first of these emerged after a year, the second only after 2 years, and still without the charitable status which would attract and enhance donations, although under the 2010 Academies Bill[15] it would become an exempted charity as soon as it became the academy proprietor. For potential donors, it was a confusing period characterized by inaction.

Understandably yet significantly, the DCSF submission to the ES Board of Governors had focused on the inter-governmental transactions and left out the local or school development. Whereas ETEE had in June 2008 revised its initial proposal to give even more importance to the school's development itself – with a sufficient schedule for a development plan with particular attention to staffing and detailing both the 'legacy' ES Type I cohorts and the stages for transition to Type III – the DCSF document, which was also presented to parents at the school, dealt principally with legalities, finance and acceptance of the European Baccalaureate. Its time frame was in two columns only: academy procedures and ES Board of Governors decisions. Moreover, it brought forward the transition proposal to September 2010 as first choice, without having a brief to consider what that would involve in the school itself. No doubt this was influenced by allocations in national budgets; it certainly bore no resemblance to the reality of the school. The financial prospect as presented was dazzling, including an offer for the British government to bear the cost of continuing secondment from other countries; it was soon to be withdrawn and revised.

Negotiations continued throughout 2009 and 2010, but each of the protagonists awaited the next move from another. Nobody had overall direction of the process. There was no agreed overriding plan. ETEE had pleaded constantly for a shadow governing body to be set up from the outset, so that it would be ready with curriculum and staffing plans to make key appointments in readiness for the transition to an academy, but this was seen as premature by those following the academies rubric, which provided for replacement rather than transformation of schools. ETEE concerns were reiterated in an interim review of May 2009, underlining the internal needs of the school and the original timelines considered to be essential for proper adjustment. Sadly, the review went without response.

However, individual issues began to be resolved late in 2009. The DCSF had identified building conversion and improvement needs before waiting for the stage at which this would be expected, and an estimate for £14 million pounds had been made in readiness. The sponsor, now having a formal organization, was assisted by the DCSF to complete the formal proposal (expression of interest, in academy terms) to the minister, and this was promptly approved in December 2009, more than a year later than had been envisaged. This set in motion the funded consultancy to develop feasibility plans for the academy, and a well-known consultancy firm, Mouchel,[16] was brought in to begin work in the new year. The date for academy opening reverted to 2011, so there would again be some prospect of completion on a very tight schedule allowing no exigencies. Meanwhile, however, the EC had decided that it was not legally possible to pass its closure funds to an intended Type III European School, and since there was now no time for or prospect of changing its regulations without delay, a Type II status was proposed instead, with transfer of funding envisaged on condition that the school would admit any Category 1 pupils from EC-employed families. This would be a breach of British regulations for admissions to schools, but it was that or nothing, and ministerial consent was given for the period of transition. Bilateral approaches were being made by British officials to their counterparts to enable continuing secondment of staff. The Board of Governors reiterated its responsibility that there should be no change in the type of education provided or the terms and conditions of the staff until that date, and required a legally binding guarantee from the British authorities to be agreed by April 2010. An excellent and reassuring letter went from the sponsor to all existing parents in December 2009. Three years after being conceived, the project could now be put through academy and European School stages toward completion, though without the phased development and staffing plans originally envisaged

The consultancy firm, Mouchel, came with a brief to have all needs for academy implementation identified, agreed and programmed within 6 months, so that the sponsor could seek final approval from the British government for the Culham European Academy. At the same time, the sponsor would have sought approval for a *dossier de conformité*[17] for the Board of Governors to approve by autumn 2010 the plans for the academy to have European Schools Type II status. All this would be too late for the academy to be included in the local admissions procedure for 2011, and there was still no academy trust in place or governing body, so admissions would be under the old arrangements until 31 August 2011.

Mouchel, appointed by the British government to work for the sponsor from January 2010 on academy planning, came in with promptly established timelines for output, including resolution of staffing structure by spring 2010 and individual contracts by summer 2010. Their task was to focus on the academy proposal, the European Schools being contextual, but meanwhile, the secretary-general of the European Schools Board of Governors, realizing that bilateral negotiations on seconded staff security were making insufficient progress, came in with a late attempt to secure national agreements as part of an overall plan. Mouchel contrived an astute proposal for admissions criteria to enable the European Academy to serve its existing wide area. They also picked up ETEE's concern that, absurdly, the European Baccalaureate was still not an authorized examination for direct British funding, and secured a quiet concession from the minister to override the examinations authority he was about to abolish anyway. Mouchel satisfied the government that the curriculum leading to the European Baccalaureate was compatible with the National Curriculum.

Inside the European School, which continued on its way, only the head and bursar were directly involved in the process of transformation. Staff representatives focused on anxieties of staff tenure, while parent representatives focused on the guarantees and reassurances that their children's education would not be adversely affected. The two deputy heads (secondary and primary) focused on ensuring that the school continued to be well run. One retired in the summer of 2009, to be replaced by an acting deputy drawn from the staff, the other was to retire in April 2011. The head, after surviving a serious accident shortly after his arrival, had courageously sustained and contributed vision to the project, but was increasingly isolated in the school as anxiety grew on the two closely issues of guarantees and staff secondments.

The *dossier de conformité* was completed and presented in the autumn of 2010 and came before the Board of Governors in December. It could still be accepted only on condition that the legally binding guarantee against possible litigation would be completed and agreed on by April 2011. Everybody wanted agreement, and frantic negotiations continued through January. However, a large proportion of seconded staff, faced with immediate decision, had concluded that it was in their interests not to continue into the proposed Type II school. So threats of parental litigation had become a reality, and the sponsor was unable to commit to taking legal responsibility for actions taken under the existing school, while the Board of Governors and DCSF had no provision to accept liability for actions taken to introduce a new one. Accordingly, on 2 February 2011, the Sponsor notified the British government and European Commission and on 3 February, parents were notified that the sponsor had withdrawn and the academy project could not continue. On the same day, the Board of Governors was notified by the secretary-general, and their original decision to proceed to phased closure at Culham would be confirmed. There was general disappointment on all sides, even among those parents who had become sharply critical. Five years of commitment, of conflict resolution and consensus building, of hope and expectation had come to grief.

Conclusion

It would be facile to conclude, as some were ready to do, that a project requiring agreement across national and European Commission authorities was doomed from the outset, or to point the finger at any one of the actors committed to finding solutions for the school. In any organizational development, human beings, whether wearing an institutional label or not, make mistakes or judgements overtaken by events, and procedures which are designed for existing systems are found not to work for new ones. That has to be allowed for in planning. Much more important is to identify what can be learned for the future, both at Culham, where an alternative project is already under way, and in any such situation, in Great Britain or elsewhere in Europe.

This was an organizational development which could and should have happened. The vision of the proposal was applauded, the objectives spelled out from the outset were recognized as achievable, the hurdles surmountable. So what went wrong that could be right next time? First, the small and initially well-knit group which took the ETEE initiative were well advised from a parallel project to hold on to the project and not let the process out of their hands. But they were not comfortable to form a legal entity which would insist on and be eligible to take on sponsorship, and wished to be free to continue informally to promote European education more widely and not be tied to a single commitment. They were relieved that their patron was approached and agreed to form a sponsorship group to advance the vision, rather than accept a corporate sponsor running a range of academies of different ethos. They made themselves available as individuals and had anticipated being more involved, but without taking on the onus of development, and indeed this involvement was at first intended. Even though they were divested of responsibility, they were bemused when the academy system took over and they were sidelined. This was the group on the ground with vision, situational awareness and hands-on capability. In retrospect, a preferable arrangement would have been for the distinguished group who eventually became the sponsor to have been seen as patrons, thereby attracting government and potential financial support, and for ETEE with the incoming head, CESPA and local stakeholders to have formed a shadow executive administration which could lead into the future governing body. Without this, there was no business plan either for institutional development or for fundraising. and nobody to pursue it on the ground.

Second, there was no one locus of authority to oversee the whole project, across Culham, local interests, the EC and the British government. From the moment in 2005 when at last the European Parliament and the Council of Ministers had taken up the idea of widening access to the European Schools beyond the service benefits provided by the EC's Human Resources and Security Directorate,[18] and to develop what would become described as Type II and Type III schools, an overarching body was needed to work with EC and national authorities, leaving the directorate to continue to fund benefits to its employees. When ETEE suggested that the project might be supported as a pilot educational development, the response was that such pilot developments were not the province of the current directorate general. The corollary was not drawn. When it became evident in 2008 that the EC could not override its own funding regulations for a Type III school, and that higher authority was needed to amend the regulations, there was no-one to go to and no-one to make the approach, with European Parliament elections and a new commission in the offing. So, too, when it became evident that no one national government official could secure agreement from counterparts to modify or even confirm their regulations on secondment to Culham if it moved from Type I status, there was no directing authority with the power to intervene. This was a prime example of where the EU should be operating above its own departments, to implement agreed policy which is beyond the scope of national governments.

Meanwhile, everyone involved at Culham was torn apart, and energies are focused on restoring confidence. A new local initiative was launched to start a 'free'[19] school, which could become a European Type III school, while the Type I school is phased out at Culham. There were still those who wanted nothing more to do with government and might have preferred a non-governmental school. Whatever emerges, there will be difficulties of hybrid site management and administration, to be resolved from the outset. There is no prospect of retrieving as much as the £14 million which would have been invested in the European Academy project and remains badly needed. But much has been learned and much more is to be learned from the academy experience, and there is much greater understanding of the issues and practicalities involved, many of them having been resolved in the course of the academy project. At the time of writing, there is new hope for Culham, and it is being pursued. It says much for the resilience and determination of current and prospective parents to have gone through serious disappointment and acrimony and to have taken this new initiative, determined also to retain the vision, management and direction of the new school. If it succeeds, it will have cleared the way for others to follow. An application has been accepted by the DfE for the establishment of a 'Europa School UK' from September 2012, and a parallel *dossier de conformité* as a Type III school is planned for the European Board of Governors, to grow as the Type I school is phased out. It will depend on restoring a good working relationship and possibly a measure of joint management with the existing school. It will also depend, as will the other Type II and III schools across Europe, on a Europe-wide network of Type II and III European Schools working together and with other schools having a strong European dimension and common features, as proposed and set out in the annex to Chapter 10, and now initiated. These will indeed be schools for the future Europe, reconciling national and Europe-wide priorities, able to link across the whole of Europe, co-operating transnationally and locally, sharing best practice and developing and representing the European dimension in every country.

Notes

1　Standard Attainment Tests, required at specified stages of schooling in maintained schools in England and the subject of constant professional dispute.

2　JET, established by EURATOM at Culham in 1978, has been the world's largest centre for nuclear fusion energy research. Its phasing out as an EU project was announced in 2002, but its future within the UKAEA awaits completion of the even larger international project at Manosque, France. See www.jet.efda.org.

3　Culham European School Parents' Association. See www.esculham.eu/Home/ExtraCurricular/CESPA.

4　Evaluation of the European Schools at Culham, Mol, Bergen and Karlsruhe and options for the future. Final report, Bureau van Dijk Management Consultants SA. See http://gudee.eu/futuree.htm.

5　For ETEE aims, composition and activities see www.etee.org.

6　Great Britain's first Steiner Waldorf publicly funded academy. See www.herefordwaldorf-school.org.

7　SSAT, an initially government-supported charity aiding and advising specialist school and academy members. See www.ssatrust.org.uk.

8   For full 2007 proposal, see http://etee.homestead.com/strategy.html.

9   See Chapter 10 for explanation of Type III European School.

10 ES Board of Governors, April 2007. Ref: 2007-D-214-en-1, access via www.eursc.eu.

11 REPORT_55126652[1]_BOG1008Culham.rtf.

12 The Department for Education and Skills was re-named Department for Children, Schools and Families. This was changed in 2010 to Department for Education (DfE).

13 Culham Languages and Sciences (CLASS) 06851858.

14 ETEE Archive, conference, 28 November 2008: The Future of the European School at Culham.

15 Academies Act 2010, Section 12.

16 Mouchel consulting service, see www.mouchel.com/about_us/default.aspx.

17 The required formal application for accreditation by the European Schools Board of Governors.

18 The EU's 'civil service commission'. See http://ec.europa.eu/dgs/human-resources/mission_en.htm.

19 Free schools are government-funded schools set up by local initiatives outside or alongside the system maintained by local authorities. They are not to be confused with the earlier connotation as internally 'democratic'.

Conclusion: the next ten years

Lynn Erler and John Sayer

In this concluding chapter, we hope to draw upon underlying themes and proposals emerging from the range of insights offered in preceding chapters and, where possible, to crystallize them into achievable objectives, whether in schools, in local and national policies or in Europe-wide initiatives.

Values for change beyond Lisbon

The social market economy appears to be the common characteristic of EU member states and many other parts of Europe. But this begs the question of priorities. Is social cohesion to be seen as a means to achieving competitive outputs in the world market, or is the market economy to be seen as leading the way to higher ends and values and not an end in itself? For educators, there is little doubt that their work centres on common values, that skills and competences are tools through which to put these values into practice, that assessment of education should have as much to do with the way skills are used as in their development per se. Competitiveness, whether of individuals or groups or states within Europe or of Europe in a global society, has to be seen as a means to social well-being and the good life. Systematized selfishness, although it has been forced into every corner of the school system, is not an educational value.

We return to the image of the school classroom as Classroom Europa. In a learning group, friendly competition can be a useful motivating tool for individual and group achievement, bringing out emulation. As soon as competition becomes an end in itself, it brings hostility and humiliation, success brings defeat, gain brings loss, the identity and progress of the learning group are compromised or destroyed, and everyone's education suffers. In Classroom Europa, if we ask why successful economies come to the rescue of those in crisis, or if we ask why everyone contributes to a stronger protective shield over Chernobyl, it is because people understand that co-operation and the common weal are ultimately more important, that it is in the interests of all, however dominant at any one moment, to restore competitiveness and well-being to the ailing and failing. The helping hand when needed is a value in itself. In the words of the doctor in Albert Camus's *La Peste* (*The Plague*), '*Il faut qu'on soit du côté des victimes*' ('You have to be on the side of the victims').

The European principle of subsidiarity has also to be restored. It has become increasingly misused as applying principally to the balance of powers between nation–states and the European Union. Following the Treaty of Maastricht, the Council of Europe (1994) found it necessary to publish a far-reaching study for its local and regional authorities of the ambiguities surrounding the notion embodied in European law, to reassert and clarify the precedence of elected authorities closest to the citizen. Teachers are even further aware that the education of children is not the responsibility of the state or the local authority or the school, but the responsibility in law of parents and guardians, whether at school or otherwise. If a school is chosen by parents to complement their responsibility and to exercise a quasi-parental responsibility for children in its care, it is responsible first and foremost to the parent, having respect for the human rights of the child, especially in cases where the parent is deemed to be failing in that responsibility. All this applies whether or not a school is maintained by a local or national authority or by a non-governmental organization. The more a school governing body, which takes responsibility for the conduct and curriculum of the school, has representation of parents, the more clearly can a school exercise its duty to the parent, to identify what its provision should be to complement what parents can themselves provide. And for teachers to reach out beyond the scope of individual families, their first task is to take the families with them. Lifelong learning begins here and must apply to all the aspirations of European education.

Education to promote European values

If subsidiarity is essentially an assertion of the primacy of the individual human being and citizen, education has a prime task to promote individual and group responsibility and active citizenship, in schools, locally, nationally, in Europe and in the world. There is a strong case for providing a focus for citizenship in the school curriculum, but this becomes futile if it is not the summation of citizenship education in all the formal and informal activities of the school, a pervading school ethos evident whether in the classroom, in the corridor, on the playground or indeed in the staffroom. So, too, there is a particular opportunity for teachers of modern languages to promote awareness and celebrate what may loosely be termed European citizenship, but again, this can best be understood and achieved as an extension of the values and attitudes explicit and implicit in the life of the school community. By citizenship in a democracy and across democratic societies, we can only understand active engagement, not just being a means of economic gains. Being filled with information and knowledge about European institutions, which can be found with two taps at the keyboard by anyone wanting to find out, is not what this is about. So opportunities for active engagement are the prime resource.

Much the same has to be asserted about education for human rights and about entering into the inheritance of a European culture both common and diverse. A multicultural society is not one which ditches traditions but one which is enriched by their variety and in which they are strengthened by having a context of comparison. That is the Europe which can contribute to human understanding worldwide. Schools are there to build the future on the richness of the past.

Perhaps the most obvious challenge for British schools is the declared aim for a multilingual Europe in which all citizens are competent in at least one other language and a substantial number in more than one. This is not just about successful marketing and exports, although it is about that as well. Using traditional parlance, it is about having life and having it more abundantly. Britons generally and the English, in particular, are impoverished as human beings by their monolingual isolation and risk being found unaccountable for quality linguistic education that expresses equity. We cannot even appreciate our native tongue without being able to compare it with others. We are being overtaken by other Europeans in appreciating and articulating the richness of English language and culture. British schools are not alone in Europe in also needing to take account of mother tongue community languages, particularly in the larger conurbations, but the starting point of discovering the languages of our nearest neighbours and the sharing of their background is vital for all.

Cross-curricular bilingual learning in whatever mixture of specialized modes is a promising way forward, and it needs preparation. The education service (and we hope that is still an acceptable description) should take a lead in this. If, given notice that in 10 years time, all future teachers of whatever subject or age group would be required to have achieved a foreign language qualification and to have maintained competence and if this directive were backed with in-service opportunities for existing teachers to revive their neglected learning and to have credit for teaching in other European countries followed by similar expectations in other major professions for access to higher education, language learning in schools would have a very different complexion. This could be achieved if school-leaving qualifications required a foreign language, as they do in many other European countries.

Support for development of European education in schools

Such expectations require development support and investment, locally, nationally and Europe-wide, from and to governmental and non-governmental services. In times of restraint, as in the current propping-up of a debt-ridden financial world no longer able to draw citizens into further personal borrowing, the most that can be expected is the effective use of existing support. The EU's budget from 2013 will affect us all. In earlier chapters, we have identified ways and means of providing and using uncostly and cost-effective resources in and across European schools: e-learning, low-cost foreign language assistant schemes, pump-priming the resourcefulness of communities themselves, support for purposeful mobility and enabling enablers.

We admire and applaud the many facets of the EU's Lifelong Learning Programme and, in particular, its COMENIUS programmes and increasing e-learning support.On these, we offer two general comments. First, because channels of communication are centrifugal, exciting and valuable funded projects go unnoticed. They may have made provisions for sustainability and outreach to those who may be looking for them, and the central databanks may have them all recorded and archived, but there is little cross-referral, for example, by the national agencies which process enquiries and applications for funding. Two examples from personal experience: When Poland acceded to EU membership and thousands left their families to earn more in more affluent western Europe, teachers in Kraków identified the need for a European curriculum which would be appropriate for the children of professionally mobile families, so that the European encouragement of professional mobility could be met without either family disruption or the discontinuity of children's education. The educators submitted a COMENIUS proposal and engaged with colleagues in Belgium, England and Italy to work on their project over 3 years. Nobody had informed them of the European Schools which had existed for half a century trying to offer precisely what they were seeking to invent. Their visit to Culham was a revelation as well as an inspiration. But how much more could have been achieved if they (or indeed the agencies which selected projects for funding) had known of and been able to build on that resource?

More recently, our ETEE conference was enriched by an unannounced visitor, the English member of a COMENIUS project ISTEPEC,[1] who had come just to present us all with the book of the project, 'Learning to Teach Europe'. Only one of the conference participants had even heard of the project before, yet its topic was central to all our concerns, and its findings would have been lost but for the personal initiative of its members. Projects like that should not depend on either personal dissemination or ploughing through central websites. It should be an obligation of national, regional and professional agencies to review and bring them to the attention of teachers. Thousands of joint European projects are being lost in cyberspace. Above all, the central European agencies must shoulder the responsibility for discovering and implementing more widely spread, effective dissemination of this vast knowledge. Creating an active and well-supported national liaison officer for the Pestalozzi Programme of teacher education in every HEI or consortium of HEIs could be a step towards spreading this knowledge to local education authorities and schools.

Development project proposals for schools range from idiosyncratic explorations to standardization, from the appreciation and celebration of difference to the transfer of good practice. This range reflects the deep-seated differences of views about being European and also different understandings of quality and standards. Standards can be understood as traditional habits, as lowest common denominators – below which schools are failing – as norms or as targets. The standard was, and is properly, the distinctive flag or figurehead raised on a pole and borne by a standard bearer as a rallying point. Formerly associated with the royal cavalry, the equivalent now might be the banners frequently used by tour guides in crowds. It has more to do with distinctiveness and aspiration than with standardization or levelling up or down. There is a case for exemplars as standard bearers, as we have argued for the European Baccalaureate. But the case for standardization, made most strongly in relation to the Europe of professional and workforce mobility, can only be realistic if it is about general direction, about frameworks within which differences can be accommodated. Support for school projects should be principally for small-scale exploratory initiatives, rather than massive schemes for generalization. The personal profile, whether for employment or for education, is a much better tool for adjusting to new contexts than the attempt to standardize. This applies equally to mutually recognized teaching qualifications, which vary so widely across Europe that the only way forward is to identify the differences and provide for induction and in-service adjustment into the different context.

Research for development

This also calls into question the rôle of educational research. In this volume, research has been illustrated which is vital to inform and point to development. A sad feature of EU funding has been the separation over many years of an educational research framework, on the one hand, and action or development projects on the other. The former has centred on such large-scale and extended research programmes that transfer to actual and specific developments has been made difficult. The current, seventh EU research programme, from 2007 to 2013, is stated to be part of a knowledge triangle of research, education and innovation, but there is nothing in it specifically to link with education or schools as such, though information technology and socio-economic and human sciences generally are included as two of nine themes. The European Research Area (ERA) has an ideas programme aiming to enhance European research excellence by promoting competition and risk taking; a people programme to improve the prospects of researchers; a capacities programme to enhance the quality of research and a joint research centre with Euratom. To practitioners, that has the ring of an enclosed introspective world, reiterating what has already been agreed on.

Furthermore, the pinnacle of educational research is generalization, and the quest for paradigms, which can then apply across varying contexts, is a priority. Diagnostic and formative research to inform development, exploratory and qualitative research are often seen as only starting points for longer-term quantitative exercises, whose findings will have been outdated by the pace of change in schools adapting to a world that has moved on. So researchers are engaged instead in assessment and evaluation, and their search for commensurability across European systems confines them to that which is most apparently measurable, such as the much disputed PISA exercise. Its generalized comparisons as league tables across national systems are of no use to schools, but are employed by governments as a justification for often unrelated kaleidoscope management – giving the system a shake-up to take credit for whatever pattern emerges. Hence the requirement in the 2011 Education Act for England for schools to take part in international assessment tests.

This is sad, for research methodology is needed for any development project as part of a cycle of mutually informing action and research. We would wish to see research more firmly tied to problem solving and action projects, and more recognition given, both from EU and from national research councils to shorter-term, illustrative, qualitative exercises of real use to schools and teachers, for example in support of multilingual, multiliterate school approaches, of teacher mobility and development needs and responses and of examples of good practice transmuted into different European contexts – with accompanying frameworks and structures for evaluation and the dissemination of findings.

Non-governmental initiatives

In the research framework and in the Lifelong Learning Programmes, there are now EU promptings for education to engage with enterprises in applying for partial funding, to involve industry as well in their search for economic support. This is all consistent with the Lisbon economic priorities of a society competitive through knowledge. However, preceding chapters have offered examples of voluntary non-governmental and non-profit organizations engaged in promoting activities and awareness of the European dimension in schools. Many such organizations, such as SEET in Scotland or ETEE in England, are small charities, and in terms of subsidiarity are much closer to individual citizens than any local authority. The EU, in particular, has been constructed of treaties and agreements exclusively with and among national governments, and its negotiation has been principally with civil servants. It has been slower than many of its member states to recognize the part played by voluntary bodies, particularly in the field of education and social care. The Körber Stiftung initiative in founding and funding the EUSTORY[2] network with history teaching associations has done more for young people across 22 countries to become aware of the richness of local histories than any inter-governmental equivalent.

The strengthening of the European Parliament's rôle in shaping policy gives greater scope for voluntary bodies to communicate concerns and influence policy making. The commission's directorates will need in the future to improve NGO access to their deliberations and to make it as easy for them to engage in shared activities as it has been for governmental agencies. Bodies representing them nationally, such as the National Council of Voluntary Organisations (NCVO) and networked across Europe in the European Network of National Associations (ENNA) should have constant dialogue with the commission and where necessary support of the kind being offered by national governments without compromising their independence. Non-union professional associations of teachers have to be similarly recognized, encouraged in their work, and given access to opportunities for shared funded development.

A European Baccalaureate (EB) framework

In an earlier chapter it has been suggested that the European Schools should come within the orbit of a reformed EU Directorate of Education and Culture, perhaps as a freestanding agency advised by an independent body also associated with the Council of Europe, and that the conduct and administration of the European Baccalaureate should be franchised to national bodies. Clearly, the next 5 years will be characterized by retrenchment and inward-looking measures to preserve the key qualities of the EB from the financial restrictions of the EU budget. During that period, the scope for expansion and wider access will be severely limited. But that makes it all the more important to build the foundations for a Europe-wide Baccalaureate and a plan for extension over the next 20 years.

Agreement has already been made for a network of Type II/III or associated European schools, with outreach to potential new members and negotiating capacities with the existing Board of Governors. By the time the numbers of associated schools exceed those of the Type I schools, a reorganization of the system will be required. The European Parliament and Council of Ministers should be asked to act on their general aspirations of the last decade to widen access to the EB. If, as might be hoped, they call for a 10-year programme to develop at least one and, if possible, two EB schools in each member country (or across the smallest) to act as an exemplar and through their network to build a model for the future, the EB can take its proper place as a significant and dynamic element of school education in Europe. Instead of affecting perhaps only one in 10,000 young people as at present, the EB would become the exemplar and framework for a general education across Europe, with a funded capacity for development and reform, working into and across national and regional systems. By 2030, the European School at Perm in the Urals should expect to be offering the EB. The International School of Iceland, currently funded by the United States embassy for its personnel, would either be matched or reshaped to a European future.

A trans-European advisory body for education

The example of the European Schools and Baccalaureate is one of many which points to a future independent body with a duty to advise on all matters related to school education in Europe, both in the EU and beyond.

No doubt there can meanwhile be some re-shaping of the European Commission, but a commission composed of directorates led by national figureheads in rotation is not conducive to capturing the imagination and commitment of young Europeans, and a legacy remains across its offices of priority given to financial and economic measures, with token recognition of the importance of education not in its own right but as a means of economic prosperity. We have to look elsewhere for fundamental change.

This could be a dimension of the Council of Europe, with its relative freedom from the politics of national and cross-national interaction, and with its capacity to reach a trans-European membership. It would have to be clearly recognizable as drawing on distinguished educators from a wide range of perspectives, akin perhaps to the consultative group which advised the framers of the Janne Report in 1972. The corollary of a body with the duty to advise is an obligation on the European Parliament and commission both to refer to it on major policy issues and either to take its advice or set out clearly for the public reasons for modifying it. This, in turn, reflects back on national and regional governments and parliaments, which should have direct access on European education policy questions.

In Chapter 8 we proposed a framework matrix of the influences on bilingual education. There the child and family formed the base of the triangle model. An alternative metaphor, coordinate with the envisaged 'platform of resources and references for plurilingual and intercultural education'[3] proposed by the Language Policy Division of the Council of Europe places the individual child as school learner at the apex of the systems and structures comprising a European education.

The following outline of actions to be taken for the future schooling of the child in Europe begins with the family as the most immediate source of support. All sources interact with one another in a variety of ways, some to mediate, others more directly.

The individual and the family

- use opportunities to relate children's everyday experience to European events, to build on shared memories and the shared excitement of popular European programmes (such as sport or Eurovision)
- ensure personal contact and exchange with other European families, and make European holidays more than cornflakes in the sun
- demonstrate continuing interest in European languages and customs, bringing the European dimension into the home
- inform the school about the child's background and work together with the school to agree on priorities and needs
- initiate and/or support coordination for development of all the child's linguistic and citizenship capacities
- inform school about local contexts and take responsibility where there is opportunity and perceived need

The school

- identify and implement with flexibility a concept of curricula and teaching for a European education which encompasses the values touched on in this book and that at the same time is appropriate for the children, the school and the context
- designate clear responsibilities for European education across the curriculum

- ensure that teachers have opportunities for experience and training in other European countries
- know about and understand the children and families that are part of the school, their heritages and their futures in relation to the curriculum and leaving certification
- work transparently with the families whose children the school is educating
- create structures for working with parents to assure quality education for equity particularly in languages and citizenship
- ensure that all children have regular communication with native speakers of the languages they are learning
- ensure that language learning is seen as a lifelong activity
- celebrate Europe Day and the European Day of Languages
- provide a valid framework for quality assessment at the school and local level
- ensure communication and mutually supportive links with other schools, with outside bodies such as NGOs and with universities for purposes of offering learners interesting educational activities through continuing teacher professional development
- pursue support that can be obtained from all levels including the EU and COE
- educate children to be critically aware of Eurosceptic media interests

National

- re-establish and strengthen local authority structures and advisory services which can support and work together at personal levels with schools and institutions for European education
- reiterate and confirm European values where they are present in schooling
- recognize achievement toward European awareness and European citizenship at local and district levels
- give specific support to local authorities, higher education institutions and schools for sustained language and citizenship education
- identify and support NGOs and other initiatives for developing active engagement in European education, particularly in languages and for citizenship
- support teacher education, initial and on-going, toward common goals in European education

Pan-national, European

- remove the curriculum and direction of the European Schools and Baccalaureate from the Directorate for Services and place them in their own body, possibly associated with a reformed Directorate of Education and Culture
- research and implement effective, person-to-person ways of disseminating what is already known and has been achieved with regard to European education

- continue to make direct use of research and researchers to identify principled responses to issues such as was done in the COE Forum in November 2010[4] which should be effectively disseminated
- actively enable the transfer of personal experience and knowledge from eastern European nation–states to western European nation–states on issues of education and European culture
- support cooperation and exchanges across nations, locales, schools and higher education institutions toward developing European education for values, languages and citizenship
- help local people study their local context for the purpose of school development toward awareness of European heritage
- support foreign language assistant programmes
- repeat the European Year of Citizenship or incorporate it into the annual European Day of Languages
- amalgamate further into the European portfolios for languages and for student teachers properties of European heritage and citizenship
- promote momentum toward making the European Baccalaureate available to all schools
- increase numbers, raise the profiles and widen the activities of national liaison officers for an expanded COE Pestalozzi Programme
- recognize, interact with and enable voluntary organizations like SEET and EUSTORY with their efforts to provide learners with meaningful experiences and knowledge
- review the effects and reflect seriously on the use of indicators and statistical representations of education

At all levels of the education sphere there needs to be frank analysis of the limited place and use for working with the results of tests in which learning is itemized or atomized to form descriptor objectives. The concept frame for this analysis must be a European education for human rights and dignity, mutual respect for different approaches to living and knowing, for linguistic capacities and for equity. Built into this is education for active, effective local, national, European and world citizenship. If we have identified the kind of society we want, we can look to design the kind of education that will be given to the children for that society. The Council of Europe has been an especial generator of ideas and guidance that reiterate these values identified as Europe's heritage. A next step is to communicate more widely and effectively what has been researched, asserted and developed for distilling in schools through teachers and teaching for learners and learning.

Notes

1   ISTEPEC, the International Studies in Teacher Education to promote European Citizenship, no. 11 9121-CP-1-2004-1-Fr-COMENIUS-C21

2   EUSTORY, the history network for young Europeans, was established in 2001, initiated by the Körber Foundation. With its coordination office in Hamburg, Germany, the network currently connects 22 civic organizations in 22 countries across Europe. All members agreed on a common document, the charter, postulating the 'disarmament of history', for tolerance and mutual understanding in Europe. See www.euroclio.eu

3   www.coe.int/t/dg4/linguistic/default_en.asp

4   www.coe.int/t/dg4/linguistic/Source/Source2010_ForumGeneva/ForumGeneva2010-Report_EN.pdf

Annex

Figure 2 Major European Events and Developments Affecting Schools 1949–2011

Dates	Key proposals, decisions, treaties, conventions, action	Bodies affected	Description, especially effects for schools	Ready references
1949	Treaty of London	COE	Founded Council of Europe, 10 signatories	http://conventions.coe.int/treaty/
1951	Treaty of Paris	ECSC	Five members, (also led to plan for 1st European School)	www.eurotreaties.com/eurotexts.html
1955– present	European Cultural Convention, strengthened by Wroclaw Declaration 2004	COE	National commitments to foster study of languages, history and civilisation of others and common heritage	http://conventions.coe.int/Treaty/en/ Treaties
1957	Treaty of Rome	EEC EURATOM	Proposals for co-operation in vocational education and (art. 128) European culture and history	www.eurotreaties.com/eurotexts.html
1957–present	European Social Fund	EEC	Supporting employment for deprived regions, minorities and migrants. Scotland, Wales and Cornwall still benefit.	http://ec.europa.eu/employment_social/ esf/
1961	European Social Charter	COE	Human rights including social rights	conventions.coe.int/Treaty/EN/Treaties/ html/035.htm
1965	Merger Treaty	EC	Merged ECSC, EEC, EURATOM	www.eurotreaties.com/eurotexts.html
1973	Janne Report	Report to COM.	Proposed EC policy to include education, European dimension and language learning. General and vocational education indivisible	EC Bulletin 10/73

Contd.

Dates	Key proposals, decisions, treaties, conventions, action	Bodies affected	Description, especially effects for schools	Ready references
1974	Ministers of Education Resolution	EC	Adopted main principles and action proposals of Janne Report, paving way for action programmes	EC Journal, C 98/2
1975	Helsinki Accords	OSCE	35-nation agreement on east-west frontiers & human rights	www.hri.org/docs/Helsinki75.html
1975	CEDEFOP	EC	Information centre, co-operation in vocational training	www.cedefop.europa.eu
1975	Sport for All Charter	COE	Revised 1992, 2001 European Sports Charter	www.coe.int/t/dg4/sport/sportineurope/
1976	Education Committee established	EC	Community Action Programme published (See later action programmes)	EC Bulletin 2-1976
1980–present	EURYDICE information network opens	EC	Open and accessible references for key data and studies across national systems	http://eacea.ec.europa.eu/education/eurydice/
1984	Fontainebleau 'Summit' Led to 1986 Single European Act, q.v.,	EC	EC/EFTA agreement on EEA and commissioned Committee for a 'People's Europe' leading to first education action programmes	aei.pitt.edu/1448
1984–present	NARIC network	EC	National centres for information on recognized academic awards in EU/EEA, most now merged with COE/UNESCO ENIC	www.enic-naric.net
1986	Single European Act	EC	Economic and social cohesion addition to Treaty of Rome, to reduce regional disparities	www.eurotreaties.com/eurotexts.html
1986–94	COMETT action programmes, in Leonardo programme 1995–present	EC	Co-operation of industry and higher education on technology training	Council Decision 89/27/EEC

1987–2006	ERASMUS action programmes. In Socrates framework 1995–present	EC	Mobility of students and their teachers. In Lifelong Learning programme 2007–present	http://ec.europa.eu/education/lifelong-learning-programme
1987–2006	ARION action programme, In Socrates programme from 1995	EC	Short Study visits for leaders in education. Opportunity for school heads	http://ec.europa.eu/dgs/education_culture/evalreports
1988	Education Council Resolution: The European Dimension in Education, cf 1993	E. C	Defined EU aspiration to improve young people's involvement, knowledge, awareness of EC and sense of being European	http://eur-lex.europa.eu
1988-99	YES I & II action programmes	EC	First Youth for Europe programme, mostly outside schools, schools involved through youth wings	ec.europa.eu/youth/youth-in-action...programme/doc78_en.htm
1988-94	PETRA action programmes	EC	Vocational training, preparation for adult life, school leavers involved	http://europa.eu/legislation_summaries/
1988-98	IRIS action programmes, taken Into NOW, 2000–present	EC	Promoting vocational training for women	www.peoplemanagement.co.uk
1990-2006	LINGUA action programme. Into Lifelong Learning 2007–present	EC	Promoting language competence in teacher education, secondary, vocational and higher education	http://ec.europa.eu/education/lifelong-learning-programme/doc94_en.htm
1990-2000	Warsaw Pact countries join COE	COE	1989 Gorbachev 'Common European Home'	
1990–present	TEMPUS aid programmes for eastern Europe higher education	EC, ETF, EACEA	TEMPUS-PHARE (Poland, Hungary, Czechoslovakia), TEMPUS-CARDS, S-E. Europe, TEMPUS-TACIS, former USSR. Including teacher education and partner schools	ec.europa.eu/education/external-relation.-programmes/doc70_en.htm
1990–	Action JEAN MONNET	EC	Promoting European integration studies in higher education	ec.europa.eu/education/lifelonglearningprogramme/doc88_en.htm

Contd.

Dates	Key proposals, decisions, treaties, conventions, action	Bodies affected	Description, especially effects for schools	Ready references
1991–1994	FORCE	EC	Promoting continuing vocational training	
1992	Treaty on European Union (Maastricht)	EU	Articles 126 and 127 strengthen community action to supplement member states on education and implement policy on training. They promote student and teacher mobility, European dimension in curriculum, European language-learning, exchange on common issues.	www.eurotreaties.com/maastrichtec.pdf
1992	European Charter for Regional or Minority Languages	COE	Protection and promotion of non-official historical, regional and minority languages	conventions.coe.int/Treaty/EN/Treaties/Html/148.htm
1993	Green Paper: The European Dimension in Education	COM	Open consultation based on 1988 Council, q.v.	COM (93) 4571
1994	European Centre for Modern Languages	COE	Graz Centre, European Day of Languages 26 September, Languages, Diversity Citizenship project	www.ecml.at/
1995	'Delors' White Paper: 'Teaching and Learning: Towards the Learning Society'	COM.	Sets out objectives of recognized skills, promotes community languages, proposes evaluation of investment in education. Second Chance Schools.	COM (95) 590 COM (97) 256
1995–2006	SOCRATES action programme (taken into Lifelong Learning Programme, 2007)	EU	Framework across universities ERASMUS and schools COMENIUS mobility, European curricular development projects, language learning, distance learning, adult education	http://europa.eu/legislation_summaries/other/c11023_en.htm

Date	Name	Org	Description	URL
1995–2006	Leonardo action programme	EU	Framework of vocational training (taken into Lifelong Learning Programme 2007)	ec.europa.eu/education/programmes/llp/index_en.html
1996–2013	EVS, into Youth in Action Programme 2000–present	EU	European Voluntary Service. For 18–30 age group, now merged in major youth programme	ec.europa.eu/youth/youth-in-actionprogramme./doc82_en.htm
1997	Towards a Europe of Knowledge	COM.	Guidelines for programme to 2006	EU Bulletin 11-1997
1998–2005	'Learning in the Information Society'	COM.	Promotion and action plan of co-ordinated activities on new technologies	COM(2001) 172, EU Bulletin 3-2001 www.delni.gov.uk/eeurope-2005
1999	BOLOGNA declaration	EU	Higher education qualifications framework, Europe of Knowledge; Europe as social and cultural area; mobility	ec.europa.eu/education/policies/educ/bologna/bologna.pdf
1999	Agenda 2000	ESF	Vocational training priorities as lifelong learning	COM(2000) 379
2000–2013	GRUNDTVIG action programme	EU	Adult and alternative education. Taken into Lifelong Learning Programme 2007	http://ec.europa.eu/education/lifelong-learning-programme/doc86_en.htm
2000	Lisbon Accord	EU	Shaped future lifelong learning programme, q.v.	www.europarl.europa.eu/summits/lis1_en.htm
2001–2013	MEDIA programmes	EU	Training and development, audio-visual and cinema	http://ec.europa.eu/culture/media/index_en.htm
2004–2013	ERASMUS MUNDUS	EU/EACEA	Promotes and attracts to European higher education worldwide	http://ec.europa.eu/education/external-relation-programmes/doc72_en.htm
2004–2013	E-Learning programme	EU/EACEA	Includes e-twinning for schools & teacher-training. Taken into Lifelong Learning, 2007	http://ec.europa.eu/education/programmes/elearning/programme_en.html

Contd.

Dates	Key proposals, decisions, treaties, conventions, action	Bodies affected	Description, especially effects for schools	Ready references
2006	EACEA created	EC/ EACEA	Education, Audio-Visual & Cultural Executive Agency, runs 15 programmes under three EC directorates	http://eacea.ec.europa.eu
2007–2013	Lifelong Learning Programma	EU	Framework for general and vocational education programmes at all levels; Budget: 13,620€	www.lifelonglearningprogramme.org.uk
2009	Lisbon Treaty	EU	Articles 165–167 on education and training	
2010	EUROPE 2020 strategy proposal	EC	'A strategy for smart, sustainable and inclusive growth'; 'Youth on the Move', digital society, competitiveness	ec.europa.eu/europe2020/index_en.htm
2010	Charter on Education for Citizenship and Human Rights	COE	Strengthens accords for education against increasing xenophobia, racism, intolerance; teaching manuals added	www.coe.int/t/dg4/education/edc/

References

Altbach, P. G. and Knight, J. (2007), 'The internationalization of higher education: Motivations and realities'. *Journal of Studies in International Education*, 11 (3–4), 290–305.

Altet, M. (1994), *La Formation Professionnelle des Enseignants*. Paris: PUF.

Arendt, H. (2006), 'The crisis in education', in *Between Past and Future*. London: Penguin Classics, 118–89.

Baetens Beardsmore, H. (ed.) (1993), *Key Issues in Bilingualism and Bilingual Education*. Clevedon: Multilingual Matters Ltd.

Baillat, G., Niclot, D. and Ulma, D. (eds) (2010), *La Formation des Enseignants en Europe: Approche Comparative*. Brussels: De Boeck.

Baker, C. (1988), *Key Issues in Bilingualism and Bilingual Education*. Clevedon: Multilingual Matters Ltd.

Becker, R., Lasanowski, V., Goreham, H., Olcott Jr., D., Woodfield, S., Middlehurst, R. and Carbonell, J-A. (2009), *UK Universities and Europe: Competition and Internationalisation*. London: UK Higher Education Europe Unit and International Unit, Research Series 3. www.international. ac.uk/resources/UK%20Universities%20and%20Europe%20Competition%20and%20 Internationalisation.pdf

Bekerman, Z. and Horenczyk, G. (2004), 'Arab-Jewish bilingual coeducation in Israel: A long-term approach to intergroup conflict resolution'. *Journal of Social Issues*, 60 (2), 389–404.

Bhandari, R. and Laughlin, S. (eds) (2009), *Higher Education on the Move: New Developments in Global Mobility*. New York: Institute of International Education.

Birzea, C. (2003), *EDC Policies in Europe: A Synthesis*. Strasbourg: Council of Europe.

Birzea, C. (2004), *Education for Democratic Citizenship Activities 2001–2004: All-European Study on EDC Policies*. Strasbourg: Council of Europe.

Borgwardt, E. (2005), *A New Deal for the World: America's Vision for Human Rights*. Cambridge, MA: Belknap.

Breidbach, S. (2002), 'European communicative integration: The function of foreign language teaching for the development of a European public sphere'. *Language, Culture and Curriculum*, 15 (3), 273–83.

British Academy (2011), 'Language Matters More and More – A Position Statement'. www.britac.ac.uk/ news/bulletin/Language_matters11.pdf

Brock, C. and Tulasiewicz, W. (eds) (2000), *Education in a Single Europe* (2nd edn). London: Routledge.

Brooks, R. and Waters, J. (2009), 'International higher education and the mobility of UK students'. *Journal of Research in International Education*, 8 (2), 191–209.

Brooks, R. and Waters, J. (2010), 'Young Europeans and educational mobility', in J. Leaman and M. Wörsching (eds), *Youth in Contemporary Europe*. New York: Routledge, 85–102.

Brown, P., Lauder, H. and Ashton, D. (2011), *The Global Auction: The Broken Promises of Education, Jobs and Income*. Oxford: Oxford University Press.

Byram, M. (1992), 'Foreign language learning for European citizenship'. *Language Learning Journal*, 6, 10–12.

Byram, M. (1997), *Teaching and Assessing Intercultural Communicative Competence*. Clevedon: Multilingual Matters.

Byram, M., Gribkova, B. and Starkey, H. (2002), *Developing the Intercultural Dimension in Language Teaching: A Practical Introduction for Teachers*. Strasbourg: Council of Europe, Language Policy Division.

Canadine, D. (ed.) (1990), *The Speeches of Winston Churchill*. London: Penguin.

Caprara, G. V., Barbaranelli, C., Steca, P. and Malone, P. S. (2006), 'Teachers' self-efficacy beliefs as determinants of job satisfaction and students' academic achievement: A study at the school level'. *Journal of School Psychology*, 44 (6), 473–90.

Carder, M. (2007), *Bilingualism in International Schools – A Model for Enriching Language Education*. Clevedon: Multilingual Matters Ltd.

Coleman, J. (1997), 'State of the art: Residence abroad within language study', *Language Teaching*, 30, 1–20.

Coleman, J. (1999), 'Social capital in the creation of human capital', in P. Dasgupta and I. Sarageldin (eds), *Social Capital: A Multifaceted Perspective*. Washington, DC: The World Bank, 13–39.

Coleman, J. (2004), 'Residence Abroad', Subject Centre for Languages, Linguistics and Area Studies Guide to Good Practice. www.llas.ac.uk/resources/gpg/2157

Coleman, J. (2005), 'Living in the Sun: Residence Abroad and University Language Learning'. Inaugural Lecture at the Open University. www.open.ac.uk/inaugural-lectures/p9_5.shtml#p0

Collier, V. P. and Thomas, W. P. (2004), 'The astounding effectiveness of dual language education for all.' *NABE Journal of Research and Practice*, 2 (1), 1–20.

Commission of the European Communities (29 September 1993), *Green Paper on the European Dimension of Education*. Brussels. http://aei.pitt.edu/936/1/education_gp_COM_93_457.pdf

Congress of Europe (1949), *Europe Unites*. The Story of the Campaign for European Unity, Including a Full Report of the Congress of Europe, Held at The Hague, May, 1948. London: Hollis & Carter.

Convery, A., Evans, M., Green, S., Macaro, E. and Mellor, J. (1997), *Pupils' Perceptions of Europe: Identity and Education*. London: Cassell Education.

Convery, A. and Kerr, K. (2005), 'Exploring the European dimension in education'. *European Education*, 37 (4), 22–34.

Coudenhove-Kalergi, R. N. von (1923), *Pan-Europa*. Vienna: Pan-Europa-Verlag.

Coulmas, F. (1991), *A Language Policy for the European Community: Prospects and Quandaries*. Berlin: de Gruyter.

Council of Europe (1950), *European Convention for the Protection of Human Rights and Fundamental Freedoms*. Strasbourg: Council of Europe. www.hri.org/docs/ECHR50.html

Council of Europe (1985), *Recommendation No. R(85)7 of the Committee of Ministers to Member States on Teaching and Learning about Human Rights in Schools*. Strasbourg: Council of Europe. https://wcd.coe.int/wcd/com.instranet.InstraServlet?command=com.instranet.CmdBlobGet&Instranet Image=605110&SecMode=1&DocId=686454&Usage=2

Council of Europe (1998), *Recommendation no.R(98)6 of the Committee of Ministers to Member States Concerning Modern Languages.* Strasbourg: Council of Europe. https://wcd.coe.int/wcd/com. instranet.InstraServlet?command=com.instranet.CmdBlobGet&InstranetImage=530647&SecMo de=1&DocId=459522&Usage=2

Council of Europe Committee of Ministers (1999), *Declaration and Programme on Education for Democratic Citizenship, Based on the Rights and Responsibilities of the Citizens.* Strasbourg: Council of Europe. https://wcd.coe.int/wcd/ViewDoc.jsp?Ref=CM(99)76&Language=lanEnglish&Ver=rev&Sit e=CM&BackColorInternet=DBDCF2&BackColorIntranet=FDC864&BackColorLogged=FDC864

Council of Europe (2000), *Project on 'Education for Democratic Citizenship'.* Resolution Adopted by the Council of Europe Ministers of Education at Their 20th session, Cracow, Poland, 15–17 October 2000. No. DGIV/EDU/CIT (2000) 40. Strasbourg: Council of Europe. www.coe.int/t/dg4/education/ edc/Source/Pdf/Documents/2004_12_Complete_All-EuropeanStudyEDCPolicies_En.PDF

Council of Europe (2001), *Common European Framework of Reference for Languages: Learning, Teaching and Assessment* (CEFR), English version. Cambridge: Cambridge University Press. www.coe.int/t/ dg4/linguistic/cadre_en.asp

Council of Europe (2002), *Recommendation Rec (2002)12 of the Committee of Ministers to Member States on Education for Democratic Citizenship.* Strasbourg: Council of Europe. http://youth-partnership-eu.coe.int/youth-partnership/documents/EKCYP/Youth_Policy/docs/Human_rights/Policy/ Recommendation_2002.pdf

Council of Europe (2003), *Declaration by the European Ministers of Education on Intercultural Education in the New European Context.* Strasbourg: Council of Europe. www.coe.int/t/e/cultural_ co-operation/education/intercultural_education/EMED21-7final.pdf

Council of Europe (2005), *Education for Democratic Citizenship 2001–2004 from Policy to Practice*; Synthesis Report on the 2nd Phase of the Education for Democratic Citizenship (EDC) Project 2001–2004. Strasbourg: Council of Europe. www.coe.int/t/dg4/education/edc/Source/Pdf/ Documents/2005_24_Rev3Synthesis2ndPhaseEDCProject.PDF

Council of Europe (2006), *Plurilingual Education in Europe: 50 Years of International Cooperation.* Strasbourg: Council of Europe. www.coe.int/t/dg4/linguistic/Source/ PlurinlingalEducation_En.pdf

Council of Europe (2010), *Charter on Education for Democratic Citizenship and Human Rights Education.* Recommendation CM/Rec(2010)7 and explanatory memorandum. Strasbourg: Council of Europe. www.coe.int/t/dg4/education/edc/Source/Pdf/Downloads/6898-6-ID10009-Recommendation%20on%20Charter%20EDC-HRE%20-%20assembl%C3%A9.pdf

Council of Europe (2011), *Living Together: Combining Diversity and Freedom in 21st-Century Europe.* Report of the Group of Eminent Persons of the Council of Europe. Strasbourg: Council of Europe. http://book.coe.int/ftp/3664.pdf

Creanza, M. A. (1997), 'La Motivazione all'Apprendimento della Lingua Inglese nella Scuola Superiore'. *Rassegna Italiana di Linguistica Applicata*, 29 (3), 97–114.

Cummins, J. (1979), 'Linguistic interdependence and the educational development of bilingual children'. *Review of Educational Research*, 49, 222–51.

Cummins, J. (2000), 'BICS and CALP', in M. Byram (ed.), *Routledge Encyclopedia of Language Teaching and Learning.* London: Routledge, 76–9.

Dearing, R. and King, L. (2007), *Languages Review: Final Report*. London: DES.

Delors, J. (1996), *Learning: The Treasure Within*. Paris: UNESCO.

De Mejia, A. (2002), *Power, Prestige and Bilingual Education – International Perspectives on Elite Bilingual Education*. Clevedon: Multilingual Matters.

Department for Children, Schools and Families (2009 update), *The European Schools and the European Baccalaureate: Guidance for Universities and Colleges*. London: HMSO.

Dewey, J. (1916) *Democracy and Education: An Introduction to the Philosophy of Education*. New York: Macmillan.

Doyé, P. (1998), 'Eine Untersuchung zum Höverstehen der Schülerinnen und Schüler der Staatlichen Europa-Schule Berlin', in M. Göhlich (ed.), *Beiträge zur Schulentwicklung. Europaschlue – Das Berliner Modell*. Neuwied, Kriftel, Germany: Hermann Luchterhand Verlag GmbH, 53–65.

Drummond Bone, J. (2009), 'Internationalisation of HE: A Ten Year View'. www.nusconnect.org.uk/pageassets/campaigns/highereducation/educationinformation/EIInternationalisiation.pdf

DSDE (1993), *The Preparation and Continuing Development of Teachers*. Oxford: DSDE.

Duparc, C. (1993), *The European Community and Human Rights*. Luxembourg: Commission of the European Communities.

Eckstein, M. A. and Noah, H. J. (1989), 'Forms and functions of secondary-school-leaving examinations'. *Comparative Education Review*, 33 (3), 295–316.

Edwards, J. (1984), *Linguistic Minorities, Policies and Pluralism*. London: Academic Press.

Étienne, R. and Lerouge, A. (1997), *Enseigner en Collége ou en Lycée, Repères pour un Nouveau Métier*. Paris: Armand Colin.

European Commission (2006), *The History of European Cooperation in Education and Training*. Luxembourg: Office for Official Publications of the European Communities. http://ec.europa.eu/dgs/education_culture/publ/pdf/education/history_en.pdf

European Communities (1997), *Treaty of Amsterdam, Amending the Treaty of the European Union, the Treaties Establishing the European Communities and Certain Related Acts*. Luxembourg: Office for Official Publications of the European Communities. www.europarl.europa.eu/topics/treaty/pdf/amst-en.pdf

European Union (2006), 'Recommendation of the European Parliament and of the Council of 18 December 2006 on Key Competences for Lifelong Learning' (2006/962/EC). Brussels: *Official Journal of the European Union*.

Extra, G. and Gorter, D. (eds) (2008), *Multilingual Europe: Facts and Policies*. Berlin: de Gruyter.

Fäcke, C. (2007), 'Sprachliche Bildung und Zweisprachige Erziehung. Überlegungen zum Partnersprachenmodell der Staatlichen Europa-Schule Berlin (SESB)', in D. Elsner, L. Küster and B. Viebrock (eds), *Fremdsprachenkompetenzen für ein Wachsendes Europa: Das Leitziel Multiliteralität*. Frankfurt: KFU, Peter Lang, 241–56.

Fisher, L. and Evans, M. (2000), 'The school exchange visit: Effects on attitudes and proficiency in language learning'. *Language Learning Journal*, 22, 11–16.

Freeman, R. D. (1998), *Bilingual Education and Social Change*. Clevedon: Multilingual Matters.

Fumat, Y. (1996), 'D'un Ensemble Confus à un Réseau de causes: Le GEASE'. *Cahiers Pédagogiques*, 51 (346), 23–4.

Furedi, F. (2009), *Wasted; Why Education Is Not Educating*. London: Continuum.

García, O. (2009), *Bilingual Education in the 21st Century – A Global Perspective* (with contributions by Hugo Baetens Beardmore). Chichester, UK: Wiley-Blackwell.

Gardner, R. C. (1985), *Social Psychology and Second Language Learning: The Role of Attitudes and Motivation*. London: Edward Arnold.

Göhlich, M. (1998), *Beiträge zur Schulentwicklung: Europaschule – Das Berliner Modell*. Neuwied, Kriftel, Germany: Hermann Luchterhand Verlag GmbH.

Goullier, F. (2010), 'The Right of Learners to Quality and Equity in Education – The Role of Linguistic and Intercultural Competencies'. Report of the Intergovernmental Language Policy Forum. Strasbourg: Language Policy Division Council of Europe. www.coe.int/t/dg4/linguistic/Source/ Source2010_ForumGeneva/ForumGeneva2010-Report_EN.pdf

Graddol, D. (2004), 'The Future of Language'. *Science*, 303 (5662), 1329–31.

Gräfe-Bentzien, S. (2001), Evaluierung Bilingualer Kompetenzen. Eine Pilotstudie zur Entwicklung der Deutschen und Italienischen Sprachfähigkeiten in der Primarstufe beim Schulversuch der Staatlichen Europa-Schule Berlin (SESB). Doctoral thesis, Freie Universität Berlin.

Grek, S., Lawn, M., Lingard, B., Ozga, J., Rinne, R., Segerholm, C. and Simola, H. (2009), 'National policy brokering and the construction of the European education space in England, Sweden, Finland and Scotland'. *Comparative Education*, 45 (1), 5–21.

Grenfell, M. (1998), *Training Teachers in Practice – Issue 9 of Modern Languages in Practice*. Clevedon: Multilingual Matters Ltd.

Grenfell, M. and Kelly, M. (2004), *European Profile for Language Teacher Education: A Frame of Reference*. Southampton, UK: University of Southampton. http://ec.europa.eu/education/policies/ lang/doc/profilebroch_en.pdf

Grenfell, M., Kelly, M. and Jones, D. (2003), *The European Language Teacher: Recent Trends and Future Developments in Teacher Education*. Bern: Peter Lang.

Harding-Esch, E. and Riley, P. (2003), *The Bilingual Family – A Handbook for Parents* (2nd edn). Cambridge: Cambridge University Press.

Hansard (2010), 'House of Lords debate, education: Languages, 28 October 2010'. *Hansard,* 721. www. publications.parliament.uk

Hawkins, E. (1981), *Modern Languages in the Curriculum*. Cambridge: Cambridge University Press.

HEFCE (2009), *Attainment in Higher Education: Erasmus and Placement Students*. London: HEFCE Issues Paper, No. 44.

Hingel, A. (2001), *Education Policies and European Governance*. Brussels: European Commission DG EAC/A/1.

Hoggan, J. (2007), 'Language Assistants: Enhancing the Learning Experience', Subject Centre for Languages, Linguistics and Area Studies. www.llas.ac.uk/resources/paper/2683

Holden, C. and Clough, N. (eds) (1998), *Children as Citizens: Education for Participation in Democracies Old and New*. London: Jessica Kingsley.

House of Lords European Union Select Committee (14 April 2005), 17th report of the session 2004–05, *Proposed EU Integrated Action Programme for Life-Long Learning*. London.

Howard, E. R. and Christian, D. (2002), 'Two-way immersion 101: Designing and implementing a two-way immersion education program at the elementary level'. *Educational Practice Report* 9. www.cal.org/crede/pdfs/epr9.pdf

Howard, E. R., Sugarman, J. and Coburn, C. (2006), *Adapting the Sheltered Instruction Observation Protocol (SIOP) for Two-Way Immersion Education: An Introduction to the TWIOP*. Washington, DC: Center for Applied Linguistics.

Ibánez-Martin, J. A. and Jover, G. (eds), (2002), *Education in Europe: Policies and Politics*. Dordrecht: Kluwer.

Janne, H. (1973), 'For a Community Policy on Education'. *Bulletin of the European Communities*, Supplement 10/73. Brussels: European Commission.

Johnston, B., Myles, F., Mitchell, R. and Ford, P. (2005), *The Year Abroad: A Critical Moment*. University of Southampton. www.critical.soton.ac.uk/LLAS%20paper.pdf.

Jover, G. (2002), 'Rethinking subsidiarity as a principle of educational policy in the European Union', in J. A. Ibánez-Martin and G. Jover (eds), *Education in Europe: Policies and Politics*. Dordrecht: Kluwer, 3–22.

Kelly, D. and Kelly, A. ([2006] 2009), *The European Baccalaureate: A Study of the Performance of European Baccalaureate Students in Higher Education in the UK and Ireland*. Luxembourg: European School.

Kielhöfer, B. (2004), 'Strukturen und Enwicklungen in der Zweisprachigen Grundschule – Eine Evaluation an der Berliner Europa-Schule Judith Kerr'. *Neusprachliche Mitteilungen*, 57 (3), 168–76.

King, R., Findlay, A. M., Ruiz-Gelices, E. and Stam, A. (2004), *International Student Mobility Study*. Sussex: Sussex Centre for Migration Research.

King, R., Findlay, A. and Ahrends, J. (2010), *International Student Mobility Literature Review*. Report to HEFCE, co-funded by the British Council, UK National Agency for Erasmus. www.britishcouncil.org/hefce_bc_report2010.pdf

Klug, F. (2000), *Values for a Godless Age: The Story of the UK's New Bill of Rights*. Harmondsworth: Penguin.

Laqueur, W. and Rubin, B. (1979), *The Human Rights Reader*. New York: Meridian.

Lawes, S. (2004), The End of Theory? A Comparative Study of the Decline of Educational Theory and Professional Knowledge in Modern Foreign Languages Teacher Training in England and France. Unpublished doctoral thesis. Institute of Education, University of London.

Lindholm-Leary, K. J. (2001), *Dual Language Education*. Clevedon: Multilingual Matters.

Lipgens, W. and Loth, W. (1988), *Documents on the History of European Intergration*, vol. 3. Berlin: de Gruyter.

Maalouf, A. (2008), *A Rewarding Challenge: How the Multiplicity of Languages Could Strengthen Europe*. Brussels: European Commission. http://ec.europa.eu/education/policies/lang/doc/maalouf/report_en.pdf.

Mackey, W. F. (1977), 'The evaluation of bilingual education', in B. Spolsky and R. Cooper (eds), *Frontiers of Bilingual Education*. Rowley, MA: Newbury House Publishers, 226–8.

Maguire, M., Ball, S. and Braun, A. (2010), 'Behaviour, classroom management and student "control": enacting policy in the English secondary school'. *International Studies in Sociology of Education*, 20 (2), 153–70.

Mailhos, M. F. (2007), 'Designing an Istepec Module'. http://python.bretagne.iufm.fr/istepec/article. php3?id_article=87

Masson, A. (ed.) (1941), *Cahiers de Montesquieu 1716–55*. Paris: Grasset.

McIntyre, D. (1983), 'Social skills training for teaching: A cognitive perspective', in R. Ellis and D. Whittington (eds), *New Directions in Social Skill Training*. London: Croom Helm.

Meier, G. (2010a), *Social and Intercultural Benefits of Bilingual Education: A Peace-Linguistic Evaluation of Staatliche Europa-Schule Berlin*, vol. 12. Mehrsprachigkeit im Unterricht. Frankfurt am Main: Peter Lang.

Meier, G. (2010b), 'Two-way immersion education in Germany: Bridging the linguistic gap'. *International Journal of Bilingual Education and Bilingualism*, 13 (4), 419–37.

Neave, G. (1984), *The European Economic Community and Education*. Stoke on Trent: Trentham Books.

The Nuffield Foundation (2000), *Languages the Next Generation: The Final Report and Recommendations of the Nuffield Languages Inquiry*. London: The Nuffield Foundation. www.ittmfl.org.uk/modules/ policy/4d/languages_nuffield_finalreport.pdf

Oakshott, M. (1989), *The Voice Of Liberal Learning: Michael Oakeshott on Education*. New Haven, CT: Yale University Press.

Ollikainen, A. (2000), 'European education, European citizenship: On the role of education in constructing Europeanness'. *European Education*, 32 (3), 6–21.

Organisation for Economic Co-operation and Development (2009), 'Creating Effective Teaching and Learning Environments: First Results from TALIS' available through www.oecd.org/edu/talis/ firstresults

Osler, A. (1998), 'European citizenship and study abroad: Student teachers' experiences and identities'. *Cambridge Journal of Education*, 28 (1), 77–96.

Osler, A. and Starkey, H. (1996), *Teacher Education and Human Rights*. London: Fulton.

Osler, A. and Starkey, H. (1999), 'Rights, identities and inclusion: European action programmes as political education.' *Oxford Review of Education*, 25 (1–2), 199–216.

Osler, A. and Starkey, H. (2002), 'Education for citizenship: Mainstreaming the fight against racism?' *European Journal of Education*, 37 (2), 143–59.

Osler, A. and Starkey, H. (2005), *Citizenship and Language Learning: International Perspectives*. Stoke-on-Trent: Trentham Books.

Osler, A. and Starkey, H. (2010), *Teachers and Human Rights Education*. Stoke-on-Trent: Trentham.

Paquay, L. and Sirota, R. (2001), 'La Construction d'un Espace Discursif en Education. Mise en Oeuvre et Diffusion d'un Modèle de Formation des Enseignants: Le Practicien Réfléxif', *Recherche et Formation*, 36, 5–15.

Parey, M. and Waldinger, F. (2010), 'Studying abroad and the effect on international labour market mobility: Evidence from the introduction of Erasmus'. *The Economic Journal*, 121 (551), 194–222.

Peters, R. (1982), 'What is an educational process?' in Finch, A. and Scrimshaw, P. (eds), *Standards, Schooling and Education*. London: Hodder and Stoughton.

Phillips, D. and Ertl, H. (2003), *Implementing European Union Education and Training Policy: A Comparative Study of Issues in Four Member States*. Dordrecht: Kluwer.

Prawat, R. (1992), 'Teachers' beliefs about teaching and learning: A constructivist perspective'. *American Journal of Education*, 100, 354–95.

Quilligan, J. (2002), *The Brandt Equation: 21st Century Blueprint for the New Global Economy*. Philadelphia: Brandt 21 Forum.

Roland-Lévy, C. and Ross, A. (eds) (2002), *Political Learning and Citizenship in Europe*. Stoke-on-Trent: Trentham.

Romaine, S. (1995), *Bilingualism* (2nd edn). Malden, MA; Oxford; Victoria, Australia: Blackwell Publishing.

Ross, A. (2008), *A European Education: Citizenship, Identities and Young People*. Stoke-on-Trent: Trentham.

Rowles, D. and Rowles, V. (2005), *Breaking the Barriers: 100 Years of the Language Assistants Programme*. London: British Council.

The Royal Society (2011), Preparing for the Transfer from School and College Science and Mathematics Education to UK STEM Higher Education: A 'State of the Nation' Report. London: The Royal Society.

Sayer, J. (ed.) (2002), *Opening Windows to Change: A Case Study of Sustained International Development*. Wallingford, UK: Symposium Books.

Sayer, J. (2005), 'Developing schools for democracy in Europe: A decade with TEMPUS', in S. Wilde (ed.), *Political and Citizenship Education: International Perspectives*. Wallingford, UK: Symposium Books, 87–99.

Sayer, J. and Jones, N. (eds) (1985), *Teacher Training and Special Educational Needs*. Beckenham: Croom Helm.

Sayer, J., Kazelleová, J., Martin, D., Niemczinski, A. and Vanderhoeven, J. (1995), *Developing Schools for Democracy in Europe*. Wallingford: Triangle Books.

Sayer, J. and Van der Wolf, K. (1999), *Opening Schools to All*. Leuven: Garant.

Sayer, J. and Vanderhoeven, J. (2001), *Reflection for Action*. Leuven: Garant.

Schön, D. (1983), *The Reflective Practitioner: How Professionals Think in Action*. New York: Basic Books.

SENBJS (2008), *Europa-Schule*. www.berlin.de/sen/bildung/besondere_angebote/staatl_europaschule/

Sheils, J. (1996), 'The Council of Europe and Language Learning for European Citizenship.' *Evaluation and Research in Education*, 10 (2–3), 88–103.

Shennan, M. (1991), *Teaching about Europe*. London: Cassell.

Starkey, H. (ed.) (1991), *The Challenge of Human Rights Education*. London: Cassell.

Starkey, H. (2002), *Democratic Citizenship, Languages, Diversity and Human Rights*. Strasbourg: Council of Europe, Language Policy Division.

Starkey, H. (2003), 'The council of Europe: Defining and defending a European identity', in M. Pittaway (ed.), *Globalization and Europe*. Milton Keynes: The Open University, 73–105.

Starkey, H. (2005), 'Language teaching for democratic citizenship', in A. Osler and H. Starkey (eds), *Citizenship and Language Learning: International Perspectives*. Stoke-on-Trent: Trentham Books, 23–39.

Starkey, H. and Osler, A. (2009), 'Antiracism, citizenship and education: European ideals and political complacency', in J. A. Banks (ed.), *Routledge International Companion to Multicultural Education*. New York: Routledge, 348–9.

Staub, F. and Stern, E. (2002), 'The nature of teacher's pedagogical content beliefs matters for students' achievement gains: Quasi-experimental evidence from elementary mathematics'. *Journal of Educational Psychology*, 94 (2), 344–55.

Sukopp, I. (2005), *Bilinguales Lernen: Konzeption, Sprachen, Unterricht*. Berlin: LISUM, SENBJS.

Surhone, L. M., Tennoe, M. and Henssonow, S. (eds) (2010), *Ventotene Manifesto*. Saarbrücken, Germany: VDM Verlag Dr Mueller AG & Co Kg.

Spolsky, B. and Cooper, R. (eds) (1977), *Frontiers of Bilingual Education*. Rowley, MA: Newbury House Publishers.

Sully, M. de B. (1638), *Mémoires des Sages et Royalles Economies d'Estat, Domestiques, Politiques et Militaries de Henry le Grand* (Modern edn). Amstelredam (sic): Lefévre, (1942). Paris: Gallimard.

Torres-Guzmán, M. E. (2002), 'Dual language programs: Key features and results'. *National Clearinghouse for Bilingual Education: Directions in Language and Education*, 14.

United Nations (1945), *Charter of the United Nations*. New York: United Nations.

United Nations General Assembly (1948), *Universal Declaration of Human Rights*. New York: United Nations.

University of Cambridge (2009), *External Evaluation of the European Baccalaureate: Final Report*. Cambridge: University of Cambridge International Examinations.

Vanderhoeven, J. (ed.) (1998), *Counselling and Prevention Work in Schools*. Leuven: Garant.

Vermersch, P. (2001), 'Conscience Directe et Conscience Réfléchie'. *Expliciter*, 39, 10–31.

West, R. and Crighton, J. (1999), 'Examination reform in Central and Eastern Europe: Issues and trends'. *Assessment in Education: Principles, Policy & Practice*, 6 (2), 271–89.

Wheelahan, L. (2008), 'A social realist alternative for curriculum', *Critical Studies in Education*, 49 (2), 205–10.

Worton, M. (2009), *Review of Modern Foreign Languages Provision in Higher Education in England*. London: HEFCE. www.linguistics.ac.uk/Documents/Worton_Report.pdf

Young, M. (2008), *Bringing Knowledge Back In: From Social Constructivism to Social Realism*. Routledge: London.

Young, M. and Muller, J. (2007), 'Truth and truthfulness in the sociology of educational knowledge'. *Theory and Research in Education*, 5 (2), 173–201.

Zydatiß, W. (1998), 'Ein Spracherwerbskonzept für die Staatliche Europa-Schule Berlin', in M. Göhlich (ed.), *Beiträge zur Schulentwicklung: Europaschule – Das Berliner Modell*. Neuwied, Kriftel. Germany: Hermann Luchterhand Verlag GmbH, 66–76.

Notes on Contributors

Paddy Carpenter Modern language teacher, adviser, deputy director of the Central Bureau (British Council), co-initiator of EU action programmes and now an independent education consultant, honoured in Belgium (Ordre de la Couronne) and France (Commandeur des Palmes Académiques).

Renée Christmann Secretary-general for the European Schools, administering both the 27-member-state European Schools Board of Governors and the Board of Inspectors for the European Baccalaureate. Background in international diplomacy, formerly principal of the European School at Varese, Italy.

Lynn Erler Research fellow, Oxford University Department of Education, teacher of foreign languages in various countries. Also past teacher and parent at the European School Culham, teacher training and research at Reading and Oxford Universities, with a focus on applied linguistics and learner cognition.

Frank Furedi Professor of Sociology at the University of Kent in Canterbury, author of several books raising issues of social capital and adult authority, including inter-generational relations, parenting and teaching, from an interdisciplinary approach through history, social sciences and culture.

Mairin Hennebry Lecturer in TESOL, Education, Teaching and Leadership, Moray House School of Education, Edinburgh University. Has taught modern languages and EFL in Swiss and British schools, and was post-doctoral research officer at the Oxford Centre for Applied Linguistics.

Jackie Holderness Teacher and teacher trainer in multilingual settings, for many years course leader of the Oxford Brookes MA in Education for international schoolteachers, has published a wide range of language teaching courses and materials and taught at Culham European School.

Shirley Lawes Lecturer in modern foreign languages Course Leader PGCE/ MFL, Institute of Education, London. She has published widely on foreign language teaching and learning and on teacher education. Previous editor of the ALL journal *Francophonie*, Chevalier de l'Ordre des Palmes Académiques.

Barbara Macleod National organizer for the Scottish European Educational Trust (SEET) since its foundation in 1993. Trained as a TEFL teacher and worked in Great Britain, Japan and Algeria before returning to Edinburgh to promote and encourage education about Europe to students at schools, colleges and universities.

Gabriela Meier ERASMUS research officer at Bath University, past translator and language teacher in Switzerland and Great Britain, Exeter University doctoral research in European studies. Research and publications on language policy and planning, multilingual education and social cohesion.

John Sayer Director from Oxford University of major EU (TEMPUS) university aid projects for education in eastern Europe. Former school principal, president, Secondary Heads Association (now ASCL), and director, London Institute of Education Management Unit.

Hugh Starkey Reader in education at the London Institute of Education, specializes in citizenship and human rights education and language teaching. Co-director, International Centre for Democratic Citizenship, with wide experience of consultancy for EU, Council of Europe and UNESCO.

Marc Wolstencroft Head of Wix Primary School, South London, sharing its premises with the French primary school École de Wix, connected with the Lycée Français. Since 2006 a joint bilingual section has been developed, with children following the National Curriculum in French and English.

Judith Woodfield Deputy head at Chenderit School, Northamptonshire, with arts specialist status. She has been the driving force behind the development of bilingual cross-curricular learning, after successful introduction of immersion language teaching at her previous school.

Martha Wörsching Lecturer in German and European studies, Loughborough University, and ERASMUS co-ordinator for student exchanges, study year abroad and English language assistantships. Widely published, and review editor, *Journal of Contemporary European Studies*.

Index